Competitive Tendering: Management and Reality

JOIN US ON THE INTERNET VIA WWW, GOPHER, FTP OR EMAIL:

WWW: http://www.thomson.com
GOPHER: gopher.thomson.com
FTP: ftp.thomson.com
EMAIL: findit@kiosk.thomson.com

A service of I(T)P

OTHER TITLES FROM E & F N SPON

Arts Administration
2nd edition
John Pick and Malcolm Anderton

Coastal Recreation Management
Tim Goodhead and David Johnson

Grounds Maintenance
A contractor's guide to
competitive tendering
Philip Sayers

Leisure and Recreation Management
George Torkildsen

Amenity Landscape Management
A resources handbook
Edited by Ralph Cobham

Managing Sport and Leisure Facilities
A guide to competitive tendering
Philip Sayers

Spon's Landscape Contract Handbook
2nd edition
H. Clamp

For more information about these and other titles, please contact:
The Promotion Department, E & F N Spon, 2–6 Boundary Row, London SE1 8HN.
Telephone 0171 865 0066

Competitive Tendering: Management and Reality

Achieving Value for Money

Philip Sayers

Head of Leisure Client Services
Stevenage Borough Council
and
Chair, Sports and Recreation Panel
Institute of Leisure and Amenity Management
Lower Basildon, Berkshire

Published in association with the
Institute of Leisure and Amenity Management

E & FN SPON
An Imprint of Chapman & Hall

London · Weinheim · New York · Tokyo · Melbourne · Madras

Published by E & FN Spon, an imprint of Chapman & Hall, 2–6 Boundary Row, London SE1 8HN, UK

UK	Chapman & Hall, 2–6 Boundary Row, London SE1 8HN, UK
GERMANY	Chapman & Hall, GmbH, Pappelallee 3, 69469, Weinheim, Germany
USA	Chapman & Hall USA, 115 Fifth Avenue, New York, NY 10003, USA
JAPAN	Chapman & Hall Japan, Kyowa Building, 3F, 2-2-1 Hirakawacho, Chiyoda-ku, Tokyo 102, Japan
AUSTRALIA	Chapman & Hall Australia, 102 Dodds Street, South Melbourne, Victoria 3205, Australia
INDIA	Chapman & Hall India, R. Seshadri, 32 Second Main Road, CIT East, Madras 600 035, India

First edition 1997
© 1997 Institute of Leisure and Amenity Management
Copyright in 'A Tender Business' (Chapter 2) is held by the University of Sydney
Copyright in 'An Evaluation for Leisure Management' (Chapter 7) is held by Jim Lynch
The quotations from Hansard (Chapter 10) are Parliamentary copyright
Copyright in 'Catering for Profit' (Chapter 13) is held by Peter Ranson

Typeset in 10½ on 12pt Palatino
by On Screen, West Hanney, Oxfordshire

Printed in Great Britain by
TJ International Limited, Padstow, Cornwall

ISBN 0 419 22440 8

A catalogue record for this book is available from the British Library
Library of Congress Catalog Card Number: 65932

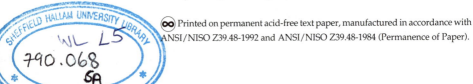 ∞ Printed on permanent acid-free text paper, manufactured in accordance with ANSI/NISO Z39.48-1992 and ANSI/NISO Z39.48-1984 (Permanence of Paper).

Contents

Preface   ix
Acknowledgements   x
ILAM   xi
List of contributors   xii

1   The contract climate   **1**
     Introduction   1
     A century of public service   5
     Philip Sayers
     Introducing CCT – the hopes and fears   15
     Geoff Nichols
     Chapter summary   20

2   A first time tender   **22**
     Introduction   22
     A tender business   24
     Ian Kwan with Simon Domberger
     Chapter summary   36

3   Contract planning   **39**
     Introduction   39
     The naturalistic landscape of Warrington   41
     David Scott
     Chapter summary   50

4   **Process and personalities**   51
     Philip Sayers

5   **Managing specifications**   63
     Introduction   63
     Building sports development into CCT   66
     Geoff Nichols
     Sports development in practice   79
     Philip Sayers
     Management specifications   80
     Chris Youngs
     Chapter summary   88

6   **Business plans**   90
     Introduction   90
     Business planning guidelines   92
     Nick Reeves
     Grundy Park Leisure Centre   96
     Philip Sayers
     Winning ways   97
     Mark Poppy
     Chapter summary   107

7   **Tender evaluation**   108
     Introduction   108
     An evaluation for leisure management   111
     Jim Lynch
     Grounds maintenance   120
     Philip Sayers
     Grounds maintenance tender evaluation   121
     Duncan Moffatt
     Chapter summary   126

8   **Performance measurement**   127
     Introduction   127
     On efficiency measurement and leisure   129
     management
     Gary Crilley, Gary Howat and Ian Milne
     The London Borough of Newham   135
     Philip Sayers
     An inner city case study   136
     Paul Martindill
     Chapter summary   144

9   Customer satisfaction   **146**
     Introduction   146
     One survey – one aim: a better service   .   148
     Stephen Howell
     Chapter summary   155
     Addendum   156

10   Conflict and collapse   **159**
     Introduction   159
     Litigation – is it worth it?   161
     Malcolm Gilbert
     Contract collapse   166
     Philip Sayers
     Extract from Hansard debate on Contemporary
          Leisure   167
     Chapter summary   173

11   Divorce   **176**
     Introduction   176
     Going bust   179
     Reg Harrison
     Emergency planning   187
     Philip Sayers
     Emergency planning for a contractor failure   188
     David Goldstone
     Chapter summary   191

12   Picking up the pieces   **193**
     Introduction   193
     From loss to profit: the DSO fights back   195
     D. Brian James
     Turnaround in grounds maintenance   202
     Philip Sayers
     From weeds to winners   203
     Michael Burgess
     Chapter summary   206

13   Profitable management   **207**
     Introduction   207
     Catering for profit   211
     Peter Ranson

| | Chapter summary | 218 |
| | Addendum | 219 |

14 Market orientation — **220**

	Introduction	220
	Client v. contractor, customers and costs	221
	Geoff Nichols	
	Chapter summary	233
	Geoff Nichols	

15 Peace in a partnership — **234**

	Introduction	234
	A hole in one: success at the golf course	236
	Steve Chaytor	
	Chapter summary	242

Appendix A: List of addresses	243
Appendix B: Outline of a tender	251
Appendix C: Glossary of terms used	253
Index	257

Preface

This is a book written by those at the sharp end of contract management. The lessons learnt from it are of value to everyone involved in, or studying, all forms of contract management. It tells of relationships born in heaven and in hell. All the difficulties and pitfalls are exposed as never before. Readers will be able to learn from examples of best, and worst, practice. This is an easy to read book.

Actual examples of competitive tendering and contract management are exposed in this book. Not just the theory, but the hard, real life actuality. No one now needs to learn the hard way. There are hopes and hype at the early stages of a contract. There are also sometimes subsequently, shattered illusions. All is told. The principles learnt from the leisure management case studies are equally applicable to all contracts.

Contributors include practising leisure managers, consultants, leading academics, a solicitor and contract managers. The people at the sharp delivery end of contracts tell their story. Their graphic accounts are balanced by academic assessments which allow a broader view of the subject. The book blends both practical and academic case studies.

In the closing decades of the twentieth century, public services in Britain were thrown into a giant political experiment. Increasingly, the provision of public services could only be undertaken by a contractor submitting the best value for money. The lowest priced bid often won. Least cost is thus guaranteed. But attention is needed to quality. Competitive tendering, compulsory contracts, externalization, privatization, are all forces at work to drive down costs and increase efficiency.

A contract is like life itself. It includes:

- birth;
- marriage, for better or for worse;
- education;
- cooperation or conflict;
- examination;
- divorce sometimes.

The book, like life, similarly follows the key stages of the tender and contract process. The chapter titles follow the sequence of a contract. The case studies highlight each key element of the contract process.

Acknowledgements

This book would not have been possible but for the willing contributions from so many who are prepared to share their own experiences. Grateful thanks are due to each and all.

The views expressed by each contributor are the views of the individuals and not of their employers, the publishers, the Institute or the editor. While every care has been taken with the advice given, the contributors, publishers, the Institute and the editor can take no responsibility for effects arising therefrom. Anyone involved in contract issues should always obtain their own legal advice and refer any part of the text to their legal adviser before taking any action.

The editor is a practising leisure contracts manager. He is also Chair of the British Institute of Leisure and Amenity Management's Panel of Sport and Recreation. He would welcome any comments on this book or suggestions for future publications.

Where necessary to protect confidentiality, contract figures and names have been changed.

The Institute of Leisure and Amenity Management (ILAM) is the professional body for leisure professionals. ILAM represents every aspect of leisure, cultural and recreational management and is committed to the improvement of management standards.

The growing importance of leisure pursuits to the quality of life demands that financial, human, physical and other resources are managed in the most effective, productive and beneficial way. ILAM, the major body involved in the pursuit of these objectives, plays a key role in the development of leisure management, through education, research, information, debate and discussion with government and national agencies.

The main objectives of the Institute are improvement of management standards in the leisure industry; promotion of the benefits of leisure and healthy lifestyles; enhancement of the quality of experience of those participating in the leisure industry; the representation, development and advocacy of professional standards; the provision of a continuing professional development (CPD) programme; the provision of a professional qualification scheme; and dissemination of information.

Activities and services provided to ILAM members include representation of the leisure profession at a national level; access to an information centre and bookshop; seminars, conferences and exhibitions; weekly mailing service; appointments service; and ILAM publications, including *The Leisure Manager, The Leisure Manager Bulletin* and a Fact Sheet series.

ILAM House
Lower Basildon
Reading
Berkshire
RG8 9NE

List of contributors

Michael Burgess MBA, DMS, MILAM Cert
Michael came to Stevenage Borough Council as Contracts Manager of the Grounds Maintenance DLO in 1991 from Buckinghamshire County Council where he had been Contracts Manager in the Grounds Maintenance and Landscape DSO. He joined Buckinghamshire County Council from the private sector in 1988.

Steven Chaytor BEd, DMS, MILAM
Steven is the Leisure Management Officer in Middlesbrough responsible for all contract and non-contract facilities plus the catering contract. He is also co-author (with colleague Phil Rogers) of the book *Managing a Leisure Management Contract* published by Pitman for ILAM.

Gary Crilley MBA, GDipRec, GDipEd, BA
Gary is now Senior Lecturer, Recreation Planning and Management at the University of South Australia. Up to 1988, Gary managed recreation facilities and services in Australia. His applied research activity is in the evaluation of public sports and leisure services, and the delivery of integrated community recreation for people with a disability. The project described also involved Dr Gary Howat, Associate Professor, Recreation Planning and Management, Ian Milne, Senior Lecturer, Recreation Planning and Management and Graeme J. Alder, Chief Executive of Leisure Australia.

Simon Domberger BSc, MA, PhD
Simon holds the Foundation Chair of Management at the Graduate School of Business, the University of Sydney. He has published some of the most influential and widely cited articles on competitive tendering and contracting in the UK, and heads the leading research team in this field in Australia. He is also chairman of CTC Consultants, a specialist in contracting and outsourcing, and has consulted to prominent organizations, both private and public. He is widely published in international journals, is the author of two books and is working on a third entitled *The Contracting Organization: A Strategic Guide to Outsourcing*, to be published by Oxford University Press.

Malcolm Gilbert, Principal Solicitor at the City of Plymouth
Malcolm is a Solicitor specializing in contract dispute work. Over the years he has developed a healthy respect for the commercial impact of litigation.

David Goldstone MILAM
David is County Officer - Sports Provision at Wiltshire County Council. He is also the Chair of the Professional Practice Committee of the Institute of Leisure and Amenity Management.

Reg Harrison FILAM, NDH
Reg Harrison is a Chief Officer at the London Borough of Croydon. He has been a Council member of the Institute of Leisure and Amenity Management for many years. He was President of the Institute in 1995–96, the highest honour to be bestowed on an Institute member.

Stephen Howell BSc, MSc
Stephen is Leisure Manager at Darlington Borough Council. In 1996 he became Senior Leisure Services Assistant at Hambledon District Council.

D. Brian James MSc, CEng, MICE, MCIOB, MIHT
Brian is Director of Contract Services with Torfaen County Borough Council and prior to entering local government DSO management ten years ago, gained substantial experience of contract management in the private sector.

Ian Kwan BEEng

Ian holds his BEEng from the University of New South Wales and an MBA from the Australian Graduate School of Management. He has worked as a project engineer for Proctor and Gamble, and is now a member of a team from a prominent European business school who wish to establish a new business school in Shanghai, China.

Jim Lynch BA (Hons), DMS, MILAM

Jim is Principal Consultant at Strategic Leisure Consultancy.

Paul Martindill BA (Hons), MILAM

Paul is the Leisure Management Coordinator at the London Borough of Newham.

Duncan Moffatt BSc (Hons), MSc, ALI, MILAM, MIEEM

Duncan is a landscape management consultant specializing in all aspects of grounds maintenance CCT issues. He has 22 years' experience in landscape management and is principal of Landscape Management Consultants.

Geoff Nichols BA, MSc, MSc

Geoff has been a Lecturer and Researcher at the Leisure Management Unit of the University of Sheffield since 1990. Prior to this he has worked as a sports development officer, a researcher for a local authority leisure department, a university researcher and an outdoor pursuits instructor. As well as CCT his present research interests are; the use of sports schemes to divert young people from offending behaviour, sports development work and the role of the voluntary sector in the provision of sports opportunities.

Mark Poppy BA(Hons), MBA

Mark is a commercial manager with a thorough understanding of the local authority market. Those skills are backed by an MBA and a proactive approach to innovative management. He is the Business Manager at the Broxbourne Borough Council

Peter Ranson FHCIMA, FCSI, FBIFM
Peter is a Fellow of the Hotel Catering and International Management Association, Foodservice Consultants Society International and Fellow of the British Institute of Facilities Managers. He is Managing Consultant at Peran Consultancy.

Nick Reeves BA, MILAM, MIHort, DMS, MIM
Nick is Director of Policy and Development at the Institute of Leisure and Amenity Management. He has worked in most areas of the leisure profession at a strategic and operational level. His career to date has included periods employed in the public and private sectors.

Philip Sayers BSc (Hons), FILAM (Dip), MIM
Philip is Head of Leisure Client Services at Stevenage Borough Council, Hertfordshire. Philip has provided advice on competitive tendering issues throughout the British Isles by lectures and seminars for some ten years. He is an author of management books, also published by E & F N Spon. Of particular relevance is *Managing Sport and Leisure Facilities: a Guide to Competitive Tendering*. He is a regular contributor to monthly publications. He was an active member of two national working parties giving advice on CCT. He is currently the Chair of the Sport and Recreation Panel of the Institute of Leisure and Amenity Management (ILAM).

David Scott BA(Hons), DipLD, MRTPI, FLI, MILAM
David played a major role in the creation and management of the much acclaimed landscape of Warrington from 1972. From 1974 until 1987 he was the Chief Landscape Architect at the Warrington New Town Development Corporation. He then joined Gillespies, where he is now a partner.

Chris Youngs DMS, MILAM
Chris has worked for East Hampshire District Council since 1986, first as contractor (until 1990) and now client. Chris has worked in leisure management for nearly twenty years in three local authorities. He is now Leisure Services Manager at East Hampshire District Council.

The contract climate

Introduction

by Philip Sayers

Contracts are a bind. Contracts bind two parties together to achieve a common purpose. Once entered into, contracts continue for better or for worse, in sickness and in health, until their natural or unnatural conclusion.

Contracts are not just a bind. They are legally binding. A sufficient transgression by one party or the other can lead to justified legal action. After all, a contract made within the law of the land is bound by that law. The natural end point of a contract is invariably agreed at the beginning. In the case of marriage this is death.

The end of many contracts occurs after an agreed number of years, or on the completion of a building project. But the best-made plans of men and women often mean that contracts finish before their agreed length. Contracts can end in bitter acrimony between the two parties – a sad fact of life. Bankruptcy and broken promises are but two ways which lead to abrupt termination. All contracts need to be based on the possibility of failure. It limits the damage at the end.

CONTRACT MANAGEMENT

Contracts are like life itself. They both have their ups and downs. If married life, or a partnership, is taken as an example of a contract, every aspect of contract management can be easily seen:

- Ideas are formed.
- In a contract, the specifications are written.
- Possible partners are sought, tested and evaluated.
- Meeting and matching takes place.
- A marriage or partnership is created.
- A contract or agreement is made.
- There is a honeymoon period.

- Both parties keep to the contract or not.
- The contract terminates.

To be a success, all contracts have to be worked at – constantly. No one ever said that marriage was easy. There has to be give and take by both sides. The frailty of human beings is that we all see our own personal giving and not our own taking. Thus contracts end up in dispute. Divorce rates rise. Contract failures increase.

COMPULSORY CONTRACTS

There is some difficulty where contracts are imposed. Some arranged marriages work very well. Others do not. They especially do not where one party is less than willing. Well, that has been the reality in Britain

Fig. 1.1 All contracts have a honeymoon period

for more than a decade. Many of the examples contained in this book are of contracts formed following a tender process enforced by central government. They derive mostly from the British experience.

Tendering worldwide

However, towards the end of the 20th century, competitive tendering and privatization practices swept the world. Britain, Australia and New Zealand, for example, followed similar tracks. Countries in Africa, and other developing countries, have pursued similar policies. The requirement to seek value for money via competitive tenders is often imposed on developing countries by Western financial institutions.

Competitive tendering and contract management had always held sway in the United States. Yet even in the States there is an ever-increasing move to privatize services. In New York street cleansing was privatized. A security force has been used to supplement the Police Department. National and Federal governments imposed their will on to the service directorates.

A huge variety of public services are involved:

- management of leisure facilities;
- grass cutting and grounds maintenance;
- catering;
- refuse and garbage collection;
- health and welfare;
- accounting and legal services.

Competitive tendering is not an easy route to take. Anguish and emotion mix with fear and elation. Hard technical analysis needs to be balanced with fine financial acumen. The bright prospects of winning a contract contrast sharply with the black shock of a possible loss. Competition brings out the best and worst in us all.

Creating contractors

Sometimes, there are no existing contractors available. Or too few. Some specialist services, like management of swimming pools, have always been carried out by directly employed staff. In Britain there were no alternative contractors ready to tender. This led to all sorts of attempts to fill the gap.

Companies specializing in the management of swimming pools and leisure centres in particular have only really appeared after the introduction of legislation making competitive tendering compulsory.

Then many companies were formed from staff who had previously been employed by local authorities.

Quite obviously, there can easily be a conflict of interests between working for a local authority and then setting up your own company. Self-interest can be a powerful incentive. Handled well, it can help everyone. Handled badly, it can lead to dubious practices, if not corruption.

How did we arrive here? Well, history has an interesting habit of repeating itself.

A century of public service

by Philip Sayers

One hundred years ago, in the late 1800s, the new local authorities in Britain were getting into their stride. They employed contractors to carry out the necessary works of laying sewers and collecting refuse. However, it became evident that local authorities could sometimes carry out the work less expensively by directly employing the labour themselves .

The weekly periodical *The Municipal Journal* has been reporting on municipal affairs for over a hundred years. In one of its earliest editions, the *Journal* recorded an interesting example of thrift. This first case study is a very early example of the new local authorities seeking value for money in a maintenance contract. In this case, a private sector contractor was replaced by local authority employed staff.

Here is an edited extract of what the *Municipal Journal* had to say.

The Surveyor and Cleansing Department of Chelsea Vestry are to be congratulated on the satisfactory way they have displaced the existing contractor. When the Vestry found that they would have to pay a contractor 4 shillings per load for the removal of dust, they wisely decided to do the work directly. It has cost them 3 shillings 3 pence per load. This represents a saving of 8¼ pence, or about 20%.

On this count there is a clear saving of £700 a year. But the advantages do not end here. The contractors' loads were more numerous and smaller. That the work has been better done is evidenced by the fact that complaints have decreased by two-thirds.
(The Chelsea Vestry, 1893 – an extract from *The Municipal Journal*)

CONSTRUCTION WORKS

The *Municipal Journal* did not limit itself to reporting on maintenance contracts. In London boroughs in the early 1890s, for example, workmen were employed directly for construction work. On one occasion, this was after a previous contractor had been defaulted. The next case study relates to a new school building at Crossness:

July 6th 1893: The school house building is modest enough in appearance. Yet, it may become historic by the fact that it is the first erected by the County Council without a contractor. It was erected by the Council's workmen in the main drainage department. In this small undertaking costing £1,652, a saving of £536 has been secured.

The Council felt it incumbent to provide a schoolhouse for the children of the workmen engaged in constructing the new Crossness sewage station. This site of the southern sewer-outfall works lies more than two miles from the nearest Board School.

The lowest tender received was £2,300, or £500 above the estimate of the architect. In view of the high excess of the tenders above the estimate, the Council concluded to dispense with the contractor and carry out the work themselves. Mr. Blashill, the superintendent architect, prepared the plan, and applied himself to the work with considerable interest. The total cost turned out to be £1,652.

It is worth noting that the cost of supervision on the part of the council was not more than it would have been if a contractor had been employed to do the work.

Mr. John Burns has been telling a *Star* interviewer his opinion of the work. 'Critics may say that the Council scamped the work,' said Mr. Burns, 'but the facts are all the other way. We had to deal with an isolated site, far from railway stations, in a miserable marsh. We had under these circumstances to buy plant and to hire men and begin a new system.'

'And just see what has happened', he continued. 'We have completed a splendid job, using the best material and workmanship, and have saved a considerable sum for ratepayers. I am delighted to be able to report that the men working for us are shrewd enough to see that the London County Council offer practically permanent employment, and they recognise the necessity of putting in downright good work. At any rate, whatever may be their motive, we get splendidly honest return in the shape of labour from them.'

The 1900s

And so it continued into the next century.

Local authorities increasingly employed their own labour for a diversity of tasks. Of particular relevance to this book are the teams of gardeners employed to look after the parks and open spaces, and the staff employed at the local swimming pools and bath houses.

Contractors were still often employed for capital construction works. Directly employed staff were mainly used for on-going maintenance works. Local authorities were increasingly seen as good employers; a job with the council could last for life. But then there was more security in many other established industries as well. Working for one employer all your life was not uncommon.

The Edwardian era

For those who did not need to earn a wage, the first decade of the 1900s in Britain was a time when high society had a ball. The fun loving Prince of Wales finally became King Edward in the earliest part of the decade, and the upper crust waltzed and gavotted its way through the years. A distinct contrast to the dark final years of the last century, and of the Victorian era.

The mass of people, however, did need to earn a wage. Their employment may have been secure, but work continued unabated. They were there to work. High days and holidays alone provided entertainment and happiness. The established ways of a century were not be overturned by a new king.

A war, mind you, was different.

The Great War

From 1914 onwards, contracts of employment were dramatically changed. The Great War of 1914 to 1918 was the war to end all wars. Or so it was said. The high and mighty in the land no longer needed to drive the mass of people into heavy industrial work in hot machine shops. Instead, they drove them to their slaughter in mud and mayhem. Public service took on a new meaning.

Some historians argue that the war came about because some mad young man assassinated Archduke Francis Ferdinand. He was the heir to the throne of the mighty Austro-Hungarian Empire. The assassination took place in a little known town under Austrian rule called Sarajevo. The town sank back into insignificance for the rest of the First World War. It was only at the end of the twentieth century that Sarajevo hit the headlines once again. Christian versus Muslim. Serbs versus Croat. Bosnia, Yugoslavia, Sarajevo, all hit the headlines again.

But in the early part of the century, Sarajevo was known for the start of the Great War. The start of great change as well. As far as contracts of employment were concerned, these also changed drastically with the start of the First World War.

Liabilities were portrayed as assets. A huge public relations campaign swung into action. Posters throughout the country showed Lord Kitchener inviting YOU, to come to the help of the country. Volunteers gave up their sweat and toil in machine shops up and down the country. They willingly took the king's shilling, and joined the army. Those who didn't were to be conscripted later. Conscription was a very different sort of contract. The end result was the same. Conditions of employment did not enter the equation.

The Great Depression

As war led to conscription, so economic depression led to unemployment. Perhaps any contract of employment is better than no contract of employment. But then again, perhaps not. The 1920s were, in their way, as traumatic as the previous decade. Homes for Heroes returning from the war was the dogma of the day. Yet it never really happened. In the 1920s there were neither homes nor jobs.

The environment for employment conditions is set by the politics and economics of the time. So it was with the Depression. During the 1920s the government of the day decided that it was time once more for Britain to be Great. The Chancellor of the Exchequer, a Mr Winston Churchill, decreed that the currency of the country was to be tied to the value of gold. Unfortunately, the pound sterling was linked to the Gold Standard at a rate which was far too high. Churchill was to say years later that it was the worst advice he had ever accepted.

Depression, unemployment, hunger marches all followed. For those who were employed, wages were meagre.

ECONOMIC STIMULATION

Eventually, the 1930s fared somewhat better. A brilliant economist, John Maynard Keynes, had argued that unemployment could be cured by the government operating an unbalanced budget; it should borrow in order to ensure adequate employment.

The government did take heed to a certain extent. Substantial public works were undertaken at the time. Employment was created by, for example, a major road building programme. The mighty port of Liverpool was connected to its hinterland counterpart Manchester, by a new dual carriageway. The road in the 1930s was compared to the already existing mighty ship canal. It was one long, straight road, an incredible example of highway engineering for the time. The private sector played its part too. Economic growth was financed from savings; homes and houses were built.

Meanwhile, on the international front, events were taking on an all too familiar turn for the worse. Conditions imposed on Germany at the end of the First World War proved too onerous. Penalties and reparations are no way to manage affairs in the long term.

Every action has an equal and opposite reaction.This is a simple law of physics and humanities. Unfortunately this simple law is relearnt the hard way every generation. And relearnt for every contract as well, for that matter.

The Second World War

The build up to the Second World War at least led to full employment. Working women no longer gave up their jobs on getting married. They were needed in the munitions factories. Public service took on its familiar nature again. Management was effortless. No one dared not obey. The very existence of the country was at stake. Motivation was taken for granted. The war had to be won at all costs. Pay was determined and not open for negotiation. There was a form of incentive pay, however. A packet of cigarettes a day was granted to those who chose to join the army Airborne Division and be dropped behind enemy lines. Amazing what we let ourselves in for, when we have limited understanding.

The 1940s were in two halves: half war, half the birth of the welfare state.The new Labour government was determined to ensure that there was no return to the redundant years of the 1930s. With Keynesian economic policies in place, and new social policies being promoted, the end of the world war this time did see a change for the better in the lives of ordinary people.

The 1950s

The late 1940s and 50s saw Europe repairing the ravages of war. Britain was busy at work rebuilding its shattered infrastructure and debt-ridden economy. It took a decade just to get rid of all the bombed and blasted buildings. The now less than radical theories of John Maynard Keynes were taking effect. Full employment brought prosperity from austerity. Soon there was a labour shortage. Britain had to encourage people from overseas countries, especially the colonies, to work in the mother country. So paternalistic, so imperialist. Even on a national scale, management styles had changed so little.

Management methods of the time were built on military discipline. The military may have much to teach everyone about logistics, critical path analysis, and supply lines, but as regards the management of people, forget it. The military have effortless authority. What is decided will be done.

Not that a war weary population cared. To do, and not to need to think, was fine for most. However, as the 1950s advanced, a younger generation that had not been traumatized by war became more dominant. The stage was set for a huge social upheaval.

The 1960s

The 1960s was a much vaunted decade. People changed. Stable societies who knew their place in the world moved to become dynamic, mobile populations. People were ready, and able, to do the things they wanted to. No longer would they accept being told what to do.

Fig. 1.2   In the 1960s the social order was changed for ever

Two pictures perhaps sum up that decade. First, the beauty of flower power people, open air concerts and psychedelic clothes. This reality for many contrasted starkly with the horrors of the Vietnam War. Yet both were characterized by people, individually and collectively, doing their own thing; or at least trying to. It was the decade of the individual, at last.

EMPLOYEE VERSUS EMPLOYER

The 1960s saw a distinct shift in employer and employee relationships. The employee was no longer satisfied with job security. With high employment, employees could move from job to job without fear of being without a job later on. Freedom found a new reality. Individual freedom gave way to collective freedom. Rigid management could not deal with forceful demands of employees.

In Britain in the 1970s the population as a whole took power into their own hands. Industrial strife became endemic. High employment led to greater employee strength. There were demands for ever-higher increases in wages. Interest rates soared and so did wages, in an ever upward spiral. Local authority workers at last saw an opportunity to have their wages increased significantly. They went on strike as never before. The fire brigade, the refuse collectors and even the gardeners in the parks all went on strike at one time or another. All demanded wage rises to balance the ever-increasing levels of inflation. This was a classic model of spiralling inflation. Increased inflation led to increased wages, which in turn led to yet more inflation.

The coal miners' strike

Management tried to manage. Workers had other ideas. Coal miners in particular flexed their industrial muscles to dramatic effect. They too went on strike. Coal supplies at power stations diminished rapidly. Electricity could not be produced and the atmosphere was tense; there was insufficient electricity to go round. To conserve supplies, planned reductions of electricity were made around the country. A three-day working week was imposed. Manufacturing production dropped, but so did electricity consumption.

Coincidentally, oil prices doubled and then tripled. This only added to the political woe. The old petrol coupon books of wartime were re-issued, nearly 30 years after the end of the war. The political humiliation of this industrial strife laid the foundations of a greater political resolve which was to find expression a decade later. Every action has an equal and opposite reaction.

The 1980s

On the verge of the 1980s a new Conservative administration was voted into government. A very different agenda was set. A first priority was to stockpile massive piles of coal at power stations to ensure that there was no return to a three-day working week. In the early to mid-1980s the most powerful and determined strike in decades failed to budge the government. The coal miners had taken on the government once too often. This time they lost. Management had reasserted the right to manage.

This was a government set on the destruction of the power held by large collective workforces. Ever greater freedom was allowed to the individual entrepreneur working in a free market environment. There was a new commercial edge as never before. Those who were successful were very successful.

Stability of employment gave way to instability. High levels of unemployment went ever upward. Yet unemployment moderated claims for pay rises. The fear of redundancy in a climate of high unemployment eventually becomes a powerful tool of management by government. Those who failed to appreciate the consequences of redundancy soon had time to ponder their plight. Months of unemployment give time in abundance. It was within this harsh environment that compulsory competitive tendering – CCT for short – was introduced.

COMPULSORY COMPETITIVE TENDERING

Quite simply, from the early 1980s, a local authority was not allowed to employ staff to carry out certain activities (for example, highway maintenance, grounds maintenance, refuse collection) unless the authority had sought tenders for the work. In other words, each local authority could then demonstrate that they were employing the cheapest labour to carry out the work. Almost one hundred years after that *Municipal Journal* article, the principle of lowest cost is still a key concern.

Rules and regulations tie the whole CCT process together. This is the compulsory element. Local authorities have no choice. It is the law.

To seek competitive tenders demanded a whole panoply of documentation. This can be summarized:

- crystallize the key essentials of the service, to suit the local authority;
- write specifications to give accurate expression to these essentials;
- advertise for contractors;
- assess the competence of contractors replying to the advert;
- seek tenders from at least three private sector contractors, if available;
- arrange tender opening and the comparison of quality and price;
- commission the contract.

Constant communication is then necessary to ensure the smooth running of the contract.

Simple. Or at least simple when written down. The tales told in this book, however, tell a different story. In Britain, all contracts are operated mainly by the same rules and regulations. But they are also operated by very different people, working in very different environments. It is the interplay of human relations which is as interesting and informative as the actual straight-forward contract process itself. No one can ever legislate for human behaviour.

A contract

To easily understand CCT, let us return to the example of life itself. Life is a good example of a contract. It has a clear beginning and a definite end. Married life, or a partnership, is a contract. Most of us have experience of married life, directly or indirectly. Even as children, we observe the good and bad in married lives around us. The whole array of contract management is there for us to see, in life and marriage.

The contract	*Life*
Conceptualization of the contract	Conception
Preparing a specification	The birth
Bidding for a tender	Education
Evaluation of tenders	Examination
Awarding the contract	The marriage
Performance measurement	Well, that's somewhat personal
Crisis	Pull together, or pull apart
Horror stories	The agony before separation
Arbitration	Counselling
Contract termination	Divorce
Review, and start again	Avoid the previous pitfalls, if you can

Of course many contracts flow from beginning to end without major mishap. Others, again and again, split apart. This book provides examples of both. The analogy with life, partnerships, and married life is evident through every contract. It gives us all an easy reference point.

To give an easy reference point for this book, the book concentrates on two contract areas:

- grounds maintenance;
- leisure management.

These are two diverse subject areas which provide a good base from which to demonstrate clearly the actual operation of all contracts. Although the principles remain the same, a maintenance contract does differ markedly from a management contract.

It is easier to be exact with a maintenance contract. Exact measurements can be given. Exact requirements of work to be undertaken can be stated, and when, where and how. Assessment is easier. A job has either been undertaken or not. For example if grass is to be cut 26 times per year, performance can be measured and monitored.

A management contract is different. Some aspects of a management contract lend themselves to measurement, e.g. the warmth of the swimming pool water. The temperature of the pool water can, and should, be regulated to an exact degree. However, it is more difficult to assess the satisfaction of the swimmer.

The grass is cut or not cut. It is an exact science. Rarely however, is the swimmer 100% satisfied or dissatisfied. So grounds maintenance and leisure management provide two good and diverse areas in which to demonstrate the contract process. The book is principally about the contract process. Technical detail relating to horticulture and leisure has been kept to a minimum. This will allow the key principles to be seen, and thus be of value to everyone with an interest in competitive tenders and contract management.

To start the first part of this book, we have an overview of the whole CCT process provided by Geoff Nichols of the Leisure Management Unit of the University of Sheffield.

Introducing CCT – the hopes and fears

by Geoff Nichols

Most local authorities did not welcome the legislation that obliged them to competitively tender the management of their leisure facilities. However, the process of CCT did offer positive opportunities.

HOPES

Local authority provision of leisure opportunities has developed since authorities were first permitted to provide washhouses and libraries in the last century. Philanthropists had donated parks and buildings many of which are still in use today, with their associated costs of maintenance. The present day pattern of subsidy associated with this historical legacy of provision[1] is hard to justify.

The clarification of objectives ...

There is a different pattern of subsidy for different facilities. In addition, the recipients of this subsidy are largely the middle class. It is they who comprise the majority of users of public leisure facilities. This led to the criticism made by the Audit Commission that prior to CCT many local authorities appeared to be confused and unclear about what their role should be in this area.[2] The service could not be effective in achieving its objectives because it did not know what they were. Clarification of objectives was one hoped for improvement from introducing CCT.

Clarification of objectives and how they would be achieved required planning at the strategic level. One outcome of this improved planning may be the more precise targeting of subsidies. Perhaps the demands of CCT would stimulate this and leisure services could be part of a new strategic vision for the public sector.[3]

... improved information, and ...

Planning in local authorities has also been criticized as being based on inadequate information. CCT could provide the catalyst for improved information systems to be developed. In preparing its bid, the direct service organization (DSO) needed to have costs centred so that costs could be related to each facility and individual sessions. In operating the contract there needed to be a much tighter control and awareness of costs than before. This alone could lead to better planning.

For its part the client needed a more detailed picture of who was using the facilities and levels of user satisfaction. Thus, to write a good initial specification, the client officer would need to know:

- patterns of use;
- customer satisfaction.

This information would also be required in monitoring the contract. Information about the management of the facilities would also need to be collected to write the contract specification. Thus, the process of preparing for CCT and operating under it should automatically produce more information that could be used for planning.

... improved efficiency

The Audit Commission, and central government, thought that local government services were often not provided as cheaply as they could have been by the private sector. By exposing the provision of local government services to market forces it was believed that savings could be made. This fitted in with the general strategy of central government to reduce public expenditure and an ideological commitment to the free market as the most effective means of allocating resources.

The major element of facility running costs is staff. It could be argued that the conditions of service of many local authority facility staff were anachronistic. They included enhanced payments for weekend shifts and evening work that were out of line with the modern leisure industry. Other leisure providers in the private sector recognized that, by the nature of their business, they had to work when other people did not.

Customer needs

The local authority still controlled prices and programming. However, it was likely that the facility manager would always have a degree of discretion to respond to changes in the market. By putting the DSO manager into a position similar to a private sector manager, more incentive might be provided to react quickly to new demands.

This is particularly relevant in the leisure industry, which is more susceptible to fads and fashion than some others. Perhaps greater flexibility to exploit market opportunities might enable running costs to be reduced while still targeting a subsidized service at those in greatest need.

Improved quality

You have to persuade people to come through the leisure centre door. Usually they have to pay to do so as well. You do not have to persuade people that they need their dustbins emptied. Therefore the quality of a leisure service, as perceived by the user, is more important. By making DSO managers more aware of their income, and the relation of this income to the number of people who use the facility, CCT could stimulate a desire to provide a higher quality of service.

FEARS

Many of the apprehensions associated with the introduction of CCT were the converse of the hopes.

Privatization

Some feared that CCT meant privatization. This depended on what they understood by privatization. Generally this fear was based on a misconception that the private sector would now be responsible for the provision of leisure opportunities. Clearly this is not the case. The facilities are still owned by the authority, which has the right to specify prices and programming.

While the service was not being privatized, there was a fear that it would be very difficult for client officers to specify a contract in a way that would ensure that the social objectives of the service were achieved. Continuing the parallel with dustbins, it is easier to write a contract that will result in a dustbin being emptied once a week, than it is to write one that specifies the management of a complex facility with multiple objectives.

Conflicting objectives

The structure of CCT set up a conflict of objectives between the client and the contractor. There was a fear that CCT could have resulted in a more market led service, but at the expense of social objectives. The client wants to ensure that a service is provided that meets certain objectives that may not be achieved in the free market.

The contractor is basically concerned with the relationship between income and expenditure. If they were able to, contractors would act to increase their income and reduce expenditure. This might involve setting up new leisure activities with the primary aim of increasing revenue and diverting resources away from sessions directed towards low income groups.

Many authorities reacted to this situation by writing a very detailed contract. But could this ensure that social objectives were achieved? Could this cope with the inherent flexibility needed in operating the service? Associated with these concerns was the fear that the service would neglect the needs of present non-users. These would include potential participants in leisure who might need encouragement to take up the opportunities, often through sports development programmes.

It would also neglect the opinions of local citizens who had a right to influence the pattern of provision and subsidy but who might not necessarily wish to use the facilities themselves. The fear was that the right to influence local decisions as a citizen, based on the right to vote, would be replaced by the right to influence decisions as a consumer or customer, on the basis of the amount of money spent.

This could lead to a move:

- away from provision led by public policy;
- towards provision based on market forces.

And if local authorities were going to act in the same way as a commercial provider, what was the purpose of their existence? Yet the emphasis on market forces as the determinants of provision was consistent with the ideological stance of central government and the language used in the Audit Commission publications.

Reduced pay and redundancy

To compete with private sector tenders, it was feared that DSOs would have to cut staffing costs. This would be achieved either by redundancies or by a deterioration in conditions of service. Staffing structures would be flattened, with fewer opportunities for internal promotion. More staff would be employed on a casual or part-time basis. There would be greater job insecurity and therefore lower morale.

This challenge to working conditions and jobs was a major fear of some traditional left-wing authorities which felt a social responsibility to provide good quality employment and were major employers in their areas. If their DSO was forced to compete with a private tender on level terms they might have to abandon this objective.

Increased costs

The deployment of officers to prepare for and manage CCT would involve extra costs. There was no evidence from previously contracted services that these costs would be offset by gains arising from competition.[4] Writing the contract specification required the skills of a senior officer. The subsequent monitoring, if it was to be done properly, required an officer with knowledge of facility management.

Deteriorating relations

The client–contractor split within departments led to animosity and misunderstanding. This was especially so where the DSO suddenly felt much greater job insecurity and was forced to make changes to conditions of employment. While a major positive consequence of CCT could be improved information systems, animosity between client and contractor could actually inhibit the flow of that information. Clearly, within the same department, the structure of CCT meant that the different sides had different objectives. Reconciling these presented a major personnel challenge.

Thus before CCT there was much speculation on the positive and negative outcomes of the process. Much of this was fuelled by prejudice, fear and suspicion. However, the compulsory element of CCT was also part of a conflict between central and local government reflecting different political ideologies and attempts to limit public sector expenditure. How did it work out and what are the lessons for subsequent tendering?

NOTES

1. Sayers, P. (1991) *Managing Sport and Leisure Facilities: A Guide to Competitive Tendering*, E & F N Spon, London.
2. Audit Commission (1990) *Local Authority Support for Sport*, HMSO, London.
3. Benington, J. and White, J. (1988) *The Future of Leisure Services*, Longman, Harlow, Chapter 10.
4. Walsh, K. (1991) *Competitive Tendering for Local Authority Services*, HMSO, London.

Chapter 1: summary

by Philip Sayers

A study of relevant events from the past can help all of us face the future. There is no reason to repeat the mistakes of a bygone era. Unfortunately, most of us have to learn the hard way, by harsh experience of life itself. The following summary is offered as an easier route:

- Contracts are legally binding.
- They have an inception and an end.
- Just like marriage.
- Often what is planned does not materialize.
- Either expectations were too high at the outset; or there was insufficient give and take during the contract.
- Partnerships can be sweet or volatile.
- Compulsion can just add to the agony.
- Competitive tenders give clear evidence of value for money.
- The best deal is on the table.
- Many countries, and international institutions, demand evidence of competitive tendering, to establish that least cost has/will be achieved.
- Human nature intervenes in all contracts.
- One hundred years ago, direct employed staff could sometimes carry out work more cheaply than contractors.
- The direct employment of staff became a feature of all local authorities.
- Up to 1914, workers knew their station in life.
- After the war, greater equality was demanded.
- The state of the general national economy greatly affects terms and condition of employment.
- Unemployment is a hard but effective tool of economic management.
- Military style management gave way to people management.
- In the UK in the 1970s, strikes led to a three-day working week.
- Every action has an equal and opposite reaction.
- The government of the 1980s ensured that a three-day working week could not, would not, reoccur.
- Compulsory competitive tendering for local authorities also became standard throughout the 1980s and 1990s.
- CCT brought real hopes and fears.
- A clarity of objectives and purpose was essential.

- For the client, as the purchaser, that means being quite clear about what is wanted.
- For the contractor, as the provider, this means delivering what is wanted and still making a profit.

This chapter provides a recent historical context from which to read the rest of the book. Look out for history repeating itself.

A first time tender

Introduction

by Philip Sayers

Competitive tendering means different things to different people. At the start of a competitive tendering process, a person is often buoyant and keen. It is often a far different person who emerges some years later. The vicissitudes of competition, conflict and concentration take their toll. At the same time, the actual tendering process itself gets refined. Lessons are learnt from mistakes made.

In Britain, there are a mass of government rules and regulations to comply with, in relation to compulsory competitive tendering. This is because the tendering process is compulsory. As we saw in the last chapter, the government wanted to be seen to be taking a tough line. Equally important, all contracts need a mass of documents (plans, specifications, conditions) to be produced to be able to seek competitive tenders. The actual range of documents is detailed in Appendix B.

In addition, all contracts and tender processes are governed by rules and codes of tendering conduct. Often these are written down, sometimes they are not. However, the intention of a tender process is always the same: to obtain a like for like comparison for a clearly stated amount of work. There are two key requirements for fair tendering:

- the client has to produce documents with exact specifications and quantities;
- the tenderers have to price the documents, without colluding with other tenderers.

So long as these requirements are provided for, then the tendering process can commence. Everything will be quite proper. If a code of conduct for the tendering process is not written down, then there will be the opportunity for misinterpretation. Worse, there will be the opportunity for misrepresentation. This is a particular difficulty with public contracts, where newspapers are looking for newsworthy stories to make headlines. Over the years in Britain, ever tighter written rules and regulations have been introduced. But at the start of CCT, the rules had to be compiled as experience dictated.

The case study in this chapter provides a fascinating account of competitive tendering in its infancy. At the time the tender process was fair, but not yet encumbered with masses of rules.

The case study is devoted to the introduction of competitive tendering to a grass cutting (slashing) contract in Bendigo, in the State of Victoria, Australia. Here, the concept of competitive contracts was as fresh as the grass to the cut. The rules of competition were as yet unwritten. Indeed, the process of this particular competition led to key rules and regulations being crystallized.

Most of us in life, have little opportunity to produce ethical guidelines. Ethics are invariably handed down from previous generations. Yet in Bendigo the participants in the competitive process were establishing ethical behaviour as they went about their first contract. They were establishing ethics for generations to come.

In this part of the chapter, Ian Kwan with Simon Domberger provide a fascinating account of contracting grounds maintenance in the City of Bendigo.

A tender business

by Ian Kwan with Simon Domberger

In August 1993 the Victorian Minister for Local Government, Roger Hallam, initiated the introduction of compulsory competitive tendering (CCT).

He established an advisory committee comprising members of local government who had extensive knowledge of CCT. Its task was to pool together previous research, to encourage submissions from councils throughout the state, and to ensure a full discussion of the issues relating to the introduction of CCT.

This resulted in the issue of an interim report on CCT to all councils for further comment. The final report was submitted to the minister late in 1993. From October 1994, new legislation made competitive tendering compulsory for up to 50% of local government expenditure within a period of three years.

THE CITY OF BENDIGO

Bendigo, Victoria's third-largest provincial city, is 150 kilometres northwest of Melbourne. It was established in 1855 and is the state's second oldest city. The 1850s gold rush was undoubtedly the city's most significant period, leaving in its wake many historic buildings and landmarks which speak of the prosperity and pioneering spirit of those times. When mining declined in the 1950s, Bendigo maintained its economy through the growth of manufacturing, unlike many old gold mining centres which became virtual ghost towns. Today, the city of Bendigo has an electoral population of over 31000, an annual budget of almost A$33 million, and employs the equivalent of 300 full-time staff.

The ordinary ratepayer of the City of Gold and Dragons would have first heard of competitive tendering when he or she saw the front page story of the *Bendigo Advertiser* on 8 November 1993. The headline read 'Councillors reject own work tender'. This was followed the next day with 'Tenderer slams unfair council choice'. Such headlines indicated a shaky start to competitive tendering for the Bendigo City Council.

True to its pioneering heritage, Bendigo is at the forefront of competitive tendering within local government, being a significant contributor to the CCT interim reports. CCT has been seen by management as a tool for:

- introducing accountability in performance;
- providing evaluation against detailed specifications;
- increasing efficiency;
- reducing costs.

However, council employees have not been as optimistic. They see CCT as a direct threat to their jobs and as an instrument for eroding working conditions.

According to the council's executive manager for recreation, 'It is a tool that I can use to ensure the staff can become more competitive, more productive. From a staff point of view, they're very insecure, jobs are more at risk. If they don't become competitive then their positions will be in jeopardy.'

This case study examines the first contract to be implemented by the Bendigo City Council. It was for the slashing of grass. It also examines how the stage has been set for letting small contracts in the future, which will inevitably be put to tender in the wake of the forthcoming legislation.The case highlights a number of fundamental points which will have to be addressed to avoid problems similar to those encountered in Bendigo.

Change comes to the City of Bendigo

Predictably, the changes that preceded the contracting process resulted in considerable anxiety within Bendigo City Council. The first wave of changes began in 1993 as a result of recommendations by a consultant that the council be restructured from the top down. The second wave saw the introduction of total quality service. This initiated substantial changes to internal work processes.

The third wave involved enterprise bargaining negotiations over working conditions with individual employees. This gave scope to go outside existing pay award conditions. The fourth wave began with the introduction of CT, which will become compulsory after the passage of legislation. The fifth wave of change, which council employees hope is final, is the amalgamation of five neighbouring councils around Bendigo to form the Greater City of Bendigo.

These changes have significantly affected the morale and motivation of council staff and have bred insecurity about their future employment. With the prospect of traditional council work being lost to external contractors, CCT has been seen as a direct threat to council jobs. The council has reassured its staff that no jobs will be lost, but employees remain unconvinced by assurances of redeployment to 'other positions' within the council for an indefinite period. A well-respected senior labourer, the parks section foreman, was very apprehensive about the prospects for council labourers, given that CCT is here to stay. The executive manager for recreation observed: 'So if he's apprehensive, then so is everyone else.'

Bendigo City Council has taken a serious and progressive attitude toward CCT by appointing a manager for CT who reports directly to the council's Chief Executive Officer (the CEO). His department remains separate and independent of the other six departments. The job of the CT manager involves developing and implementing strategies concerned with the introduction of CT for works and services provided by the council, for administering, managing and representing the interests of the council in future contracts, and for other engineering-related management support work.

Moving to competitive tendering

Grass slashing in reserves and parklands in and around the city has traditionally been a council service offered to its ratepayers. The work was done in an *ad hoc* fashion, primarily driven by ratepayer complaints and a schedule which lay in the hands of the operator. This job was formerly undertaken by one council employee, who early in 1993 left the organization after 10 years' service. It was decided not to replace this position with another council employee as the job was identified as a good opportunity to initiate the process of CT.

This service was seen to be a good test case because no job would be lost regardless of the outcome. For the first time work traditionally done in-house was to be exposed to competition. This required the production of detailed specifications on which tenderers were to base their bids.

THE TENDERING PROCESS

The parks section of the council falls under the umbrella of the recreation department. The executive manager for recreation, like the CT manager, reports directly to the council's CEO.

Data collection

The CT manager in conjunction with the parks manager initiated a data collection programme to provide information for the technical specifications required for the tenders. The parks manager commissioned two of his associates, the works officer and his subordinate, the foreman of reserves maintenance, to do some preliminary work to determine the actual sites where the previous work had been undertaken. This was necessary because specifications for grass slashing had never been documented before. No one except the previous operator had ever known where all the sites were. Eventually 125 sites were identified.

Declaration of interest

This preliminary data collection stage occurred during February and March of 1993. No further work was done on the tender specifications for some months. When the work resumed, the works officer and foreman prepared some estimates of how long slashing at these sites would take. Shortly afterwards the works officer indicated to the parks manager that a relative of his was interested in submitting a tender. At this point the CT manager was informed and the works officer was removed from the data collection programme. The major part of the data collection programme was completed by the foreman and another member of the parks section, the senior parks officer. These data were relayed to the CT manager.

Tenders sought

On 7 October of the same year, the CT manager finalized the specifications for the tender process. On 9 and 16 October, the council advertised in the local newspaper calling for tenders for 'the slashing of grass at numerous locations within the City'.

On 18 October a pre-tender meeting was held to discuss the specifications and to clarify any problems prospective tenderers might have. Although the meeting was not compulsory, it was stated that 'prospective tenderers are strongly encouraged to attend'. Some changes were made and documented, and a copy was sent to all those who attended the meeting and also to all interested parties who could not attend. At the meeting it was publicly announced that the City of Bendigo itself was going to submit an in-house tender.

The tendering period closed promptly at 4 pm on 21 October and the council procedures for the opening of tenders were strictly adhered to and documented. Seven tenders in total were received and opened at 4.20 pm by a presiding council member in the presence of the CT manager and parks manager.

Division of responsibilities

The City of Bendigo itself had decided to submit an in-house tender as it was the traditional owner-operator of this service and had the equipment to do the job. The team leader was the executive manager for recreation. The parks manager, however, had no involvement in the in-house or any other bid, given his own involvement in setting the tender specifications and subsequent assessment of tenders.

THE SELECTION PROCESS

After submission, the tenders were assessed by the CT manager and the parks manager. A report prepared by the CT manager summarized their assessment. It was contained in the council's ordinary meeting report dated 8 November, the same day that the council decided to award the contract to an external contractor. Table 2.1 is the summary provided in the report.

Table 2.1 Report summary of tenders (Australian$)

Tenderer	Section A site slash	Section B site slash	Section C site trim	Estimated total annual expenditure
Contractor 1	2 142.00	4 660.00	–	47 238.00
Contractor 2	2 144.00	6 896.00	2 162.50	69 322.00
Contractor 3	2 796.50	8 389.50	1 735.00	82 445.50
City of Bendigo	3 001.81	8 089.16	2 142.18	84 119.97
Contractor 4	3 051.00	9 328.50	2 409.75	93 069.00
Contractor 5	3 037.00	10 575.00	1 800.00	97 983.00
Contractor 6	7 420.00	25 138.40	12 040.00	265 768.00
Average of conform-ing tenders (2 to 5)	2 806.06	8 655.63	2 049.88	85 387.89

Note that the average included only five bids because it was found that the bids submitted by contractors 1 and 6 were based on an under-estimate and an over-estimate of the work involved. Consequently they came in too low and too high respectively when compared with the detailed cost analysis made by the CT manager prior to the call for tenders.

For the five acceptable tenders, the CT manager made what he thought were fair and factual assessments of the tenders and finished with a recommendation that the City of Bendigo's in-house bid be awarded the contract. However, on 8 November the council met and decided not to adopt this recommendation. Instead it awarded the contract to an operator by the name of L & P Grass Maintenance (contractor 2).

Sudden press interest

Clouds of controversy began to gather over the council's decision. The following day the *Bendigo Advertiser* published a front page story covering the awarding of the contract under the headline 'Councillors reject own work tender'. The gist of the story was that Bendigo City Council had rejected its own tender in favour of one from a private business, L & P Grass Maintenance, which was operated by a city council employee, the parks works officer.

The tender was A$14 000 lower than any of the others considered by the council. However, the works officer had carried out the initial tasks of identifying the scope of works to be included in the grass slashing contract and was also involved in preliminary costing for the project. On completion of this analysis, the officer had indicated that a relative of his was interested in submitting a tender for the work. One councillor was concerned that it would appear that this business had a 'particular advantage'.

The following day, in another article in the *Bendigo Advertiser*, one of the failed tenderer's described the council's newly adopted competitive tendering process as 'rough'. If we had access to that sort of inside information then maybe things would have been different for us, he said.

The facts behind the stories were as follows. When the tender submitted by L & P Grass Maintenance was initially assessed, it was discovered that the principals of this bid were the works officer and his wife. The works officer did not attend the pre-tender meeting personally. However L & P was represented at this meeting by a relative of the works officer, a fact of which no one present was aware.

L & P Grass Maintenance submitted a tender two days after the pre-tender meeting signed by the relative who had attended. The works officer had given no indication to any one among his supervisors or associates prior to the close of tenders that he was going to submit a tender. During the initial tender assessment stages the principals of L & P's bid were identified, but the CT manager was advised by the CEO to continue the assessment process. The works officer had indicated to the parks and CT managers that he would resign from the council if he was awarded the contract. He did so on 8 November after hearing of the council's favourable decision.

INSIDER ADVANTAGE?

The works officer had bought a tractor three days before winning the contract. However, the newspaper did not report that the works officer was also involved with grass slashing for a neighbouring shire as a private contractor. He had won this contract about a month before winning the Bendigo contract and had ordered a new tractor and slasher to do the job. These arrived before the closing date of tenders for the Bendigo contract and were inspected by the CT manager. Following Bendigo Council's decision, the works officer ordered a second tractor and slasher specifically for his new contract.

The media coverage focused on the issue of whether L & P Grass Maintenance had an 'insider advantage' over the other tenderers because of the works officer's involvement in the preliminary data collection programme. The media's source of information was the ordinary meeting report. This report, prepared by the CT manager, made an assessment of all the tenders, which stated for L & P Grass Maintenance that:

> [The works officer] carried out the initial task, of identifying the scope of works to be included in this contract and was also involved in the preliminary costing for the program. On completion of the analysis work, he indicated that a relative of his was interested in submitting a tender for the work. At this point all direct involvement of [the works officer] ceased. He did not acknowledge until the tenders were opened and assessed that he had submitted a tender personally.

It was assumed to be common knowledge that parks personnel would help to identify the scope of work prior to tendering, even though some were closely involved in the City of Bendigo's in-house bid. 'We first had to find out what were the sites', the CT manager said. 'The works officer did his consultation with the foreman and came up with the list. We did this early on and didn't get back to it for some months. The works officer told me about his relative as we started getting back into it.'

The CT manager and the parks manager both confirmed that the data collection programme was completed by the senior parks officer and the parks section foreman.

The works officer was initially hesitant in providing a justification for not disclosing his interest in tendering. At first, his reason was that his relative was originally going to submit a bid but pulled out after doing so. Later on, he admitted that if he had publicly revealed his intention to submit a tender then he would have been considered disloyal and a bad example to his colleagues and associates. In describing his apprehension, he said on the day he resigned that he deliberately did not go back to the depot where he worked because he was afraid of the criti-

Fig. 2.1 The tender made the headlines. More was to follow

cal reaction he thought he would receive from his associates. He thought they would accuse him of 'bailing out' or 'jumping ship'.

The executive manager for recreation confirmed that this could certainly have been the case. He said the works officer was a very well-respected staff member whom his associates trusted and, considering the widespread suspicion about CCT, if someone like the works officer openly made known that he was tendering for traditional council work then it would be seen as disloyal.

Nevertheless, all the tenderers appeared to be generally satisfied with the whole process. The executive manager for recreation who represented the in-house bid said 'from an outside tendering point of view, the process was pretty good'. In reference to the notification of changes to specification after the pre-tender meeting, he added that he 'thought this was more than fair'. Another external tenderer made similar comments praising the well thought out and well-executed technical specification.

THE RECOMMENDATION

The CT manager said that his recommendation to the council was based on ethical grounds. He was strongly influenced by the fact that it wasn't until after the close of tenders that it was realized the works officer was involved directly with the L & P Grass Maintenance tender. The CT manager and two other tendering parties all felt that the works officer should have made his personal interests publicly known at the pre-tender meeting, as the City of Bendigo had done. By not doing so the officer raised doubts over the integrity of his own bid as well as of the CT process itself.

'I was concerned for the public perception of the process', the CT manager observed. 'A lot of people run with perception rather than fact. In my mind it would be received by the press in the way that it was. If I had recommended [L & P Grass Maintenance] then it would be perceived that something untoward had happened.'

Open selection criteria

There was general agreement among the tenderers that the technical specifications were the best that they had seen, and were indicative of the quality of service, performance and professionalism to be expected of contractors then and in the future. The tender documentation included a statement of selection criteria against which tenderers would be assessed. These criteria were also verbally communicated to the prospective tenderers at the pre-tender meeting. It was up to the CT manager to apply them in the selection process.

The CT manager argued that for a small contract such as this one, a fully documented selection process was not necessary. He was of the opinion that only contracts valued in the next order of magnitude, or greater, required a team of people to assess the tenders. 'Perhaps I acted a bit beyond my duties by bringing that [ethical issue] up', he admitted, 'but the council certainly said we accept your recommendation, but we can't see where he has done anything wrong. That's true, theoretically he hasn't.'

He conceded that the works officer had no advantage over the in-house bid or any of the other tenderers. In fact all of the tenderers interviewed agreed that L & P Grass Maintenance was no better off than they were.

Best value

L & P Grass Maintenance's bid was the lowest of all the acceptable bids. Their bid was 18.8% below the average, the equivalent of two months of extra service. The monetary difference between L & P's and the City's bids was about A$14 000. In the ordinary meeting report it was stated in regard to L & P Grass Maintenance, 'the price submitted is certainly on the low side of the average price, which indicates that the tenderer will have to run a very lean operation.'

TENDER ANALYSIS

This was determined from a cost analysis carried out by the CT manager, which included everything – a new tractor, a slasher, blades, labour, fuel, supplies, maintenance, insurance, etc. The CT manager said L & P could fulfil its commitment for the price quoted but would have to watch its costs closely.

Although he felt that the council was not exposing itself to any unnecessary risk, he could not really say it was a wise business decision considering that L & P Grass Maintenance was a new business with no proven track record. 'From my cost analysis I could envisage he could do it for that price. That's not to say it was a wise business decision for L & P', the CT manager said.

Despite some risk, there were a number of other options available to the council if the contract had to be terminated. 'I was also confident', the CT manager explained, 'that if he did get himself into trouble, there are enough qualified contractors that I could pick up the phone and have the contract up and running for next month.'

An external tenderer concurred with the CT manager's assessment of L & P's low tender price. He calculated if he took on the contract at the price quoted, he would have to run almost at cost with little allowances for breakdowns, broken slashing blades, etc. 'He'll need to be working with his fingers crossed the whole time, hoping nothing goes wrong.' He was concerned that L & P's contract was not financially viable and that the council had not taken this selection criterion fully into consideration. The council's decision was based only on the fact that L & P could do the job at the cheapest price. He felt that L & P would run into serious cash problems to meet its immediate commitments.

The tenderer confirmed that he priced his own bid as a stand-alone tender. In other words, the revenue from the contract would cover the full capital and running costs of his equipment and labour.

IMPLEMENTATION

Although the City had lost the contract, the parks section of the recreation department was made responsible for implementing and maintaining the contract's specifications. The executive manager questioned the reality of saving A$14 000 considering the time and effort required to set up the new contract and develop new working relationships. The costs of monitoring should also have been taken into account when evaluating the savings.

The foreman's responsibilities were expanded to include liaison between L & P Grass Maintenance and the council, and to maintain the performance level according to the specification. Ironically, the executive manager explained that problems were arising not because the (now) former works officer was unfamiliar with how to deal with the council. The opposite was the case.

The former works officer knew the people in the council and the council's formal system of operation so well he would bypass the foreman and deal directly with the council department concerned in the hope of saving time. However, this frequently resulted in confusion.

L & P Grass Maintenance's tendered price was indeed low. The executive manager for recreation explained how small contractors could work whenever they wanted, for however long they wanted, for however much they wanted, and with whomever they wanted. They did not have to pay penalty rates, storage of equipment costs, substantial overhead costs, or on-costs such as superannuation. However, the disadvantages of small operations are that they are less flexible with the use of plant and equipment and may be unable to cope with peaks in demand.

The executive manager for recreation did not feel that the City of Bendigo Council had been adequately prepared to take on CT. He thought that the City's cost estimates were reasonable compared with the average published in the ordinary meeting report, but that they were hampered by the structure of the wage awards. He believed that the City team was further disadvantaged by not having anyone with whom to negotiate terms and working conditions to make the bid more competitive.

Losing this first contract was a major blow to the morale and confidence of the council labour force. The only consolation, described by the foreman was: 'Like I said, no one lost their job.' This view was shared by the Municipal Employees' Union representative, a maintenance carpenter also in the parks section.

CONCLUSION

Following the council's decision on 8 November to award the contract to L & P, a motion was referred to the Objectives, Policies and Evaluations Committee which said: 'That any employee intending to submit a private tender for the council works or services advise the manager, competitive tendering, as soon as notice is made of those works and services which are to be put to tender.' The motion was carried.

The grass slashing contract has now been in operation for over six months. The quality of the work has been judged by the parks section manager to be outstanding. To date no complaints have been received from ratepayers. The reasons for the successful outcome appear to be due to the systematic evaluation of the work using measurable performance objectives, and the contractor's considerable efforts to adhere to the contract specifications.

Chapter 2: summary

by Philip Sayers

The case study in this chapter allows a clear insight into the very first tender, for a grass slashing contract, to be implemented in the City of Bendigo. Key points from the chapter include that CCT was seen by management as a tool for:

- introducing accountability in performance;
- providing evaluation against detailed specifications;
- increasing efficiency;
- reducing costs.

However, council employees have not been as optimistic. The process was as follows:

- An independent CT manager was appointed.
- The manager was required to represent the interests of the council in contracts.
- Data collection (e.g. the sites and their location) was undertaken by the works officer and his subordinate.
- Subsequently, the works officer said that a relative of his was interested in submitting a tender.
- The works officer was removed from the data collection programme.
- A pre-tender meeting was held to discuss the specifications and to clarify any problems prospective tenderers might have.
- Some changes were made and documented.
- A copy was sent to all those who attended the meeting and also to all interested parties who could not attend.
- At the meeting it was publicly announced that the City of Bendigo itself was going to submit an in-house tender.
- The average bid price came in at A$85 387.
- However, bids submitted by two contractors were based on an underestimate and an overestimate of the work involved.
- Consequently they came in too low (A$47 238) and too high (A$265 768).
- The CT manager made what he thought were fair and factual assessments of the tenders.
- His recommendation was that the City of Bendigo's in-house bid be awarded the contract at a cost of A$84 119.

- The council met and decided not to adopt this recommendation.
- It awarded the contract to the lowest acceptable tenderer, at a cost of A$69 322.
- The press reported that the city council had rejected its own tender in favour of one from a private business which was operated by a city council employee.
- Yet, the tender was A$14 000 lower than any of the others.
- The works officer had indicated that he would resign from the council if he was awarded the contract. He did so after hearing of the council's favourable decision.
- The media coverage focused on the issue of whether the works officer had an 'insider advantage' over the other tenderers.
- The works officer was slow in publicly revealing his intention to submit a tender as he would have been considered disloyal and a bad example to his colleagues.
- All the tenderers appeared to be generally satisfied with the whole process.
- There was concern that the contract was with a new business with no track record.
- If the contractor did get into trouble with the work, it was considered that there were enough other qualified contractors to take on the job within a month.
- The council revised its rules to require any employee intending to submit a private tender ... to advise the CT manager as soon as notice is made of those works.
- There was a successful outcome to the contract. Quality is outstanding.

The reasons for the successful outcome appear to be due to:

- the systematic evaluation of the work;
- the use of measurable performance objectives; and
- the contractor's considerable efforts to adhere to the contract specifications.

CONTRACTING AND OUTSOURCING
Where, why and how?

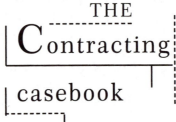

THE

Contracting

casebook

Competitive
tendering
in
action

This important book sets out, in easy-to-read form,
the evolution and outcomes of several contracting
experiences. Why were some great successes, yet
others failed? Written and edited by leading contracting experts, this book provides valuable lessons
and tips about the art of contracting in Australia.

Edited by Simon Domberger and Christine Hall,
Graduate School of Business,
University of Sydney.

Available from AGPS Press
fax +(612) 6295 4888, or
from bookshops.

ISBN 0 644 43124 5

Contract planning

Introduction

by Philip Sayers

Contracts are long and complex affairs. With contract documents, it is easy to get lost in the minutiae of detail. It is too easy to lose sight of what the contract is all about – to lose sight of the wood because of the trees, as the saying goes.

Any contract which is a success is based on clear objectives. Everyone needs a visible goal and needs to know what the contract is about. Clarity, prior to the birth of the contract, is of paramount importance. There is real danger in taking the easy route; buying a ready-made contract from someone else. Each local authority places different degrees of importance on different aspects of maintenance and management.

Some authorities are happy for grass to be cut once per month. Other authorities require almost once per week. So, a little time is needed at the outset of the contract to decide the key parameters. All the detail and contract documentation can then flow. Get the concept right, and there is every chance the contract will be right.

The next full case study of a specific contract covers Warrington New Town. The New Town movement was given great impetus in Britain after the end of the Second World War in 1945. It was all part of repairing the damage. Bombed out houses in London were replaced by new homes in a necklace of new towns some 30 miles or so from the capital city.

THE BIRTH OF A CONTRACT

The New Towns offered a fresh, clean and green lifestyle. They were an attractive alternative to poor inner city housing where whole populations of people were crammed into too few houses. The environment of new towns was very different from the cities. Grass, trees and shrubs were key elements in the landscape design process. The architecture of the town was invariably complemented by a landscape architecture specific to that town, a landscape which was designed around and within the special geographical and geological features of the landscape itself. In particular in the early new towns, grass abounded. Grass was a perfect antidote for people moving from bombed and cramped city environments.

The success of the post-war New Town movement led to other new towns being developed elsewhere in the country in later decades. These new towns, too, were provided to help overcrowding in nearby cities. Such was the case of Warrington New Town, in Lancashire.

But at Warrington New Town a very different approach to the landscape was adopted from that employed in the first generation of new towns. It was appreciated that landscape design, and the subsequent maintenance, go together. Standard grass everywhere not only looks boring; it also costs more in the long run. So at Warrington, a more naturalistic design and maintenance concept was adopted. Here it was decided to move away from the mechanistic approach of cutting grass six, or twenty-six, times per year. The naturalistic approach worked. And it worked well. The reason that it worked was because someone had thought it all through at the outset. The objectives were clear.

The case study is provided by David Scott. His role in the creation and management of the much acclaimed landscape of Warrington began in February 1972. From 1974 until 1987 he was the Chief Landscape Architect at the Warrington New Town Development Corporation, prior to joining Gillespies, where he is now a partner.

The naturalistic landscape of Warrington

by David Scott

Warrington was an established industrial town situated in the Mersey river valley between Manchester and Liverpool. In 1968 the government confirmed the designation of a New Town Development Corporation, which was given the task of expanding Warrington and its employment base by developing four new districts. One of the greatest development challenges to the Corporation was to be the reclamation of large derelict military establishments, abandoned over a period since the end of the Second World War: Risley Royal Ordnance Factory, Padgate Transit Camp and the United States Air Base at Burtonwood.

CONCEPTS

In 1973, the outline plan for Warrington New Town was approved by the Secretary of State. It promoted a positive approach to the development of a landscape structure. The main aims were:

- improving the environment;
- improving the image of the town.

Bold concepts had to be devised to ensure landscape restoration of derelict sites.

Particular importance was placed on the conservation of areas of ecological importance, including woodlands, copses and hedgerows. Extensive shelter belts, woodland planting and mounding were proposed to reduce the visual impact of the exposed character of many areas.

Much of the planning of the New Town was undertaken by multi-disciplinary teams. The role of a landscape architect was seen at an early stage as being essential to the process. The allocation of a clearly defined landscape use, coupled with adequate finance, had to be fought for by initiative, persuasion and by convincing other disciplines that money spent on landscape was money well spent.

This chapter briefly describes the creation of this new landscape framework, primarily on despoiled land, and its management, largely based on ecological principles.

A cost-effective landscape

At an early stage in the planning of the new landscape structure for Warrington, we began to explore relatively new, low-cost maintenance techniques. This was in contrast to the more traditional methods which were in general use elsewhere.

Most local authorities in Britain had a tendency to close mow and edge grass areas, to plant more decorative trees and shrubs and to select certain areas of town for formal bedding displays. Such operations had resulted in workforces made up of skilled gardeners (to grow bedding plants and prune special trees and shrubs) and relatively unskilled grass-cutters and general labourers. They seemed to have little experience of the specialist ecological and silvicultural skills required for the maintenance of the semi-natural parkland, mass shrub planting and new forestry plantations which we were proposing for the Warrington landscape.

Most of the traditional urban landscape had been laid out when Britain was a leading industrial power and very wealthy. Times, however, were changing. Towns and cities could no longer afford to spend on landscape maintenance at the same levels as previously. Expensive traditional techniques meant the concentration of resources on a very few areas of the town for a limited time of the year. Attempts to continue as before on reduced budgets had led to inequality. Prestige sites, sometimes in the more affluent areas, were being maintained to a high standard. However, at the same time, maintenance of sites in the more deprived areas was sadly lacking. This problem was evident in very many authorities.

It was my view that money spent on greenhouse heating, annual bedding plants, shrub and rose pruning, handweeding for relatively few shrubberies and regular mowing of large tracts of grass, could be better spent on achieving a major impact with mass tree and shrub management throughout the town. This would require a new attitude towards landscape management. Only in this way could real cost savings be achieved. There would be a need to change the attitude of the general public towards a highly manicured landscape and to encourage an acceptance of managed natural landscape.

THE OBJECTIVES

The objectives were to maintain the new landscape in a more cost-effective manner and to develop a style of landscape that was substantially cheaper to implement, maintain and manage than traditional styles.

A NATURAL APPROACH

Urban landscapes based on ecological principles were becoming well established in Holland and, to a lesser extent in Germany, while there was a rapidly expanding interest in Sweden. In these countries, as well as here in Britain, this development represented a practical attempt to solve both the question of the social relevance of landscape and the ever-increasing problem of landscape maintenance costs. What was required was a social, dynamic landscape based on 'ecological' principles to help compensate for some of the decaying landscape of the urban areas.

The vision at Warrington was to provide a backcloth of landscape, incorporating linked open spaces threading throughout the town. This has now been achieved by the development of a system of linear parks along the existing streams and waterways. These features provide a background to the large public parks, and link to other landscape elements such as:

- parkways;
- woodland shelter belts; and
- adjoining countryside to provide a continuous landscape setting.

The linear parks now define the major development areas and extend between elements of the district distributor road system. The woodland shelter belts provide a continuity of setting for individual residential areas and a means of controlling the micro-climatic conditions in the bleak and exposed areas of the town.

The linear parks have been supplemented by district parks, each of around 20 hectares, providing formal team sport and play areas, park pavilions and other facilities. The district parks were located on the principle that no home should be more than 1.2 kilometres away.

A main aim in the development of the structure was to minimize the environmental problem of road noise, by developing landscape buffer zones adjacent to the primary and district distributor roads. The zones adjacent to the primary roads have been developed as 'parkways', providing a pleasant landscape setting for the driver as well as protection against noise for adjacent land users.

THE IMPLEMENTATION

This was a radical departure from traditional horticulturally-led landscape practices. The planning of much of the new landscape in Warrington has been inspired by nature, and influenced by forestry practices, wildlife conservation and a desire to create usable landscape for recreation, education and children's play.

In the Birchwood district a demolished ordnance factory was remarkably transformed in just over a decade, from a bleak expanse of rubble

and compacted subsoil to a thriving residential area. The most dominant characteristics of this area are its woodlands and meadows and the
sense of nature on the doorstep.

The planning of the new landscape structure in Warrington involved
two main phases:

- identifying and preserving areas of existing vegetation;
- integrating a new system of parks and woodland belts into the
  planning of housing, industry, roads, community and commercial facilities.

The linked woodland belts were designed to form a 'web' around developments. The woodlands enclosed district 'cells' for residential,
commercial, industrial and educational land use.

Continuity and linkage of the woodland belts define the extent, indi-
viduality and territory of each land use and reduce the perceived scale
of development. The wider belts serve as corridors for main footpaths,
providing a continuous 'thread' of landscape running through the residential development. These 'greenways' lead the pedestrian into the
parks and ultimately to the rural fringe, to form a natural physical link
between the countryside and the immediate home environment.

Early establishment

Wherever possible landscape development preceded all other development so as to achieve environmental improvements in advance of
new residential and employment areas. Advance planting was one of
the most important principles in establishing Warrington's new landscape structure. The landscape planning policy aimed to commence
planting of the woodland belts three to six years before the adjoining
housing areas were occupied. This early planting helped play a major
role in creating a 'green', established and sheltered environment for
the early residents. The new woodland structure was established using
indigenous species typical of the region.

MAINTENANCE AND MANAGEMENT

Following the commencement of major landscape implementation in
1974, the board of the Development Corporation was persuaded to
recognize that the ultimate quality of these well designed and executed
schemes depended on a comprehensive maintenance and management
policy, if the investment associated with them was not to be totally
wasted within a few seasons.

In 1974 the board therefore approved the establishment of a directly employed landscape maintenance unit, nursery and plant-holding area, together with a small mobile forestry unit. From comparatively small beginnings the two direct labour units, collectively called the Landscape Management Service, grew to meet a growing and extensive commitment to carry out landscape maintenance and management.

The majority of the landscape capital schemes, in particular the larger schemes, continued to be implemented by local landscape contractors who were developing in size and experience. This was largely due to the scale of landscape work being put out to competitive tender by the Development Corporation.

Community involvement

As the naturalistic landscape and major parks steadily developed, Britain's first Urban Park Ranger Service was established in Warrington New Town in 1979. Although the landscape has now been transferred to the local authority, Warrington Borough Council, each of the main parks still has a ranger team, based in a park pavilion or cabin. The rangers' task is to help and encourage the public to use, enjoy and care for the parks and the wider landscape of the town. They achieve this through organizing events in the parks in conjunction with the community.

As part of an environmental education campaign, a good deal of contact was made with new residents and local schools through newsletters, leaflets and personal contact. This 'after sales service' was considered to be essential in order to protect the original investment, by gaining the respect of the users. It also helped the community to use and enjoy the landscape to the full and ensured that the potential for education was realized. This process is on going through the Borough Council's Ranger Service.

VOLUNTARY COMPETITIVE TENDERING

In April 1981, to achieve economies of scale, the Department of the Environment (DoE) decided to merge the New Town Development Corporation of Warrington with the neighbouring New Town Development Corporation of Runcorn. This seemed eminently sensible, especially as both new towns had contiguous boundaries. The Department then decided to reduce the numbers of Corporation staff in line with Government privatization policies and a voluntary redundancy scheme was introduced.

As a consequence, by April 1982, the Development Corporation's landscape direct labour was reduced by approximately 50%. Yet the number of completed landscape projects was still steadily rising. It was inevitable that a large proportion of landscape management work would have to be awarded to private contractors, following competitive tendering.

Due to the inflexible nature of the direct labour organization's bonus scheme, it had proved difficult to manage specialist landscapes (e.g. woodland edge planting belts and wildflower meadows) with the in-house workforce. Thus tender documents for the management work had been drawn up by the Development Corporation's ecologist, and, after competitive tendering, the work had been awarded to private contractors. This was the first step in the move towards the privatization of the grounds maintenance operation.

Client meets ...

Because of the experience gained by the ecologist, he was encouraged to set up a Contract Management Unit, charged with the task of managing several major landscape areas of the town using private landscape contractors. Certain supervisory staff, who were considered suitable, were transferred to this new unit from the direct labour force. They were retrained in the management of landscapes by private contract. Procedures were drawn up and new maintenance contract drawings prepared in relation to sites previously managed by in-house direct labour.

... the contractor

From 1982 onwards, the size and number of landscape management and cleansing contracting firms increased rapidly to meet the demands of the Development Corporation. In any one year, up to 25 contractors were employed on various contracts throughout Warrington and Runcorn. The policy was one of dividing up the cake, rather than putting all the eggs in one basket. Although this was more administratively demanding, it ensured quality workmanship coupled with competitive pricing.

This increasing reliance on private contractors for landscape management and landscape cleansing continued until the demise of Warrington – Runcorn Development Corporation in September 1989. All staff in the direct labour organization were made compulsorily redundant. From that date the Commission for the New Towns (CNT) took over responsibility for the New Towns' estate. Gillespies were

Fig. 3.1 Costly bedding displays have no place in a natural environment

appointed by CNT, until April 1994, to administer the majority of land-scape management contracts in both the Warrington and Runcorn New Towns, covering a total area of 340 hectares. Since September 1989 all landscape management and cleansing work had been carried out by private contractors following competitive tendering.

TRANSFER OF THE NEW TOWN LANDSCAPE ASSETS

Towards the demise of the Development Corporation, negotiations on the transfer of the New Town's landscape assets began to take place with the appropriate local authorities, namely Warrington Borough Council and Cheshire County Council, the latter being the recipient of highway land and sub-regional landscape developments, e.g. country parks. Similar negotiations were also taking place with housing associations regarding the transfer of housing landscape assets and also with the Woodland Trust in relation to woodlands owned by the Development Corporation.

The 'hard' and 'soft' elements which contributed to the landscape were identified, in order to provide a detailed analysis of their management costs. These elements included 'soft' features such as:

- amenity;
- meadow and rough grass areas;
- banks and ditches;
- herbaceous and groundcover planting;
- specimen trees;
- water bodies;
- ornamental shrub planting; and
- naturalistic structure planting.

It also included hard features such as:

- walls;
- various types of paving;
- play areas;
- boardwalks;
- site furniture.

Following this, routine landscape maintenance and refurbishment operations were defined. Each landscape parcel was surveyed, using a combination of on-site survey and analysis of the landscape management contract drawings. All landscape elements for each parcel were then:

- identified;
- quantified;
- and a lifespan assessment made.

Every site was broken down into its individual parcels, and measures derived for all their constituent elements.

Following protracted negotiations between CNT, Warrington Borough Council and the DoE, transfers of land took place on 1 April 1993. Since that time the Borough Council has managed the landscape using a combination of direct labour and private contractors, working to drawings, specifications and quantification contained in a series of comprehensive landscape management plans.

LANDSCAPE MANAGEMENT PLANS

In preparation for the transfer of the New Town landscapes, landscape management plans were drawn up by Gillespies on behalf of CNT. This was with a view to handing them over to Warrington Borough Council and the Woodland Trust, at the time of transfer of management responsibility. These management plans were considered essential by the Borough Council in order to support the successful long-term establishment of Warrington's new landscape and achieve cost-effective landscape management.

Each management plan was a site-specific document prepared to guide the local authority's landscape managers in the future planning and management of all the major parks, together with the New Town's overall structure, planting and ponds. A similar document was prepared for the Woodland Trust in relation to Warrington's mature woodlands.

The management plans were designed to be flexible documents outlining the long-term strategy for each major park, as well as planting and ponds. Each plan took the form of a written statement detailing:

- the method, timing and aim of maintenance and management operations;
- location plans;
- detailed landscape management drawings.

Specific items covered in the plans included a general description, site history, implementation details, design intentions, management objectives, long-term requirements, maintenance operations and schedules of quantities.

FURTHER READING

Greenwood, R.D. (1983) Gorse Covert, Warrington: creating a more natural landscape, *Landscape Design*, **136**, 35–8.

Greenwood, R.D. and Moffatt, J.D. (1982) in *An Ecological Approach to Urban Landscape Design* (eds. A. Ruff and R.J. Tregay), Department of Town and Country Planning, University of Manchester, pp. 40–59.

Tregay, R.J. and Gustavsson, R. (1982) *Oakwood's New Landscape: Designing for Nature in the Residential Environment*, Sveriges Lantbruksuniversitet and Warrington and Runcorn Development Corporation, Warrington.

Tregay, R.J. and Moffatt, J.D. (1980) An ecological approach to landscape design and management in Oakwood, Warrington, *Landscape Design*, **134**, 33–6.

Scott, D. (1983) *Handover of Open Space to Local Authorities*, paper given to JCLI Conference, Liverpool, July 1983.

Scott, D. (1991) The greening of Warrington, *Landscape Design*.

Chapter 3: summary

by Philip Sayers

In many towns in Britain, the use of minimal-maintenance techniques in the urban area has, until recently, been discouraged due to predictions of unfavourable public response. Some people still consider natural plants and long grass to be synonymous with neglect. But with the need to minimize expenditure on landscape management and the growing awareness of conservation, a natural approach to urban landscape design and management is essential.

A main aim is to reduce the scale of highly managed grassland, particularly those grass areas which are expensive to maintain due to their character, size and slope. Much of this grassland can be replaced with woodland, to screen and break up the scale of the built-up area. This not only leads to longer-term cost savings, but also greatly improves visual quality.

In recent years maintenance budgets for the naturalistic landscapes of Warrington have indicated that the cost of managing them has been dramatically reduced in comparison to conventional 'horticultural' landscapes. Operations are less frequent and intensive but are more dependent upon skilled and timely management decisions.

With the increased and challenging workload generated by the New Town's landscape, Warrington Borough Council has recruited and retrained staff with expertise in the management of natural habitats. One of the biggest problems facing the council in the future will be training staff in different methods and convincing them that much of the landscape management needs to have an 'ecological' rather than an 'horticultural' basis.

The success of the Warrington landscape has been increasingly recognized, both throughout the UK and internationally. As well as receiving several Civic Trust, Landscape Institute, and other awards, the New Town was awarded a Certificate of Merit by the Council for the Protection of Rural England 'to place on record its appreciation of the excellent work of the landscape team'.

In 1991 Gillespies received a Landscape Institute Award, for the management of the 50-hectare Sankey Valley Park in Warrington. This success was repeated in 1993 when the practice received the award again for the preparation of a comprehensive management plan for the 340-hectare Warrington Forest Park: an amalgamation of several parks, woodlands, water bodies, open space and roadside landscaping threading through the built environment of Warrington.

Chapter Four

Process and personalities

by Philip Sayers

Tendering is not just a formalized process. People are involved too. And with people, come their personalities. The influence of key people can, and should, drive the whole process forward.

Invariably, most people are working towards the best outcome possible; in their eyes. This creates a difficulty. What one person sees as a good way forward, another may consider to be disastrous. Conflict between people can often be explained by the fact that any two individuals are driven by different circumstances. Sometimes the tension between individuals can be very creative and lead to excellent results. At other times, the tension just produces a negative atmosphere.

This chapter offers an excellent example of negative management. Events and people combined to produce a harrowing result. No one could rise above the melee. Everything everyone did just made matters worse. There was no magnanimity. Unfortunately this type of experience has been all too common for those involved in CCT contracts. Sad, destructive, damaging, yet very real. People can get in the way.

PERSONAL AMBITION

Let's admit it, we all have our own agendas and career paths. We all seek opportunities to exploit new avenues, whether it be at work, at home, or perhaps in sport. All too often, however, we are not open with our hidden agendas. Thus the scene is set for conflict.

A major change like competitive tendering, or a new contract, presents endless opportunities for a wide range of people to exploit their own hidden agendas. We saw an example in an earlier chapter.

The case study in this chapter derives from a number of actual contract experiences. Because it is about a contract that went badly, and derives from a number of contracts, all names are fictitious. It is an amalgamation of stories given to the editor. For any reader who may take personal umbrage at the case study, please let it be understood that this case study is not about you or your work situation. Everyone involved in contracts is bound to identify with the situations shown in this case study. The chapter is about real life CCT contract situations.

It highlights how people work together to address external threats. Initially they all worked well. Their methods of preparing for the contract was a model to follow. It was only under pressure that everything fell apart.

THE TENDERING SET UP

Before CCT, the town of Workingham spent just over £1 million per year on maintaining all the parks, playing fields, open spaces and verges within the borough boundary. Fifty gardeners were employed. A few more were employed on a casual basis during the peak months of May and June.

The population of the town was 100 000. There was a substantial industrial area in the town which provided about 50% of the jobs within the borough. Perhaps because of the hard indoor manufacturing industry, the town's people took great pride in their parks and open spaces. The roundabouts always had very colourful, seasonal flower displays. The gardens were always well trimmed.

To provide this service, the council employed four office-based staff. They were:

- John Saunders, parks manager;
- Anthea Turnbull, deputy parks manager;
- Andrew Staithe, technical assistant;
- Evelyn Hew, clerical assistant.

John had been with the council many years and was now in his 40s. He dealt with the councillors on policy issues, and day to day matters which involved their constituents. John always attended council committee meetings. He always made it known that he never took holiday between Easter and the beginning of August. Thus he was always present during the busy peak months. The council could, and did, rely on John to maintain standards.

Anthea was in her 20s, very keen to progress her career, and saw the council as a stepping stone. She resented the slow, yet sure, management style adopted by John. She was unaware that this very steady style was what councillors expected from John. That would have irritated her even more.

Andrew had only left college a year previously, and was still learning the ways of management. He designed all the flower beds. He arranged for plants to be grown in the municipal nursery each year. He also ensured that there was sufficient work during the winter months to keep the men outside employed and so improve the town at the same time.

Evelyn was the clerical assistant who took all the bookings for the parks, and saw to all the time sheets and bonus sheets, invoices and all the other paperwork.

A team effort

They worked well together as a team. Realizing the implications of CCT, they purchased contract documents from the Institute of Leisure and Amenity Management, and set about tailoring them to their own requirements.

John looked after all the conditions of contract, the tendering arrangements and formalities associated with the tender process. This involved him working in close liaison with the council's solicitor. Anthea adapted the specifications. She used her own experience, and enlisted the help of all the parks foremen. This not only involved the foremen in the CCT process, but also gave Anthea valuable local information. Andrew measured every single shrub bed and piece of grass in the borough with the help of outside surveyors. Evelyn worked overtime to cope with all the extra typing.

They thus adopted a classic division of labour:

- the manger looked after the overall process and the formalities;
- the technical specifications were prepared by the deputy;
- the technical assistant produced the bills of quantity.

Meanwhile, on the advice of the Chief Executive, the council formally agreed on a contractor and client division of responsibilities. The client side of the operation continued to report to the parks sub-committee. John, Andrew and Evelyn retained their jobs and titles, but they lost direct control of the labour force. This made John somewhat uneasy. He liked direct control.

COMMERCIAL PRACTICES

As a matter of policy, the council appointed a direct service organization (DSO) board to oversee all contracts from a contractor's point of view. Anthea was appointed contracts manager (parks and grounds maintenance).

Anthea was very keen on her new job and set about it with vigour. She started by training the foreman and charge hands about commercial practices. She felt well placed to do this. Her father had been a grocer. She had therefore grown up with an inside knowledge of cash flow, and the need to make profit at the end of each working day and each working week. New paperwork systems were introduced which linked the rate of work exactly to the quantity of work. But it was uphill work with the foremen.

Yet Anthea was quite clear about the necessity for the new systems. It was absolutely essential to determine the actual costs incurred in undertaking the existing work. This would then allow accurate prices to be included within the tender in due course.

Competition

There was competition. The in-house team had to bid against three outside contractors. One company was a Dutch company just commencing work in grounds maintenance contracts but with a long horticultural pedigree. The next company was a national grounds maintenance contractor who was getting bigger by the month. The third contractor was more regional, having commenced grounds maintenance contracts in a nearby town some ten years previously. All tenderers, including the DSO, were intent on winning.

The tender process

The tenderers kept the client officers busy. At the pre-tender meetings, all the tenderers asked many questions. Without Anthea now to help, John and Andrew had to work doubly hard to reply fully to all enquiries. They copied all replies to all the other tenderers. The many questions asked by the tenderers unsettled John to a certain extent. He began to feel a little unsure about the quality of his contract documents. He had nagging doubts that the specifications did not include everything.

On the day of the tender opening, four plain envelopes were received by the council before the closing time of noon. At a quarter past noon the Mayor opened all four envelopes. The Assistant Chief Executive logged all the prices tendered.

The DSO had submitted the lowest tender. John was relieved. With the DSO winning, he felt easy that the work would be carried out as in the past. However, he was concerned at the very low DSO tendered price.

Redundancies

Anthea was also pleased to learn that she had won the contract. In fact she was delighted. All the staff joined her in a small champagne celebration. Some had a beer. Everyone wanted to share in the success.

Anthea was quite satisfied with the low price. She had to be. After all, it was her price. She knew exactly what she was doing. She intended to reduce the number of casual staff employed during the summer. She was also relying on natural wastage to reduce the number of permanent staff. Nevertheless, in the two months between the tender opening and the start of the contract, Anthea made herself very unpopular. She asked the DSO board to agree to four early retirements. The board members thought that they should have been involved earlier. They resented being told after the event.

The contract commenced on the 1 January – an odd date to start a grounds maintenance in the northern hemisphere. However, that was the date which was stipulated in the Act of Parliament.

The first three months went well. Client, contractor and council were all satisfied. The financial year ended in March. Thus the contractor had a short three-month financial year. A profit of £15 000 was declared. Anthea was ecstatic. She threw a small party for all the staff after work on a Friday evening. John, now as client, was slightly peeved by this profit. He felt he had somehow been ripped off. Because the party was purely for contractor staff, he was not invited.

The next three months, up to July, were not so easy. They were the peak months of maintenance. It was also a very wet spring that year. The grass grew quick and lush. With reduced staff, it was proving difficult to meet all targets. Grass was not cut as often. It grew ever longer. Of more concern to Anthea, however, was the fact that the working teams continued in their old ways. They did the work they had always done. They did not work according to the contract documents. They carried out some work for which the contractor would never receive payment. Instead of waiting for a variation order, the teams would carry out the work as in the old days.

NON-PERFORMANCE

Meanwhile, John was getting complaints about the grass not being cut. Large swathes of grass were being left behind. This was because the grass had been left to grow too long before cutting. Children were making haystacks out of this grass. Worse, they were then tramping clumps of long, wet grass it into their homes. Complaints increased. In his time-honoured fashion, John spoke kindly to Anthea about the difficulties and the need to improve.

Defaults in theory ...

Anthea tried cutting the bonus payments to force everyone to work according to the contract. The unions complained. Councillors got involved. At the same time councillors were receiving complaints from residents about lack of performance. They then complained to both Anthea and John. The mayor demanded action. John realized he would have to use the default system provided for within the contract. He looked up the documents.

The default clause stated:

> Where works have not been carried out according to the contract documents, a rectification notice will be issued to the contractor. The contractor will be required by the rectification notice, to rectify the defect or deficiency within 48 hours. Failure to do so will leave the contractor liable to the issue of a default notice. If the works subject to a default notice are not undertaken to the entire satisfaction of the supervising officer within five working days, then the supervising officer will be at liberty to employ another contractor at the expense of the first contractor to undertake the works. Furthermore, the accumulation of twenty-five default points in any one month period, will lead to the termination of the contract.

John reread the paragraph. It seemed quite clear. It also seemed relatively easy to action. He then thought of the hundreds of bits of grass around the borough which may or may not have been cut according to the contract documents. It would be quite legitimate to issue twenty-five rectification notices tomorrow. He pondered on the issue overnight.

He had to be seen taking decisive action. The councillors expected nothing less. Furthermore, he was annoyed. When he was in charge, this poor state of affairs would never have happened. Yet, he wanted to be fair. So, next day, he served five rectification notices.

... defaults in practice

Anthea was inflamed. She maintained that the service delivery was little worse than in previous years. The work programme had only slipped by three weeks. It was just unfortunate that it was a wet spring. Moreover, the grass cutting was being carried out much more cheaply than previously. In addition, she felt bitter. After all, it was the contractor who had to do all the work. John and his colleagues could sit in the office.

Anthea went to see John immediately. There was a very bitter dispute. Evelyn left for an early lunch. She could not stand the upset. Andrew was not in the office. He thus did not know of this row until later in the day.

On that morning, Andrew was visiting sites where grass had not been cut according to the contract. He also had being reading the default procedures. As the technical assistant now, he felt that it was his job to

Fig. 4.1 Conflict and confrontation divert attention from work to defence building

maintain standards on behalf of the residents of the town. Just before lunch, at the same time that Anthea and John were having their set to, Andrew called into the grounds maintenance depot and issued his first five rectification notices.

John cancelled the notices after Anthea's remonstrations. John also rebuked Andrew. In future, Andrew was to report to John before issuing defaults. He told Andrew that the issue of defaults was confrontational. That was not his management style.

Although Andrew learnt from Evelyn about the row, he did not know what the row had been about. In view of his humiliating rebuke, he did not care to ask anyone.

Resentment

Tempers cooled over the following weeks. Work output improved. Anthea, shaken by events, took on more casual staff. By the autumn the contract was working relatively smoothly. There was now, however, an underlying resentment between the client and the contractor. The formal monthly meetings between the client and contractor were packed with everybody watching everybody else. Instead of there just being Anthea and John at the meetings there were more than half a dozen people. Andrew now attended, and Evelyn took minutes. The senior supervisors from Anthea's team attended. They were all making sure that no one was making a move which would be detrimental to their own interests.

By December, Anthea was just about breaking even. She threw a small party for her own staff. She did not invite the client officers to the party. They joked about contractors inviting the client out to slap up Christmas dinners. Anthea did not even rise to the bait. She still had a further three months of this financial year to try and turn in a profit.

BUREAUCRACY

In January, a council policy decision infuriated Anthea. Due to cash limitations imposed by central government, the council was put into a financial straightjacket. The council responded by placing a freeze on all vacancies and all uncommitted expenditure. No posts were filled. No new machines were purchased.

But Anthea had allowed many vacancies to accrue to save cash. She intended to advertise in January and appoint in February and thus have a full complement of staff. This would allow her to complete the winter schedule of work and make a flying start into the new grass-cutting season which started in March.

Anthea complained that this new policy was not fair. This would not happen to a private contractor. How could she manage a contract if she did not have the resources? Her complaints got her nowhere. The freeze remained.

It was a warm, wet spring that year. By April it was not possible to maintain the grass and grounds to the stated frequencies. The work was not being undertaken due to the freeze on staff. Complaints flowed. John still tried to hold the line. He refrained from issuing rectification notices.

ANNUAL DSO PROFITS

Then, in early May, Anthea announced the provisional trading results for her first full financial year. To everybody's amazement it showed a £50 000 profit. John was aghast. Here was a contractor making a profit out of a service which that contractor manifestly was failing to deliver. His attitude hardened.

The simple truth was, however, that the large profit was due entirely to the freeze on recruitment in the last two months of the financial year, and the lack of expenditure on new machines.

Matters got much worse, as spring turned into early, warm, wet summer. Without sufficient staff and no new machinery, it was impossible to cut the grass frequently enough. Anthea concentrated her staff on the high profile sports facilities like the bowling greens and the cricket wickets. General grass cutting was abandoned to a much reduced cutting frequency. As more staff left, Anthea gave up any pretence of keeping to any schedule.

CONTROL MECHANISMS

Meanwhile John was preparing his explanations for the external auditor. He knew that there was to be a special study this year on the first year's CCT contracts. With the profit which the contractor had accrued, and the known inadequate delivery, John felt very unsure of his approach to the external auditor.

And now, the contractor was not performing. John had no alternative. He used the default procedure. First he issued rectification notices. The contractor could not, and did not, rectify the deficiencies. Default notices followed. Then alternative contractors were employed to do some of the work. The work undertaken by this new contractor eased the pressure on the in-house contractor.

Punitive defaults

Regrettably, due to a lack of communication, the second contractor sometimes doubled up on works undertaken by the in-house contractor. A piece of grass would be cut twice within one week, where the specification required it to be cut once in two weeks. Local residents who had complained that their grass had not been cut in weeks, found their grass cut in the morning by one contractor and in the afternoon by another contractor.

Not only did this infuriate Anthea, but to rub salt into the wound, the in-house contractor had to pay for all the other contractors. The cost was punitive. John thought that Anthea could afford it. More important he believed that she should pay. It was her fault. But the use of outside contractors clearly hurt both parties. Anthea and her team lost financially. John lost credibility due to the lack of control over the two sets of contractors.

Weekly, there were blazing rows between Anthea and John. But John continued playing it entirely according to the book. Rectification notices were issued, followed by default notices, followed by bringing other contractors in to do the works. The number of complaints mushroomed. He spent at least half his week just responding to residents' complaints attempting to get works done.

Personal injury

Not only was John maddened by all the difficulties, he was also deeply upset. Everything he had held important in his working life, was being trampled underfoot. He was working 70 to 80 hours every week. Yet he remained appalled by the mess which lay around him. His pride in his career was in tatters.

By August, John was off work on sick leave suffering from stress. At the same time, Anthea's accounts were radically in the red. Residents were totally dissatisfied with the service, and councillors were continually criticizing. And yet, council policy in relation to the freeze on posts remained.

THE DSO VIEW

Anthea summarized the principal difficulties in a candid report to the Direct Services Management Board:

- The in-house contractor was still considered part of a local government set-up.
- There was no autonomy.
- The contractor was bound up in red tape.
- There was no chance to act commercially.
- The staff freeze had led directly to standards of work not being maintained.
- It was ludicrous to employ outside contractors when in-house contractor could do the work more cheaply.
- There was an essential need for the in-house contractor to be treated like a private contractor.

The direct services management board took umbrage at the tone of the report. They considered that they were running the contract, not Anthea. Furthermore, they had to take account of all the government's many requirements. Grounds maintenance was only a small part of a larger picture.

Anthea, now defeated, gave in and let the inevitable happen.

At the end of that financial year the grounds maintenance contract declared a substantial financial deficit. There was a possibility of the DSO being closed down after being audited by the government. The full financial impact of the client's actions only now became totally apparent for all to see.

Councillors on both the DSO board and the client parks sub-committee were appalled by the actions of John and Anthea. The councillors saw the rows and lack of cooperation. The absurdity of the financial situation was hidden by the constant smoke from the client and contractor officers. 'A curse on both your houses' was the view of the councillors. They only had one course of action open to them.

MEDIATION

A consultant was employed to check through the mess. First the consultant was require to assess the financial consequences of the actions of the client and whether these actions had been justified. The consultant was also asked to verify if all works performed by Anthea had been paid for. Some works had been clearly undertaken by the DSO team which had not been specified. If the works were required to maintain previous standards (the stated aim of the contract), then additional payments were justified to the contractor.

The consultants and the council's Finance Department became closely involved with the contract that second summer. There was no other option. There had been some dramatic staff changes.

John retired early on grounds of ill health. Anthea moved to the private sector. She became the contract manager for three nearby towns. Andrew was placed in Anthea's position. He rapidly changed his tune.

Chapter 4: summary

This chapter gives a clear illustration of the process of competitive tendering, from a client and contractor viewpoint. It also graphically illustrates some of the inherent difficulties with public sector management. Some of the key lessons from the chapter are now summarized:

- Initial preparations for the CCT contract required a formal division between client and contractor within the council.

- The council officers drew up specifications, after studying industry standard documents from the Institute of Leisure and Amenity Management.
- Plans, maps were drawn up and all areas of grass were measured and quantified.
- A DSO board was set up.
- The parks sub-committee was left as client.
- The client officer was a middle-aged manager who was set in his ways.
- The contractor manager was young, with plenty of good ideas.
- She was determined to ensure that all work was accurately costed.
- To win the tender, she cut costs by reducing staff.
- Bonuses were only to be paid on work undertaken.
- The old staff continued with their old ways and undertook work which had not been ordered by the client, and thus the contractor did not get paid.
- The first spring was warm and wet, the contractor fell behind with the work, complaints followed and the default procedure was used.
- There was an immediate polarization of views between the client and the contractor.
- Attitudes hardened, working relationships became confrontational.
- Defaults are divisive.
- Both parties get blamed when things go wrong and are not sorted out.
- A consultant was needed to mediate in the end, to allow justified payments to be made to the contractor.
- The government changed the funding arrangements to the council, as always.
- A knee jerk reaction by the council made the contract virtually unmanageable.
- A council operated contractor can be much more restricted than a private sector contractor.

Although people often act with the very best of intentions, the results of their actions may be the opposite of those intentions, especially in an uncertain world. When things go wrong there are two options; be ever so reasonable, or allow relationships to degenerate into conflict. Depending on the circumstances, either option can be right. Experience with the first round of CCT contracts tends to show that things can go badly very quickly. An ability to think through the consequences of all actions is needed if disaster is to be avoided.

Managing specifications

Introduction

by Philip Sayers

All contracts change as they grow and mature. Childhood is similar. Growing up is all about adapting to constant physical and mental change, and in an ever-changing environment. So it is with contracts. For success, changes and alterations to a contract need to be accommodated easily and smoothly.

To a certain extent, change can be easily accommodated in a maintenance contract by issuing variation orders. These are quite literally an order to vary the works being undertaken. For example, following residents' requests, a variation order may be issued to cut the grass more frequently in one area of the town. In a grounds maintenance contract, there is an endless stream of variation orders. The contract needs to be varied to take account of the ever-changing growth patterns of nature.

In this chapter, we examine the growth and change of contracts. The development of sports is the example chosen to illustrate the key issues. By looking at sports, we also see the interactions within a management contract.

A management contract is different from a maintenance contract. For example, if casual swimming is reducing in popularity over the years, perhaps increased fun sessions are needed. But is the reduction in popularity due to the inefficiency of the contractor, or some national pattern? Managing a leisure centre, sports hall, swimming pool and the like requires careful and constant assessment of customer requirements. People's use of leisure time changes continually. Each year brings its own particular fashion or craze. This affects the environment in which the contract is operating, and in turn affects both client and contractor.

There is too, the need everywhere to develop and promote sport and the benefits of physical activity. As we all know, activity makes the heart grow stronger. In a contract situation, both client and contractor need to agree the change.

The theory ...

For a leisure centre or sports hall; development of sports is a key requirement. A structured approach to the development of sport:

- helps the customer;
- increases attendance;
- increases income.

More importantly, a proper approach to sports development obviously
fulfils the purpose of providing the sports hall in the first place.

Central to the process of sports development is the belief that everyone should have the opportunity to reach their potential, with the only
constraints being their interest and ability. This means ensuring that
sporting opportunities exist for everybody, regardless of age, gender,
ethnicity or ability.

... and the practice

Within CCT, local authorities were allowed to keep sports development
on the client side of the authority. Simultaneously with the introduction of CCT, many authorities were undergoing spending cuts.

Not only does this chapter highlight sports development, it also
provides a graphic example of the division between:

- the client, or purchaser;
- the contractor, or provider.

This division of responsibility is the basis of all contracts.

There is a further interplay in respect of sports development. Developing interest in a sport is hard work. Initially there may be few
participants. However, the pump-priming nature of sports development
will (if successful, which most programmes are) lead to increased use.
And of course, increased income. Therefore a sports session of no particular interest to the contractor initially may later become of key
financial interest.

So given these many varying aspects of sports development, given the
pressures of producing CCT specifications and tenders, and given the
sheer gamesmanship employed in the whole process, the scene is set for
widely differing interpretations and applications of sports development.

In this first part of the chapter, Geoff Nichols surveys the methods
adopted for the introduction of sports development within a CCT environment. He has made specific studies on the impact of CCT on sports
development within leisure contracts.

In the second part of the chapter, there follows an example of good practice. The case study relates to the implementation of a sports development specification into a leisure management contract at East Hampshire District Council in southern England. Example specifications, the method of pricing, and the tendering background is given. The tendering environment or backcloth is all important in determining the nature of each and every contract.

Building sports development into CCT

by Geoff Nichols

The following account of the methods by which the needs of sports development have been built into CCT is based on the experiences of 12 leisure departments. All employ sports development officers. It shows the strengths and weaknesses of the two major approaches and draws conclusions for the next round of contracting.

Client-side initiatives for new sports sessions are most likely to come from the sports development sections. Through these the client side was able to develop the service and achieve flexibility within the constraints of a contract. However, the lessons learnt from the first wave of tendering are also relevant to authorities with no specialist sports development officers (SDOs) in which new initiatives will have to come directly from the client officer.

The needs of sports development had to be adequately protected in the contract specification in the event of the contract being won by either the DSO or a private company. In doing this a balance had to be struck between protecting existing sessions and allowing for flexibility. There was a need to protect existing and potential sessions that contributed to all stages of the sports development continuum.

The sports development continuum moves:

- from foundation;
- to participation;
- to performance;
- and then excellence.

There was also a need to ensure sports development could offer a flexible service.

The key problems, as perceived by one SDO, were:

- How do you put a philosophy into a specification?
- The emphasis of our work changes all the time.

In other words, sports development has certain objectives to meet. The best way of meeting them will continually change over the period of the contract.

PREPARING FOR CCT

The degree of involvement of client sports development sections in the preparation for CCT varied. It was difficult in authorities where the sports development section had only recently been established. Here, the political profile of the sports development section within the department was low. So, too, was the section's contribution to contract preparation.

Involvement was also made difficult by the haste with which some of the first contracts were prepared. In some authorities complacency and inexperience were also contributing factors. Some authorities were concerned not to let commercially sensitive information escape to potential bidders.

Here preparations for tendering were conducted in relative secrecy by a few officers. In these instances involvement of the sports development team might only occur near the end of preparations for contracting. By then, there was little opportunity for them to make a significant contribution.

The sports development sections were more likely to be consulted if they were large and well established, had a strong political profile in the department, and if the client and chief officer were supportive.

DIFFERENT APPROACHES

There were two major ways of meeting the needs of sports development within CCT. First, the required sports sessions could be specified in detail by the client at the outset of tendering. Thus the contractor would be then required to deliver.

Second, a client sports section could be given a budget with which to buy its way into facilities. There are strengths and weaknesses of both approaches and the most satisfactory contracts involved a combination of both.

Via the specification ...

A comprehensive specification of sports sessions was usually based on what was being done before CCT. A thorough specification would include details of the:

- time;
- venue;
- facilities;
- payment arrangements.

It would include a clear specification of responsibilities between client and contractor including details such as who was responsible for collecting charges, for promotion and for providing instruction.

In practice the thoroughness of the specification varied. There were bound to be considerable lessons learnt from this first experience of contracting. And there were. For example, the Sports Council found that most contracts did not specify the minimum number of people that should be attending certain sports sessions. They argue that you might specify that sessions should be put on but unless this is supported by specifications of target attendances there is no guarantee the client will achieve what it wants.

And what is wanted is ever-increasing participation in sports and physical activity by an increasing proportion of the population. Increased use by young, fit people is only a small part of the picture. An increase in physical activity, whatever the nature of the activity, is beneficial to the large majority of the population.

However, the first round of contracting revealed that a lot of authorities did not have detailed information about their users. The Sports Council's National Information Survey specifically identified this lack of information which local authorities had about their users. This meant that tightly specified targets for use might be unrealistic in the first round of contracting but that it might be possible to build them in next time.

Client officers felt that a thorough specification was a strength. A thorough specification was more likely to protect the service if the contract was won by a private contractor. This depends on the extent to which the objectives of the contractor, whether the DSO or a private company, differ from those of the client. This will be discussed later, but the conflict of objectives was not as great as was perceived before CCT.

... or via a separate client budget ...

The second method was to allocate the sports development team a budget within the client section with which to negotiate use of facilities.

This gave the sports development teams a great deal of flexibility. Individual arrangements could be negotiated with facility managers for different types of session. For example, if a session was being set up that was likely to become a regular part of a facility programme and contribute to the facility's income the costs of setting it up might be shared between the sports development team and the contractor. The sports development team would not pay for the facility, but the centre manager would keep the income.

If a session was being introduced to fill a particular gap in the sports development continuum, for example a specialist coaching course, then this might not be expected to contribute to the facility's income.

In these cases, the sports development team might negotiate a hire charge for the facility, meet the cost of putting on the session and keep any income.

If a session was to become a regular part of the facility's programme it was important that the facility manager was fully involved in its planning because he or she would be the person who would be responsible for it in the long term. In this case the facility manager would want to agree a price for participants that would at least match the revenue that might be obtained from alternative programming.

On the other hand, if the sports development team was hiring the facility and keeping the income they would set the prices. For one-off special events, for example a summer coaching scheme, the sports development team and contractor would plan the event together, sharing costs and sharing the income. The range of permutations of sharing costs and income was a practical way of dealing with the varied needs of sports development work.

While the flexibility of this approach was its major strength it required each new session to be negotiated individually between SDO and facility manager. It required a sports development's budget to be adequate to allow it to provide the required service. It also stressed the importance of a good working relationship between SDOs and facility managers.

... or a mixture of both

Naturally there is a third way. Some contracts used a combination of both approaches and this was a good way of balancing the need to protect existing sessions and allowing for development.

A basic specification of regular sessions would be combined with a variation budget that enabled the sports development team to negotiate access to facilities. Some contracts used aspects of one approach or the other but did not adequately develop the specification to protect the interests of sports development. For example, some contracts specified times and venues for sessions but left the price paid by participants to be negotiated.

In some cases there was an imprecise attempt to specify prices.

For example, one authority specified that rates should be 'at a price that is not prohibitive to disadvantaged groups'. In practice the greatest difficulty the SDO had was in negotiating a price he felt was acceptable to the people in his target groups. Because sports development is continually starting new and different sports sessions, it was difficult to specify all prices in the contract. In some cases the sessions

Fig. 5.1 A poor specification leads to uncertainty

might fall within general categories for which prices had been specified in the contract. Often this was not the case, and a price had to be
negotiated. If this was so client officers could still influence prices if
they wished by stipulating in the contract that prices of any new sessions
should be agreed by them.

　　The most inadequate contracts were those where the requirements
of sports development had not been built into the specification or those
where a private sector bid winning the contract had exposed how poorly
it had protected sports development needs.

Conflicting interests

Even in the most comprehensive of contracts the major sources of difficulty were where the interests of client and contractor conflicted.
However, there were also many instances where they converged,
although these were not always fully exploited.

　　Within CCT the contractor is now primarily concerned with his financial performance. As one client officer described his DSO manager:

- His attitude has changed completely ...
- His idealism has gone out of the window ...
- He is now looking for pounds and pence.

The conflict of interests in sports development is most apparent when the SDO is trying to establish new sessions at peak times. The contractor is interested in the opportunity cost, the revenue that he loses as a consequence of accommodating the new sports development session. This has made it virtually impossible for sports development sections to introduce sessions using facilities at times of peak demand, such as weekday evenings. At these times the facilities can be filled by the contractor much more profitably. Examples include keep fit sessions and five-a-side football.

If sports development use of these facilities at these peak times has not been specified in the contract it will not be possible to negotiate access because it will be too expensive to compensate the facility manager for the loss in revenue.

One SDO reported, 'we don't even try to book the centre on Wednesday nights as it is full of aerobics classes'.

This has been a problem for sessions towards the top end of the sports development continuum that require specialist facilities. These sessions may use voluntary instructors who work in the day. Thus evening sessions are the only time that they have available for coaching. The essential need for evening use of a facility is intensified when, say, the course is aimed at school-age participants. National coaching foundation courses have been adversely affected in this way.

Another example was a proposed swimming session for Asian women, which would have required exclusive use of the pool. This would either have required existing users to be excluded, with the consequent loss of income, or that the pool be opened at an additional time, with the extra costs this involved.

A further area of conflict has been over pricing. This is especially true of sessions which have not been tightly specified and are a matter for negotiation between SDO and facility manager. The facility manager will be keeping the income from the session. Here a sports development objective of equality of access for all income groups could conflict with a facility manager's objective of profit maximization. A sports development officer reported that there had been some drop out from his sessions in which he had to raise prices after negotiation with facility managers.

In general there is no strong evidence to show that prices for local authority leisure facilities represent a significant barrier to participation. However, this may be more important to low income groups who are frequently the target of sports development activities.

Fig. 5.2 ....the clash: cash versus coaching

Converging interests

On the other hand there are many instances where the objectives of sports development and facility managers converge. The most significant of these is where a sports development session will raise extra income for a facility by encouraging use at a time of slack demand.

Some sports development officers reported that before CCT the facility manager regarded an approach from the sports development team as more hassle. Now they regarded it as extra income. Therefore the managers were much more enthusiastic about becoming involved. In an authority where an SDO had only been appointed after the introduction of CCT the facility managers primarily saw him as a way of marketing their centres, and approached him to do so. This may be completely compatible with sports development objectives.

In Sheffield the sports development promotion of diving and tennis programmes brings in considerable income to the related specialist facilities. The participants in these activities can afford to pay a price that is compatible with the facility managers' objectives.

There were other ways in which the interests of sports development and facility managers converge, although these were not always recognized in practice. Extra income could be gained from catering and other aspects of secondary spending. New users of the facility would increase its profile in the local area and possibly lead to additional use at other times.

For example, in one authority the sports development team had introduced an ante-natal swimming session in a pool. This did not contribute to the manager's costs. The pool was already open and staffed. It did, however, introduce new people to the facility. Specific sports development sessions could lead to extra income through sponsorship. In one authority events for disabled participants and a drugs awareness day were financed by sponsorship. These events could also enhance the facility's image.

Sometimes facility managers seemed unwilling to be swayed by consideration of these extra benefits. Sometimes sports development officers did not emphasize them sufficiently in negotiations. In the first round of contracting the potential conflicts between client and contractor were often overemphasized. The convergence of interests was often not fully recognized.

SOCIAL OBJECTIVES

The degree to which the authority has social objectives of leisure provision that conflict with those of a market-led service will vary with political control.

In one authority the social policy objectives were limited to promoting use of its facilities by the rural population. A sports development officer was appointed to thus promote the use of facilities. He had a budget to subsidize the travel costs of rural participants. However, there was no subsidy for other sports development sessions that he set up. At these sessions participants paid a rate negotiated between the SDO and the facility manager. The contract made no reference to this. On the other hand an authority with broader social objectives did tightly specify sessions for particular target groups. This prevented the facility managers from developing more commercially oriented sessions.

FINANCIAL CONSTRAINTS

Where a leisure department had experienced financial cuts during the course of the contract these might affect sports development directly and indirectly.

If sports development budgets were cut, there would be less money to buy into facility time. In this case a sports development unit with a large proportion of its facility usage built into the specification was less exposed than one that relied on negotiation and paying for the bulk of its time on an *ad hoc* basis. An indirect impact of financial constraint was that if facility managers were under greater financial pressure they might attempt to charge more for the use of their facilities and ask for higher prices from customers.

For example, two of the SDOs interviewed said that negotiations with facility managers were harder when the managers had been given tighter financial targets.

Financial constraint has encouraged facility managers to be more active in exploring market opportunities and this means that the opportunity cost of giving up time to a sports development session might be perceived as greater. For example, a sports centre which formerly had spare capacity in the morning might now have it filled with aerobics classes. Thus whereas before a sports development session would have meant extra revenue, now it would displace more lucrative use.

On the other hand, where sports development sessions would increase revenue, financial constraint would encourage the facility managers to cooperate to develop them. Thus there is greater impetus to set up sessions that the facility manager can take charge of once they are established. This has improved the work of SDOs to the extent that they are now more prepared to leave an established session and move on to set up a new one.

School swimming

As a consequence of financial constraints some sports development units have altered their programmes to include some that raise extra revenue. For example, some authorities have exploited the growing market for children's swimming lessons as the implications of local management of schools reduces the amount of swimming offered in schools.

Some sports development sections have now targeted sessions at more wealthy areas of the community to generate income. This need not necessarily conflict with sports development objectives. In response to higher charges from leisure centres some sports development sections have moved programmes to where they can hire cheaper facilities, such as schools. This may enhance their work through networking with other organizations.

Thus the impact of financial constraint has not always been negative. Sometimes it has encouraged positive changes in sports development work. The impact has been less on sports development sections who rely least on use of leisure centres. These sections have been least affected by CCT.

PROFESSIONAL RELATIONS

The preparations for CCT in many authorities have strained the relationships between the client side and the DSO. The DSO may have had to accept changed conditions of service or job losses to become competitive. They have resented the loss of job security, especially compared to the client. Sports development, in the large majority of authorities, has been retained on the client side. Thus where there have been poor relations between client and contractor these have impeded sports development officers' ability to negotiate with facility managers. In one such authority the SDO summed up the relationship as 'one of mistrust'.

The problem is greatest in authorities where preparations for CCT have left the most antagonistic relationships. These have been in authorities where the approach to CCT could be described as extremely reluctant compliance rather than in those that had taken a positive approach. The clear conflict of interests and the need to negotiate individual sessions has put greater emphasis on the need to establish good working relationships.

'Ease of booking depends on the working relationship with that particular duty manager or officer', said one SDO. 'We don't use the spec. We depend more on our working relationship', he explained.

THE NEXT ROUND

Several steps need to be taken by sports development officers in preparing for the next round of contracting.

1. They should get involved in preparing for the next round of contracting at the earliest stage possible to ensure that their interests are represented.
2. The present arrangements for building the needs of sports development into the contract should be reviewed, especially to identify areas where sports development needs are not adequately met.
3. If the needs of sports development are inadequately met because there is a conflict of objectives with the contractor, then the sports development team should calculate how much revenue the contractor would lose if the contract was altered.

For example, if the sports development team wanted access to a facility at a peak time how much revenue would the contractor lose from the displacement of existing sessions? This would be the amount by which the management fee would have to be increased if the sports development session was tightly specified. Alternatively, it would equal the amount that the sports development team's budget would have to be increased to enable them to buy into the use of the facility.

In either case the cost of meeting a sports development objective is now defined in terms of the sacrifice to the contractor's objective of profit maximization. This is the 'opportunity cost' of putting on the sports development session.

4. Having calculated the cost of meeting the social objectives of sports development that conflict with market-led objectives of the contractor, the sports development team should then work out if there is a cheaper way of achieving the same objective.

    For example, could a session be run at an alternative facility, such as a school? Could sponsorship be found to compensate the facility manager for loss of income? Sports development should also go back to its objectives and decide exactly how important this one is in relation to the cost of achieving it.

    Another example is where a sports development section was considering putting on an archery session at a leisure facility on a weekend morning. This was part of a strategy to develop certain focus sports. This would have displaced activities that would generate more revenue. The sports development team had to ask themselves whether this session was the best way of achieving their objectives. Furthermore, if it was, were these objectives worth it?

5. The sports development team should then decide the best combination of specified sessions and variation budget to meet their objectives. This will vary in each instance. Whichever methods are chosen they need to be justified with reference to the sports development team objectives. This is especially important when these conflict with market-led objectives and the cost of achieving them has been identified. This means that the sports development team is clear about:

    - What it wants out of the contract.
    - Why it wants it.
    - How it wants to achieve it.

6. Whichever method of specification is selected it needs to be detailed enough to ensure that the agreed objectives of sports development will be met whoever wins the contract. Again, this is most import-

ant in areas where social and market-led objectives conflict. Several DSOs expressed reservations about how well their interests would have been protected if a private company had won the contract. At present they relied partly on the goodwill of DSO managers and the support of senior officers.

7. In negotiating with the client officer for the new contract arrangements the sports development unit will need to respect the contractor's position and be prepared to compromise. The sports development team should be clear about where the areas of perceived conflict are and consider jointly ways of reconciling them. They should also stress, wherever relevant, the benefits to the contractor through increased income, sponsorship and enhanced public profile.

8. Whatever is specified in the contract there will need to be subsequent negotiations with the contractor. These may be to alter specified sessions or to negotiate access for new ones. The relationship with the contractor and individual facility managers will be very important. The process of preparing for the next round of contracting should be handled in a way that minimizes the inevitable tension between client and contractor and lays the foundation for a good working relationship in the future.

CONCLUSIONS

Both of the major ways of incorporating sports development into the contract have their advantages.

- A tight specification of sports development sessions will protect them best where there is a conflict with market forces. Also sports development may be less vulnerable to financial cuts during the period of the contract. Even within a tight contract anything can be renegotiated. However, the time and effort of doing this will still reduce the sports development team's flexibility.
- On the other hand a system that relies on individual negotiations for sessions, supported by a variation budget, is the most flexible. This system will allow sports development to shift resources around different facilities.

A key influence on deciding the approach to specifying the needs of sports development is the degree to which the objectives of sports development and facility managers conflict. This will reflect the degree to which the authority has social objectives of provision that conflict with a market-led service.

While the conflicts do exist and need to be addressed, there are many areas in which the interests of sports development and contractors converge.

One SDO pointed out that by focusing on the conflicts, 'there is a real danger that due to CCT, sports development can be seen as just a welfare service. This is not so as it covers a wide range of levels and types of activity.'

Sports development in practice

by Philip Sayers

The next part of the chapter studies the start of the implementation of the Sports Development Plan at East Hampshire District Council. The area of the council covers urban and rural settlements near the south coast of England.

The plan was developed by Chris Youngs, the Leisure Services Manager, together with consultants Knight, Kavanagh and Page. Chris Youngs is Leisure Services Manager of East Hampshire District Council. He has worked for the council as contractor for nearly five years, then for over five years as client. Chris has worked in leisure management for nearly twenty years in three local authorities.

Knight, Kavanagh and Page are perhaps the UK's leading consultancy on sports development and related management issues. They have worked with a number of local authorities on development strategies and specific planning for compulsory competitive tendering.

Management specifications

by Chris Youngs

CCT has tended to emphasize the need to look after existing customers. It is easier to concentrate on known customers, rather than extending the reach of that customer base to include a wider range of people from the community.

As a result of both the CCT specification, and the tight financial targets set by the council, the recreation contractor operates as a business. Thus there is an over-emphasis on income generation and perhaps less attention given to other aspects of service provision.

It was therefore agreed that with the new CCT contract, the specification needs to be constructed in such a way as to ensure that the contractor is focused upon:

- encouraging use of centres by new people and groups;
- offering a broader range of opportunities to cater for both new and existing users;
- income generation.

Any assessment of value for money and the determination of appropriate performance indicators needs to be built around this focus. In other words, within existing resources, the contractor should be seeking to make space for, and then attracting, more and new people into the system to take part in sports and activities at a wider range of levels.

Key service objectives are:

- to give a wider range of people the chance to take part in sport;
- to target people from specific communities within the district;
- to give people the chance to take part in a wider range of sports;
- to give people the chance to improve and develop their skills in a range of sports by offering opportunity to take part (and be taught/coached) at a wider range of levels of those sports.

In effect, sports centres should operate as part of a network of sports development activity. Sports centres need to be linked to work in the community; in schools, in voluntary sector sports clubs and at other venues. Sports development can be defined as:

A process by which interest and desire to take part may be created in those who are currently indifferent to the message of sport; or by a process by which those not now taking part in sport, but well disposed, may be provided with appropriate opportunities to do so; or by which those currently taking part may be enabled to do so with meaningful frequency and greater satisfaction, thus enabling participants at all levels to achieve their full potential.

In East Hampshire there is a tendency to use the terms; 'sports development' and 'outreach' interchangeably. Sports development was not included in the last round of CCT. The specification for the last round of CCT was, in common with many other local authorities, largely based upon what was going on in centres at the time. This was not, in itself, inherently developmental. However, getting the contract specification for the next round of CCT right is vital. It will frame the operation of sports facilities for the next five to ten years.

RATIONALE

One of the main blockages to implementation of effective sports development in centres is the fact that much of the available space (particularly at traditionally busy 'peak' times) is occupied by users/user groups that either do not or cannot provide for developmental activity. The objective of these specifications is to increase the levels of defined developmental activity within the programme of centres. The key objective being to balance the role of centres between:

- provision of a basic (static) service to the community,
- being part of a dynamic process,

via which a wider range of people are given the opportunity to enter, participate and progress in sport.

Development

In order to do this, it is necessary to identify what is to be classified as developmental activity. Equally as important, it is necessary to identify what is not. The contractor will, in collaboration and negotiation with the client, therefore be required to achieve an overall gross increase in the number of programme hours devoted to developmental activity. The increase in hours will be in given ratios, for both peak and off-peak hours. Initial and on-going targets for the implementation of such changes are stated to be achieved during the period of the contract.

Development can be defined as:

- coaching, particularly young people, at a range of levels, and offering them clear opportunities for progression within the programme;
- development of clear linkages with schools and utilizing sessions run in facilities to accommodate/encourage continuous demand from school age children;
- provision of coaching/club-based activity into which young people can 'graduate';
- club activity which is clearly geared to assisting and developing talented performers;
- club-based activity where there is a clear emphasis on introducing new people to the sport and allowing them the opportunity to develop;
- activity sessions clearly designed to attach and accommodate currently under-represented user groups (care should be taken to ensure that such sessions do not stagnate);
- activities designed to ensure that people who have made the 'breakthrough' are then encouraged to progress to other organized (or casual) activity within centres; e.g. progression from a women's morning to involvement in a badminton or squash league;
- active promotion of schemes designed to enhance the participation habits of people; an example would be organized casual badminton where, for limited periods of time people can turn up – on their own - and be organized into informal singles and doubled matches.

Non-developmental activity might be the term used to describe, for example:

- casual badminton bookings;
- casual five-a-side football bookings;
- club block bookings where there is no development basis.

Block bookings where there are no junior coaching programmes are also non-developmental. Another example is where there is very little change in the composition of the group taking part, or where there is no real evidence of a systematic process of raising standards of performance.

PERFORMANCE INDICATORS

Performance indicators are simply means of assessing progress made towards the achievement of given objectives. Indicators need to be meaningful to the objective to which the specific indicators relate. The indicators also need to be clear, correspond to, and interrelate with, other objectives being set.

Table 5.1 Example specification: development of young people

Objective: to develop participation among young people

Requirement	*Minimum level of performance*
Increase in gross number of junior admissions to centres	Agreed percentage increase each year (initial target to be set for developmental activities at a percent-age, to be agreed with the client by the end of the first six months of the contract period)
Meetings with individual heads of PE from all secondary schools in the district and sixth-form colleges (minimum target attendance numbers to be agreed)	Two per annum
Collective meetings with primary school teachers/representatives from all schools (minimum target attendance figures to be agreed)	Two per annum
Allocation of on-going liaison responsibility for specific schools to specific members of staff	Two meetings of group (by end of year) Three meetings per annum (from year two onwards)
Full programmes of 'dry-side' twilight sessions to be running by end of year one	Minimum of one hour of coached activity on each evening provided at both centres between the hours of 4–6 pm Monday to Thursday evenings during term time
Development of new curriculum linked minitwilight activity programmes at both centres (in a minimum of two different sports – linked to 'focus sport' programme – to be agreed)	Five new programmes (i.e. a mum of ten weeks at one hour per week) per annum, at each centre, over the period of the contract

Progress indicators are requried for each and every specification
Appropriate progress indicators are discussed in the text

Setting and measuring performance can, in many aspects of operation, be substantially enhanced by the use of a swipecard-based computerized booking and admissions system. However, even without such a system, it is possible to measure a range of delivery-based factors when assessing progress made towards the achievement of given objectives.

A number of the objectives cited and the performance indicators related to them are interconnected. The development of a particular programme may thus enable the contractor to meet several of the requirements stipulated.

Contractor performance needs to be measured and assessed at three meetings per annum. At these meetings, the client will review performance over the previous period. Furthermore, there will be a detailed discussion about on-going or new developmental programmes planned for the following period. The client's contribution to the initiation, promotion or underwriting of such work will also be determined at such meetings within given, predetermined parameters.

SPECIFICATIONS

Based on the principles already outlined, a specification for young people can be prepared.

Development of participation in sport among young people is key to the creation of sporting habits in the young. This can provide a platform enabling them to continue and progress in sport to achieve their maximum potential. At the core of sports centre operation should be a commitment to work to attract as many young people as possible from the district to take part in sport, irrespective of the area that they live in or their social or financial position.

PROGRESS INDICATORS

Progress indicators are essential to an on-going management contract. There is a need to measure, for example, the setting up and absorption of schools into a scheme – whereby information is regularly channelled to teachers and young people via an agreed process.

This will be noted and measured via agreed market research into:

- teacher awareness of centre programmes;
- children's awareness of centre programmes;
- measured attendance from (specific) schools.

This will need to be followed up with specific targeting work, as necessary.

Another progress indicator would be the setting up, operational use, and demonstrable impact of, a programme planning group to advise on complementary programming options for sports centres, e.g. the assessment of the number of new initiatives that have resulted.

This would be measured via:

- addition of specific activities to holiday activity programmes based upon expressed need/interest;
- introduction of new after school activities in centres – based upon expressed needs/interests;
- running of introductory/feeder sessions in schools;
- the levels of response of young people to specific short-term marketing/advertising effort;
- the on-going impact on participation resulting from a concentration on attracting young people.

A progress indicator would also be needed to assess the implementation of improved systems at the sports centres to assess overall numbers of young people making use of the facilities, how they found out about activities attended and which schools they come from.

Suitable measurements would be:

- the increased numbers of young people taking part in activities at the centres;
- schools-based surveys;
- feedback from teachers at individual and group meetings.

COACH DEVELOPMENT

Coaching and coach development is integral to sports development. Specific targets can be set either for the contractor working on its own or as a mechanism to encourage the forging of links with voluntary sector sports organizations in the community. The contractor will, at the start of the contract period receive up-to-date information about the current state of play in the district in the context of coach qualification across a range of sports. In the context of the contract specification these will include main curriculum sports, sports presently carried out in sports centres, sports with development potential in the district and others as agreed with the local sports councils.

Other progress indicators for the development of sports coaching can be measured at the end of each year of the contract period by:

- gross number of attendances on each course;
- gross number of Sports Council recognized qualifications achieved;
- number of teachers qualified in different sports;
- number of contractor employees qualified in each sport;
- number of nominated community based individuals qualified.

Table 5.2 An example specification for the development of sports coaches

---

Objective: To ensure that the contractor offers coach training and development opportunities throughout the contract period, particularly in the sports which the contractor is involved in developing, and those which are relevant to schools and the voluntary sports sector in the district

Requirement	*Minimum level of performance*
The contractor will ensure that people are given the opportunity to attend qualification based coach training courses in each of the sports in which a development programme is operative. This will consist of providing (or ensuring that people have access to) at least one Sports Council recognized/approved course per sport per annum. Except where, by prior agreement with the client, an alternative form of updating/refresher type course is offered	Contractor to ensure that a minimum of eight people (resident in, or likely to apply the skills acquired in, the district) are recruited onto each course in each sport each year

Contractor to run qualification courses in at least two recognized different levels of Sports Council recognized qualification over the contract period |
| The contractor to run a Sports Council recognized qualification based coach training course for one sport which is not part of the development programme | One course per annum. Contractor to ensure that a minimum of eight people (resident in, or likely to apply the skills acquired in, the district) are recruited onto each course offered |
| The contractor to liaise with representatives of local sports (including via the local sports councils) to determine priorities for such courses | A representative of the contractor to attend each quarterly joint sports council meeting |

Progress indicator would be the number and levels of Sports Council recognized based sporting qualifications of local people to be significantly increased/improved over the contract period

---

PRICING THE SPECIFICATION

Having produced the specifications, the next step is to require the tenderer to submit a price. This is easy with, say, grass cutting. A price can be submitted per acre or hectare cut (in accordance with the specification) and like for like prices will be submitted by each tenderer.

It is not so easy for management contracts. It is even more difficult for sports development. There is a lot of in-built variability, as we have seen. East Hampshire District Council was quite clear as to the methods it would employ to ensure value for money, and actual delivery.

The council asked tenderers to submit expenditure and income details which deliver all the elements of the specification. The council evaluated tenders by the use of an evaluation matrix including elements of:

- risk;
- quality;
- price.

The council weighted each element according to the importance placed on each. In regard to sports development, the Council asked tenderers to provide information on:

- the strategies;
- the resources.

that they would employ in the sports development requirements as shown in the specifications. These proposals were evaluated in terms of both quality and price.

Thus the Council is assured of engaging a contractor who is able to deliver.

Chapter 5: summary

by Philip Sayers

This chapter has been about specifications, and sports development specifications in particular. However, the principles involved are equally applicable to all contracts, especially management contracts.

Within a management contract, delivery of services like sport development can be difficult. It can be doubly difficult within the confines of a CCT contract. Some key aspects of the chapter include:

- Management contracts are difficult to quantify and specify.
- Sports development is a good example of a difficult management contract.
- Client and contractor pursue different objectives e.g. profit, service.
- Clarity in the contract reduces subsequent client and contractor conflict.
- There are three options for sports development with CCT:
    - leave it to the contractor, but specify it in detail first;
    - leave it with the client who can then hire the sports hall etc. as required;
    - a mixture of both.
- The client pays whatever the option:
    - via the tendered price if the programme is included in the specification;
    - or via the hire fees for the one-off activity programmes.
- CCT does lead to strained relations and mistrust between client and contractor.
- For financial viability, the contractor has to achieve fair payment.
- For success, the willing cooperation of client and contractor is essential.
- Where there is a convergence of interest, this is worth exploiting; for example, midweek daytime sports programmes are in the contractor's slack period.
- Financial constraints make managers more active.
- Alternative and cheaper accommodation can be hired elsewhere, e.g. schools.

Preparing for new contracts allows a total and holistic view to be taken. And there can be no excuses in a second time tender not to take account of the experiences from the first years of the contract:

- Preparations for future contracts need to start two years before contract commencement.

- Full details should be specified.
- Full details allow both contractor and client to cost the programme accurately.
- All specialists should be involved in preparing specifications.
- Objectives need to be clear.
- An example is: to give a wider range of people the chance to take part in sport.
- Income generation is another example.
- To be effective, objectives need to be linked to measurable targets.
- Good targets include counting the number of increasing attendances.

Good tender practice for management contracts states that tenderers should analyse the specifications of the client. Then each tenderer should state:

- their strategy to achieve the objectives stated in the specifications;
- the resources to be allocated to the objectives;
- their proposals for measuring that performance.

That way, everyone (client, contractor, and customer) is tied together from the outset.

Business plans

Introduction

by Philip Sayers

A 'tenderer' only becomes the 'contractor' after winning the tender competition. After that the contractor only stays in business if a profit is made. Contractors also need to satisfy their customers. These two over-riding requirements apply equally to private sector contractors and public authority in-house contractors.

By law in the United Kingdom, local authority contractors have to make a rate of return on capital employed of at least 5% each year, or for some services like leisure management, at least break even. Failure to achieve this rate of return, or break-even situation, leaves the contractor liable to be closed down by government edict.

This is the same way that the receivers would close down a private sector contractor, where the contractor was insolvent. Actually it is harder for the local authority contractor. The rules require the 5% return (or a break-even situation) in each and every single year of the contract. A private sector contractor can decide to carry a loss for a year or two. Provided the contractor is financially solvent, no-one will attempt to force the contractor out of business.

So, it is quite clear contractors have to:

- win the tender in the first place;
- make an annual profit;
- keep their customers happy.

To this end, a whole range of business principles and practices are applied. In essence, the contractor has to be:

- commercial;
- competitive;
- cost conscious;

in all the work which is undertaken. After all, a contractor who has won a tender is saying that he can operate that contract, more cheaply and more cost-effectively than any other contractor. He is the best. The tender competition was the proof. That is some reputation to live up to.

It has been said, perhaps unfairly, that anyone can win a tender. However, delivering the service for a 5–10 year period, profitably and successfully, is a different task.

This chapter concentrates on business practice. First, basic business plan guidelines are highlighted. Then the case study gives a fascinating account of putting these business planning principles into practice in a management contract. Adopting these classic business principles, a local authority won a large leisure management contract. The contract was for a leisure centre which had, until then, been operated successfully by a major leisure management private sector company.

There are many different ways of preparing and structuring a business plan. However, the principles tend to be similar from one plan to another. Nick Reeves, Director of Policy and Development at the Institute of Leisure and Amenity Management, sets out the principles in the first part of the chapter. Nick has worked in most areas of the leisure profession at a strategic and operational level. His career to date has included periods employed in the public and private sectors.

Business planning guidelines

by Nick Reeves

WHAT IS A BUSINESS PLAN?

A business plan, sometimes known as an operational plan, is a document which outlines an organization's key objectives and its management strategy for achieving them over a defined period; normally three to five years. This is presented in the context of the organization's history, status and current operating position.

Why prepare a business plan?

The process of putting together a plan, is as important a management function as the final document itself. The process enables an organization to take a critical and objective look at itself. Areas of weakness and strength are identified and realistic targets are set for achieving objectives.

Business planning should involve both the managers and the key employees of an organization. It should create a situation where employees and managers share and work towards the same objectives.

A business plan is an operating tool which should help the management team run the organization. Defined and agreed targets are set. Performance and achievement can then be monitored. A plan provides the framework within which specific decisions and directions can be taken. As a result these decisions should be more focused, effective, consistent and mutually supported.

Also, where appropriate, a business plan communicates ideas to others outside the organization. It additionally provides the basis for business development. Without a plan, an organization can deviate from its priorities, and become ineffective.

Who should read a business plan?

A business plan is primarily a document for internal use. However, it may be made available to others who have contact with the organization, e.g. potential partners, investors and funding bodies. A plan should be primarily directed at and owned by employees and managers.

Structure of a business plan

There is no standard structure for a business plan. Each document is necessarily tailored to each individual organization. However, good plans share certain characteristics. Above all, they should be clear, concise, practical and consistent about organizational and performance targets. They must reflect the organization's ultimate objectives. A workable plan must be realistic about the resources available, both financial and human.

THE BUSINESS PLAN ITSELF

The purpose of a business plan is to enable an organization to move forward effectively. This usually requires an analysis of the organization's past and current situation as well as its future plans. Organizations should therefore include the following items in a business plan.

Executive summary

The executive summary sets out and highlights the key features of the business plan. It is probably the most important section of the document.

The mission statement

The mission statement defines the organization's functions, vision and organization-wide objectives. For example, the mission statement of a local authority leisure services department might be:

> To deliver the highest possible range and standard of leisure services to its customers, thereby improving their recreational opportunities and quality of life, within the resources allocated by the council.

> The mission statement is often developed by the senior management team. It is then their responsibility to detail the plans and budgets necessary for implementing these objectives.

Strategic priorities

This should include analysis of:

- contractor policies;
- the current activities of the organization;
- the current staffing and other resources (e.g. premises, vehicles, stocks, etc.);
- how it has come to its present position;
- what has happened in the previous year in key areas that will affect future planning i.e. sales, pricing, productivity, competition, finance;
- a review of previously set targets;
- obstacles which have prevented the achievement of targets in the past.

'SWOT' ANALYSIS

This analysis is an effective way of focusing staff on their work.

- **Strengths**: what the organization does well, e.g. its recent successful achievements.
- **Weaknesses**: what the organization does less well, e.g. its unresolved problems and issues.
- **Opportunities**: circumstances which the organization can take advantage of, e.g. a new leisure activity.
- **Threats**: circumstances which could undermine the organization's achievement of its objectives, e.g. competitors, economic climate.

TASKS AND TARGETS

Once a mission statement and strategic priorities are agreed the organization is then in a position to identify the tasks which need to be undertaken for the key objectives to be implemented. These should be set out in quantifiable terms. For instance:

- to increase customer attendances by $x\%$;
- to reduce customer complaints by $x\%$;
- to reduce utility costs by $x\%$;
- to reduce staff turnover by $x\%$.

Having identified these targets the organization should then be in a position to evaluate its performance against them. Larger organizations should consider establishing individual targets for each unit/department and relate them to the organization's overall objectives.

It is not good practice or helpful to employees to set non-quantifiable targets, such as 'to market the organization' or 'to provide museum outreach services'. Performance targets must be measurable and indicators should be defined in the plan.

The future

When looking at an organization's future it is useful, in addition to setting targets, to consider in detail:

- customer profile and expectations;
- the likely difficulties in achieving these targets;
- how these difficulties could be overcome, e.g. through a marketing strategy;
- an analysis of the implications of failing to achieve targets;
- translating objectives into figures;
- the assumptions underlying the figures, i.e. inflation, funding levels, attendance, productivity;
- the internal resources (particularly personnel) necessary to achieve objectives;
- performance review (frequency and method).

Appendices

These should include:

- an organization structure chart;
- income and expenditure accounts for the past three years and the following three (assumptions could be included here, on the next three years);
- cash-flows for the three year projections;
- balance sheets.

Finally, there should be a sensitivity analysis. This should consider the effect on the organization's finances were any of the key assumptions to change. It should relate to the analysis of the implications of failing to achieve targets.

A GUIDELINE

The business plan will reflect the image and management culture of the organization especially to those not familiar with it. The document should therefore be accurate, succinct and readable. The business plan is essentially a working document and everyone in the organization must not only be aware of it but understand and feel ownership of it. The business plan (as with any text) should be constructed in a style appropriate to the target readership. A plan aimed at a potential investor will be different from that which is intended for the Leisure Services Committee of a local authority, or the contractor's management board.

Grundy Park Leisure Centre

by Philip Sayers

The last part of this chapter focuses on business planning in practice.

This case study highlights the Grundy Park Leisure Centre at Cheshunt in Hertfordshire. This is an area of the country where London at last gives way to semi-urban towns and villages.

The Grundy Park Leisure Centre is owned by the local authority; Broxbourne Borough Council. It was opened in 1990. The council, from the outset, was keen to encourage private sector management, as this was council policy.

The council went down the CCT route early. At the time there was no immediate compulsion. The council however, did not bid.

The winning tender was submitted by Civic Leisure. This company had expanded from operating health and fitness centres in London to running leisure management contracts. The contract to operate the Grundy Park Leisure Centre was for a five-year period. The Leisure Centre included two sports halls, swimming pool, fitness factory, catering and bars and associated facilities. Civic Leisure introduced a quality health suite, and ran the contract successfully for five years.

Towards the end of the five years, the council considered whether to extend the contract, or go out to tender again. They decided to test the market and go out to tender. This was in line with their general philosophy and policies.

It was also decided to submit an in-house bid. This was led by their DSO manager, Mark Poppy, who was a commercially aware manager with a thorough understanding of the local authority market. These skills were backed by an MBA and a proactive approach to innovative management.

Broxbourne Borough Council is a Conservative administration which fully supports the ethos of open competition on a level playing field. It has been at the forefront of local government and management change and wants to deliver a high quality service for all its customers.

Winning ways

by Mark Poppy

The Leisure DSO was established on 1 April 1994 with the aims of tendering for all leisure related contracts within the Borough of Broxbourne. We had a simple effective philosophy:

- commercially minded;
- community orientated.

We built this philosophy into our business plan and bid for the leisure management contract. What follows, are its key extracts. The business plan was designed to build confidence in those who read it as part of our tender submission. It also gave us a clear path to follow, if we won – which we did.

The DSO management team are experienced in achieving the bottom line, the management style and performance shown in the non-tendered facilities. We will manage Grundy Park Leisure Centre as a commercial business to the benefit of the department, the council and local community.

At the same time the DSO has a social awareness and perspective, which is compatible with the economic success of the centre. By pursuing both objectives we believe we are unique among the potential contractors bidding for Grundy Park Leisure Centre. We can offer the best management team with the most relevant policies and operational practices for achieving success for the centre, client, council and community of Broxbourne.

MISSION STATEMENT

As the commercial section of the Leisure Services Department, the DSO mission statement is closely linked to the leisure department's own one. It is: 'to secure leisure contracts and deliver the highest quality standard and range of leisure services to its customers, within specification and within the tendered price'.

The leisure DSO's goal is to develop and work with the leisure department and Broxbourne Council in achieving its overall objectives.

A 'PEST' AUDIT

A market auditing technique known as PEST (political, economic, social, technological) was used to find out centre's position in the marketplace.

Our analysis of the political perspective included:

- the impact of local government reorganization;
- changing legislation in relation to competitive tendering;
- how Transfer of Undertakings (Protection of Employment) Regulations 1981 (TUPE) will affect contracts;
- the future of cross boundary tendering.

It was equally important to have our plan set in the existing, and future, economic climate. This was:

- a general decrease in council resources;
- increase in the competitiveness of private contractors bids;
- effect of the national lottery on funding;
- possible effect of the new VAT rules.

Being a 'cash over the counter' leisure management contract, every attention was needed to the customer and the general social perspective. Account was taken of:

- an ever greater choice for customers;
- customers becoming more discerning in their spending;
- greater competition for the leisure pound;

Technology could help us as well through:

- improved management information required to track business;
- the effect of IT on business development and control.

SWOT ANALYSIS

A SWOT (strengths, weaknesses, opportunities, threats) technique was used to take a fresh perspective on the centre's internal and external operation. Our intention was to have it in place before the contract award.
Our internal strengths included:

- committed, enthusiastic, motivated staff;
- professionally qualified staff;
- departmental and corporate support.

Our external strengths could be summarized:

- good working relationship with the client;
- reputation for good management – for example other borough facilities.

Meanwhile, our major internal weakness was:

- little time to establish the business and DSO from scratch.

We were also under no illusions as to our external weaknesses:

- limited public and resident awareness of the borough and its leisure facilities;
- non-statutory status making the service contracts vulnerable to budget reductions;
- strength of local and national competition;
- sensitivity of population to discretionary spending on leisure facilities;
- local government administrative processes.

Opportunities

We had a number of internal opportunities to give us encouragement:

- a number of leisure contracts coming up for renewal;
- new management determined to achieve success;
- a good working relationship with the client officers;
- via internal reorganization, work with other departments;
- the need to achieve surpluses for the DSO board.

There were also external opportunities:

- potentially, a growing market;
- rising incomes with greater opportunities for discretionary spending;
- financial problems in adjacent authorities had led to reduced leisure provision, thus creating market opportunities;
- the shift towards a more health conscious and active population;
- education reform, providing opportunities for access to school facilities.

Threats

The DSO business was not without internal threats:

- legal restrictions on trading outside borough boundaries;
- limited planning time horizons due to local government reorganization;
- reduction in client resources, which would affect the level of business available.

We also took a long, hard look at external threats:

- increased leisure facilities in adjacent areas;
- economic uncertainty;
- high levels of unemployment which reduced disposable income;
- local government reorganization threatening disruption and the future role of leisure;
- growth of facilities management companies in the private sector;
- competitive pricing.

STAFF RESOURCES

It is often said in the leisure business that staff are the principal asset of the organization. For the leisure DSO this is not just a platitude but an integral part of our management style. The DSO approach is based on six key principles, which can be called the six Ts. They are all inter-related. Each has equal importance. They create synergy when implemented together. This was a model developed by myself as part of the MBA course (Poppy, 1993).

Team

The management culture is to encourage and motivate the team by giving them greater responsibility and ownership of the areas of work in which they are involved. The team is flexible to cope with change, motivated to achieving goals, and is given responsibility and account-ability to succeed.

Trust

Developing a culture of trust is vital in ensuring that the centre's goals are achieved. This culture can be established by fostering confidence in the staff. Formal and informal communication and consultation pro-cedures are established in order for people to feel free to express their views and therefore build trust.

Talking

Communication at all levels and between all levels is vital to success. Formal and informal communication will be encouraged. Being more involved in the decision making process, and feeling able to contribute to it, will generate a greater degree of involvement and ownership for all staff.

Targets

DSO employees must, within their area of responsibility, have clear targets which relate directly to those of the centre. Each contribution will be recognized through the performance appraisal system.

Thanking

If the centre is to get the best from its staff, it needs to create an atmosphere of encouragement whereby people know that if they do a good job, this will be positively recognized. They must also understand that poor performance will not be tolerated.

Training

Staff at all levels require training in order to improve performance and adapt to a changing environment. The DSO will set up a training programme for each member of staff.

Implementation

This philosophy gives an indication of the management style of the DSO and the environment in which staff operate.

The DSO bid was compiled with the assumption that TUPE applied to the contract. In other words, we intended to (and did) take over all existing staff on their existing terms and conditions. By employing the existing staff, we were thus also able to ensure continuity of service to our customers. Each member of staff was met individually. We tried, and succeeded, in placing individuals in positions which matched their experience, skills, qualifications and potential.

The management structure was built to ensure as few layers of management as possible between front line staff and managers while ensuring control at a senior level of all the centre's activities. Ownership and responsibility for key operational areas was given to individuals.

Customer care training was organized for all staff, and staff uniforms gave the centre a corporate identity.

MARKETING

Marketing is important in any contract. It is especially important, and obvious, in a leisure management contract.

The DSO attaches great importance to effective marketing, which is given a very high profile at Grundy Park Leisure Centre. We see marketing as a vital link in the value chain which all adds to the leisure experience of all our customers as well as helping us reach our income and customer targets. We propose to increase marketing budgets by over 25% to £50 000 per year. [Please note, all figures are illustrative. Real figures of cost and income are not given in this book, to protect commercial confidentiality].

The DSO marketing plan was compiled specially for use at Grundy Park Leisure Centre. We believe it will help us generate our prediction of £1 million income. By taking this approach, it is unlikely that we will suffer from any form of marketing myopia. The whole of the marketing plan will be constantly monitored and any changes fed back into the process.

It is the DSO belief that research is the point where marketing begins. As a management team, we need to talk to consumers, analyse their needs and create an experience based on this information. Only then will the centre's programme and development of facilities become customer orientated.

Our research includes:

- surveys;
- postal questionnaires;
- drop in days;
- user discussion groups;
- suggestion box;
- information desk;
- customer forums.

The DSO management team see the marketing mix as the nuts and bolts of the marketing plan. By addressing each element of the mix this will allow the management team to cover all relevant aspects of the centre's marketing operation.

Pricing

The pricings set by the client are the maximum. These prices are the cornerstone of our income generation. We ensure that the prices we set within the contract framework, are realistic and competitive.

Promotion

How we tell our customers about our activities is a vital element of the mix. It is also a major expenditure item and will therefore need to be carefully planned and controlled.

People

The impression our staff give to customers is crucial. The easiest way to destroy the marketing of the centre is to have staff who are not aware of their importance or their role in marketing. Appearance, manner and demeanour make or break a 'centre' and have to be continuously monitored.

Product

This refers both to the actual activity that we are selling and to the way in which it is presented to the customers. Research and training will allow us to improve the quality of our product as will the introduction of customer charters to ensure the product is delivered in a professional way.

Place

Basically this is ensuring that the activity is put in the best location for it to be of the best advantage for customer ease of use; for example, the location of the crèche.

Physical environment

The conditions within which service delivery will take place e.g. air temperature, water temperature and cleanliness are critical for customers. If we do not get this right every time, then however good the marketing is, we will not produce the desired results.

Process

How the customer gets to use a facility is of vital importance. It needs to be kept as simple and easy as possible, hence the number of receptionists employed, and the need for training on the computer system.

Each element of the seven Ps is vital to the overall marketing plan. And each element is given equal importance by the management team together with constant monitoring of the business.

STRATEGY

The DSO realizes that although it is a facility for the 'whole community' the market is made up of various segments, for example, health, coaching, social. The purpose of segmenting the market is to identify those segments which:

* are adequate in size to justify committing resources, e.g. health and fitness users;
* have potential for future growth and increased value, e.g. swimming lessons;
* are not dominated by competition, e.g. crèche facilities;
* need our services, e.g. the council's target groups.

Our strategy will be flexible enough to respond to niche markets as well as provide a general service.

INCOME

The income target of £1 million will be achieved by breaking it down into achievable elements each of which will be the responsibility of key staff. This empowerment of staff will lead to increased ownership and motivation and be a direct performance measure.

The income target of £1 million is made up from various sources. The income projection for general admissions and spectators is £15 000 and is the responsibility of the programme manager. A marginal increase is planned by:

* an increase in the number of events;
* attracting more visitors to the centre.

The hall hire projection is £100 000, and is also the responsibility of the programme manager. Increase in income is anticipated from:

* an increase in badminton use, particularly during off-peak times;
* targeting lunchtime use and the early evening sessions (the after-work slots);
* negotiating with local clubs for increased use during current 'dead times', e.g. Friday and Saturday nights;

- increasing the amount of school use via our connections with the local schools;
- working with the over 45s and youth development officers to increase usage by these target groups.

Income projection for squash is £40 000, the responsibility of the programme manager. Income increase is estimated from:

- increase in the amount of organized competition leagues, ladders, etc.;
- working with John Warner Sports Centre to pick up excess demand at this site;
- liaison with the leisure development officers to organize courses for all ages and abilities, thereby increasing the number of potential users.

The bars, catering and vending facilities are the responsibility of the catering manager. The net income here is estimated to be £50 000.

Attendance and income targets exist for all aspects of the centre's activities including:

- crèche;
- swimming lessons etc.;
- sports courses;
- aerobics;
- memberships;
- fitness suite;
- shop.

All have income targets to achieve. All have a member of staff responsible to ensure the targets are achieved. Some targets are set to decrease. This is to take account of a likely reduction in income due to a known factor. The decrease is kept to the minimum attainable.

EXPENDITURE

As with income, the expenditure level of £950 000 is achieved by breaking it down into achievable targets for key staff. This empowerment of staff leads to increased ownership and motivation. The targets give direct means for performance assessment. This in turn, results in expenditure levels being managed successfully.

The expenditure level for electricity and gas, for example, is under the control of the maintenance manager. Expenditure of £100 000 per year is estimated. Key factors include:

- an anticipated reduction in prices following negotiations with the utility companies;
- an energy review of the facility;
- a review of all tariffs;
- possible increase in consumption due to increased use of the centre, following from the success of the marketing plan;
- staff training, which emphasizes energy conservation, e.g. closing doors, switching off lights.

All areas of expenditure are itemized with costs and placed under the responsibility of one manager. Other areas of cost include:

- water rates;
- telephones/office equipment;
- marketing;
- licences;
- repairs and maintenance;
- head office expenses, e.g. accountancy, wages, administration.

Chapter 6: summary

by Philip Sayers

The theory and practice of business planning has been outlined in this chapter. The first part of the chapter concentrated on the theory and principles associated with business planning. These included:

- the need for an executive summary;
- the purpose of the mission statement;
- a critical analysis of strategic priorities;
- SWOT analysis;
- the importance of setting achievable tasks and targets;
- and the need to constantly monitor and check them.

The second part of the chapter outlined some of the key elements of the business plan prepared for the successful tender of the Grundy Park Leisure Centre. The plan was able to win the contract and act as a practical document in subsequent day to day management.

The actual business plan for the Grundy Park Leisure Centre can be summarized as:

- company policy relating to provision of leisure;
- staff and training;
- health and safety;
- marketing;
- operation of the centre;
- technical operation and maintenance;
- catering/bars operation;
- income generation;
- expenditure levels;
- capital investment;
- benefits of working with the DSO.

More importantly, the principles of business planning were successfully put into operation at Broxbourne, for the benefit of the customer, contractor and council.

Tender evaluation

Introduction

by Philip Sayers

A very clear distinction needs to be made between:

- tenderer evaluation, i.e. assessing the company tendering;
- tender evaluation, i.e. assessing the tender submitted by the tenderer.

Evaluation of all tenders needs to be thorough, objective and searching. This is even more true of British CCT tenders.

In Britain, there is a legal obligation to accept at least three external tenderers. This can be a recipe for disaster. If, three (or fewer) external contractors apply to be included in the tender competition, then all three have to be invited to tender. This is regardless of their suitability. This is the very harsh edge of a competitive tendering regime which is compulsory.

Tender evaluation has never been more essential. Get it wrong, and the consequences will last throughout the length of the contract.

Duncan Moffatt, who has contributed the second part of the chapter, stresses the importance of tender evaluation very succinctly. He says, 'It is false economy to accept a seriously underpriced or under resourced contract bid. This is especially true where most contracts are over four to six years in length'.

Acceptance of underpriced or under resourced tenders is highly likely to lead to:

- corner cutting;
- claims;
- reduced standards;
- increasing complaints;
- increased monitoring.

Invariably a rapidly deteriorating client – contractor relationship will result.

This applies whether the underpriced tender is from a DSO or a private contractor. DSOs seriously failing to make their 5% return on invested capital, or losing money, may well force a retender midway through the contract.

For DSOs, this will be enforced by the Secretary of State. For private contractors, the threat of bankruptcy, or actual bankruptcy, will lead to (often very sudden) termination of the contract.

Traditionally, the detailed evaluation process has fallen into two distinct parts:

- technical: assessing the tenderer's proposals for delivering the service;
- financial: an accurate assessment of the commercial viability of the bid.

TECHNICAL EVALUATION

Each tender needs to be examined in the following categories:

- staffing: numbers, calibre, experience;
- management structure;
- operational procedures;
- marketing plans;
- understanding of the work;
- innovation and flair.

It is then necessary to score each tender in each category. A simple way would be to give marks out of 10 to each category. Thus one tenderer may score 6 out 10 for staff, while another may score 8. A method of scoring encourages a greater objectivity in the evaluation. Subjective judgement has to be avoided.

FINANCIAL EVALUATION

The tender offers must be examined for:

- arithmetical accuracy;
- an analysis of the costs included;
- acceptability of the profit margin;
- the sufficiency of the contingency sum;
- the credibility of the income forecast, especially in leisure management contracts.

Before starting an analysis, a model needs to be prepared. For example, the sufficiency of the contingency allowed within any one tender, needs to be compared to what is accepted as a normal contingency, say 5% on a small contract.

Thus all rates, prices and sums submitted under separate headings can then be recorded against a predetermined estimated range. An entry that is seen as extreme in value (i.e. outside the range) should be examined in more depth. Reasons need to be found. An interview of all tenderers is advisable, especially for a management tender.

With any contract, you need to know with whom you will be sharing the next few years. Time spent on evaluation is time well spent. It can save much time and upset as the contract becomes operational.

The first part of the chapter highlights a specific tender evaluation for a leisure management tender.

Mike Coughlin, the Head of Leisure Services at Elmbridge Borough Council, involved a specialist leisure management consultant. The case study is provided by the consultant.

An evaluation for leisure management

by Jim Lynch

Leisure management was the first local government white collar management service to be subjected to CCT. It is therefore understandable that the initial approach to contracting was greatly influenced by experience gained in the blue collar fields of refuse collection, grounds maintenance and so on. This was reflected in the language of the documents and included emphasis on rectification and liquidated damages. There was an in-built assumption that by specifying enough detail you could safely award a contract to the cheapest bidder.

It swiftly became apparent in a management contract that something more was needed – something over and above the 'cheapest is best' approach. A purely technical approach seemed purpose built to award contracts to Cowboy Leisure Ltd.

So consultants Strategic Leisure Ltd were commissioned by Elmbridge Borough Council to develop a tender evaluation model for leisure management. It would enable them to select the best rather than the cheapest contractor. The Elmbridge experience is used here as a case study. It sets out the theoretical basis of the model, the practicalities of applying it and how it withstood a subsequent challenge.

ELMBRIDGE

Elmbridge is a medium-sized local authority in north-west Surrey where the main towns are Esher, Weybridge and Walton-on-Thames. At the time, the authority was Conservative controlled. The leisure facilities for tender were:

- package A: a large dry sports centre and a 33 metre swimming pool;
- package B: the lettings service for outdoor facilities, public halls and allotments.

The authority's policy was to encourage competition to the maximum extent. For instance, the DSO was supported, but received no favourable treatment. As a consequence, tenders were advertised well in advance of the formal requirements of the CCT legislation.

We anticipated that this would generate a considerable amount of contractor interest. So it proved. Almost two dozen expressions of interest were received. Of these, 15 were shortlisted. This substantial shortlist came about through a combination of internal legal advice and the view taken that no contractor could be excluded because of having no track record. This was in accordance with the Council's pro-competition policies. In those days before the contractor market had matured, we felt it prudent to include rather than exclude potential contractors.

FINANCE ...

Given the long shortlist, it was clear to us even at that early stage that the approaches of the various contractors were likely to be very different. This concentrated our minds on the evaluation process.

As with many decision making processes, the internal debate is easily summarized afterwards. However, this summary does not necessarily reflect the hours of discussion at the time.

Having full regard to the legislation, DoE circulars and guidance, we believed that we had the ability not to award on the basis of price alone. There had to be a quality element in the evaluation. On the other hand, we felt we would not award a contract to the highest quality contractor irrespective of cost. There had to be a judgement on value for money. In automobile terms we shied away from the Skoda, could not afford a Rolls Royce and instinctively felt we would be happy with Rover, Volvo or Audi.

Fig. 7.1 .... a purely technical approach is purpose built for Cowboy Leisure Ltd...

... OR QUALITY?

After lengthy discussion, we placed the balancing point between finance and quality at 35% to finance, 65% to quality. We then had to decide what we meant by quality. After more lengthy discussion, 65 quality points were divided up under the following headings. These headings were in accordance with the service specifications:

- staff proposals;
- programme;
- health and safety;
- marketing;
- technical competence;
- management.

This arrangement meant that finance was the single most important issue. However, a contractor's submission could not afford to ignore non-financial considerations.

With respect to finance, we anticipated two possible problems:

- a contractor would cut costs below those required to run the service properly;
- an apparently attractive bid could be submitted through including an unrealistic level of income.

VALIDITY

We therefore chose to adopt the criteria of validity of projections. The tenderer gained most marks for exceeding current performance by up to 15%. Thereafter marks reduced as income projections increased. A similar but reverse process was applied for expenditure.

Once the evaluation model had been constructed it was agreed with internal audit, and submitted to District Audit (the authority's external auditors). Subsequently it was formally agreed by the council through the Leisure Services Committee.

Open and accountable

At this stage, a further decision was taken which proved to be of immense importance. We believe this now represents accepted best practice. This was the inclusion of the assessment criteria and evaluation model within the documentation supplied to tenderers.

The bidding contractors were asked to submit information in a format reflecting the evaluation headings to facilitate comparison of their bids. The better contractors chose to do so and to build their submissions according to the relative weightings of each category. The feedback we obtained from tenderers was that they greatly appreciated knowing the rules of the game from the outset.

This practice has now been adopted by many authorities concerned with a fair and equitable tendering regime. It is also a requirement of European Union legislation that where the 'most economically advantageous' bid is to be selected (as opposed to the cheapest), the criteria for such a judgement must be made known in advance.

By making assessment criteria known in advance, a tendering authority is making a legal or government challenge to a tender award less likely. This is simply achieved by being seen from the outset to be open in its assessment. However, despite this common sense approach, it is disturbing to report that some authorities are still regarding evaluation models as confidential.

Informal discussions

The 15 shortlisted companies were invited to submit requests for information and clarification and to attend an individual surgery. These were informal question and answer sessions. The company and client were starting to get a feel for each other. These meetings were expressly not part of the evaluation process. This allowed the more canny contractors to test some ideas and creative approaches. It also allowed us to reassure one bidder whose only question was; 'is this a stitch up for the DSO?'

Questions and answers from the surgeries and written enquiries were circulated to all potential bidders. The tender documentation was modified where appropriate.

Invitations

At this stage, three of the 15 companies withdrew; it appeared that they had no real idea what leisure management contracting involved. Twelve formal invitations to tender were issued and 10 weeks were given for the preparation of bids. Again, to encourage competition, contractors were given freedom of access to the facilities and to information held by the client during this period.

From these 12 invitations, six tenders were received. The six were of very different style, approach and quality.

In size, they ranged from three full box files to only 15 sides of A4 paper. Within these, marketing plans ranged from a single paragraph to 10 pages plus visuals. Other material submitted ranged from pages torn from the specification to glossy photocopies and computer graphics.

The most complete documents included:

- financial data and working papers;
- management and bid philosophy;
- management objectives;
- detail set out as per assessment criteria;
- procedural documents;
- health and safety procedures;
- marketing plans;
- programming proposals;
- references.

Just as the written documents exhibited a wide range of style and quality, so did the financial submissions. The spread of bids for the four-year contracts was almost exactly £1 million in difference. The bids varied from a payment to the council of £500 000 each year; to a subsidy to be paid by the council to the contractor, for the same sum!

It was at this stage that we became very thankful the evaluation model had been prepared in advance. Work then commenced on putting it into practice. Once the tenders had been read, one submission was immediately discarded as being a qualified tender. In other words the tenderer would not necessarily stand by his bid. This point had been discussed, explained at the surgery and followed up in writing. You can only take a horse to water ...

ASSESSMENT

Having studied the submission, further questions and areas requiring clarification were raised. Each tenderer was written to with these questions. In the main, they all provided detailed and comprehensive answers. On receipt of these responses the assessment began in earnest.

Four individuals, two client officers from Elmbridge and two Strategic Leisure consultants, independently scored each of the five remaining contractors on the previously agreed comparative basis. This was carried out at separate locations to ensure independence. An assessment workshop was then held at which the four team members brought their judgements together. Although there were some areas of disagreement, the scorings were consistent to a good degree. After some discussions and debate, and very little argument, we reached a consensus on the score for each contractor and hence a recommendation for the best company.

Recommendation

We recommended that the contract for the management of the indoor facilities (package A) be awarded to DC Leisure for an annual payment by the council of almost exactly £100 000, and that the lettings contract (package B) be granted to the DSO for an annual payment to the council of £313 500.

Not the lowest tender

This was despite a bid being received from contractor X for a total payment to the council of £528 000 for both contracts.

The evaluation process had scored contractor X low. There were questions on the validity of his income projection and the allowances which had been made against several cost headings. The submission had also not been as good as DC Leisure's, or the DSO's, on several quality aspects; including managerial resources and operational procedures. As a result, this submission had achieved fewer marks than the successful tenderers.

The Elmbridge Borough Council Leisure Services Committee accepted the evaluation team's recommendations after a detailed presentation. The contracts were awarded and began in the September as planned.

In line with the council's policy of openness, the unsuccessful tenderers were given a detailed critique of their submissions. This was also in line with the Institute of Purchasing and Supply's guidance notes *Debriefing Unsuccessful Contractors*. In particular, the financial information given in Table 7.1 was supplied.

Following the debriefing letters sent to the unsuccessful contractors, the council received a letter from contractor X challenging the award of the contract. The company, perhaps understandably, felt that they had made a most attractive financial proposal to the Borough Council and should therefore be awarded the contract.

This challenge came despite the great pains we had taken to set out the evaluation model. The implications had been quite explicit. And yet, under the quality versus finance weighting, the council's ability to determine quality and accept a best bid did not appear to have been accepted.

Table 7.1 Analysis of tenders (£)

Contractor	Contract A Indoor facilities	Contract B Outdoor facilities	A and B * Indoor and outdoor
Contractor X	+ 140 500	+ 353 500	+ 528 000
DC Leisure	− 100 000	No tender	N/A
DSO	− 854 300	+ 313 500	− 494 000
Contractor A	− 725 000	+ 298 000	− 169 300
Contractor B	− 280 402	No tender	N/A

*Some economies of scale available
+Indicates a payment to the council;
−indicates a payment from the council.

A LEGAL CHALLENGE

The company copied their letter to the Department of the Environment asking them to investigate. Oddly, as Elmbridge had bent over backwards to encourage competition, contractor X alleged anti-competitive behaviour on the part of the Council rather than a breach of its fiduciary duties. Their complaint led to a DoE request for full information to be forwarded to them at their headquarters in Marsham Street, London. This was complied with within six weeks of the request being received.

Nothing then happened for almost eighteen months.

At the end of this period, during which both DC Leisure and the DSO had been achieving financial results very much in line with projections, Elmbridge contacted the DoE to enquire on the progress of their investigations. A brief message was received to the effect that no further action was contemplated!

Further informal contact was made with the DoE. We learned that as the council had clearly stated the procedures it intended to adopt, and had stuck to them throughout the evaluation process, it was perfectly acceptable to discount the lowest bid.

A major factor in the council's favour was that it had made the evaluation criteria known to all tenderers in advance. Contractor X's allegations of anti-competitive behaviour were, therefore, dismissed. It is of interest to note that some years later, contractor X was in the hands of an administrator, following a winding-up order applied for by HM Customs and Excise. The company's debts were variously reported to be between £1 million and £2 million.

THE ASSESSMENT MODEL

Since 1991, the Elmbridge model has been used by a number of local authorities to guide their tendering process. On some occasions, it has been used following direct contact with the council, on others through authorities working with Strategic Leisure. On yet others, some councils have simply used imitation as the sincerest form of flattery and copied the model lock, stock and barrel.

Looking back, it is rewarding to see how much we got right first time by adopting a common sense and customer centred approach.

The specification set out minimum programme requirements and asked that the contractor show how these would be achieved. Outside these core elements the contractors were given room to demonstrate flair and imagination and to gain a competitive edge over their rivals. By looking at a wide range of factors, we were able to gain a clear view of the best contractor having set out clearly beforehand what 'best' meant.

Refinement

In working with other councils subsequently, we have expanded and developed the model to suit individual circumstances. In particular, we have incorporated the concept of 'hurdles' into the process. At Elmbridge, marks were awarded up to a maximum in all categories. In theory, a contractor could achieve zero in, say, health and safety, and yet by the excellence of the submission in other areas, they could still be awarded the contract.

Minimum standards

Many authorities were unhappy with this possibility. So we set minimum standards in some, if not all, categories. Where these minimum requirements were not met, health and safety being an excellent example, the council could then reject the bid. In other words, the bidder had not cleared the evaluation hurdle.

In discussing this model with clients and others, much comment has been passed about assessing validity. Validity is seen as being more important than the absolute size of the bid, especially with regards to income. The advent of TUPE and the generally good level of knowledge of facility costings has made evaluations of income projections doubly important.

The technique we adopted at Elmbridge was to check, check, and check again and if in doubt to ask for further information from the bidder. From subsequent experience, we could look to see whether there was a logical link in the business plan between:

- market analysis;
- promotional plan;
- income projection.

Too often these three elements appear to have been drafted by three separate individuals and do not make a coherent whole.

DANGER: BEING OVER-OPTIMISTIC

Further experience since Elmbridge, with DSOs and private contractors, has shown that most contracts that go wrong do so through over-optimism on income rather than inadequate control of cost.

Projections of sports court utilization rates of over 100% are not unknown. Some business plans expect droves of customers on even the wettest Thursday mornings in the middle of winter. Common sense projections based on local knowledge, professional experience of similar facilities and a realistic sense of risk should be allowed to guide your assessment of projections.

Unrealistic income projections

If in doubt, look elsewhere in the bid to see what leeway the contractor has left to manage a way out of trouble. An optimistic income projection accompanied by a generous cost estimate gives some room for manoeuvre. Unrealistic income projections, and expenditure cut to the bone, is a recipe for disaster.

In detailing the experience at Elmbridge, we have attempted to describe briefly the process by which the best of the bidding contractors were chosen for the council. Clearly, what was best for Elmbridge need not necessarily be best for Bootle, Bolsover or Westminster.

However, we are confident that the thought processes which defined `best' and then translated this into a rigorous model can be applied everywhere. Our subsequent experiences with non-leisure services such as housing, also convince us that the technique is equally applicable to other fields.

Grounds maintenance

by Philip Sayers

The second part of the chapter displays tender evaluation principles applied to a grounds maintenance contract. The importance of accurate comparisons is stressed.

Like leisure management, it is easy for a contractor to put in a low bid. Subsequently delivering the service without going bankrupt is quite something else. No one wants to be in a position where a contractor goes bust. The details are supplied by an consultant with long and in depth experience of tender evaluations.

Duncan Moffatt is a landscape management consultant specializing in all aspects of grounds maintenance CCT issues. He has 22 years experience in landscape management and is principal of Landscape Management Consultants.

Grounds maintenance tender evaluation

by Duncan Moffatt

The purpose of tender evaluations is to ensure the bills of quantity and ancillary tender information have been completed properly. First a check is necessary to ensure that no arithmetical errors have been made in the tender.

It is also essential to be satisfied that all submitted rates are viable and sustainable, and that specifications and conditions have been fully cross-referenced and site conditions assessed.

Ancillary tender information needs to be checked for viability. Notably:

- proposed staff resourcing levels;
- realistic working method statements;
- proposed plant and vehicle resourcing;
- TUPE information (where relevant).

All other forms need to be checked that they have been completed correctly, especially the form of bond or form of parent company guarantee.

It is essential that evaluation is carried out thoroughly, objectively and not in an anti-competitive manner, and that additional costs added to tenders are not only 'allowable' but accurate. It is necessary to bear in mind that, for instance, 'Authorities should be ready to provide the Secretary of State with a detailed account of prospective redundancy costs should they be asked to do so'.

A full tender evaluation on a £500 000 per annum multi-disciplinary grounds maintenance contract is likely to take a minimum of three to four weeks, and possibly longer, if actuaries are required to assess the comparability and shortfall (if any) of a private contractor's pension scheme. This requires objectivity, experience and competence at all stages.

EVALUATION

The evaluation process can be broken into six elements.

Arithmetical checks

Checks on the arithmetic of the tendered prices are normally carried out by the Finance or Treasury Department. It is essential that the method of dealing with errors is detailed in tender conditions. It is normal to amend errors in extensions or multiplication. However, omissions or errors in decimal places in submitted rates are invariably left and contractor has to 'stand by the error or withdraw'.

The actual principles of arithmetical checking do vary from authority to authority. It is important that a consistent approach is taken.

Schedule of rates

Schedules of rates are just that. They are the rates or costs of a list of jobs to be undertaken. Typically, schedule of rates (SoR) items will cover 'one-off' jobs. An example would be tree felling or removal. The rates quoted by the tenderer are often separated from the main bill of quantities.

This leads to a major problem with SoR sections produced by a large number of authorities. The problem is that the SoR section either is not entered in the contract sum, or uses very small units of measurement, or in many cases both. Either of these aspects can lead to serious rate loading. This could cost an authority dearly whenever SoR operations are instructed and ordered.

Such rate loading should be avoided. To analyse the competitiveness of SoR prices as part of the overall tender, SoR sections should be banded. Then, the same operation should be priced for small, medium and large measures. To achieve this, an SoR model needs to be prepared. This will compare a given number of rates for jobs to be undertaken.

The SoR model must be drawn up prior to tender opening, sealed and deposited with the Legal Department. It is basically a selection of operations from the full SoR. The prices submitted by each tenderer for these selected SoR items are added to that tenderer's measured bill tender. Thus the SoR is taken into account at the tender evaluation stage to assess the overall bid competitiveness.

The selection of items for the SoR model must not be based purely on historical data, or else the DSO, or current contractor, will be deemed to have an unfair advantage. Other methods of selection should be used, e.g. by numbering every schedule of rates item and selecting 20% for the model by using random number tables.

Government circulars (e.g. Circular 10/93) state that contractors should be informed of the details of the model if they request it, i.e. how it has been formulated and how it will be used. To give precise details of the actual operations that form the model would obviously defeat the whole purpose of the model.

Financial checks and TUPE

Checks on the financial bond and, if necessary, further financial checks on any contractor whose financial health was suspect at the select list evaluation stage should be undertaken.

On full TUPE tenders, detailed checks will need to be made by actuaries on comparability of the proposed pension scheme if the lowest bid is from a private contractor. Any shortfall between the current DSO pension scheme and the contractor's proposed scheme will need to be assessed and added to that tender.

There are ancillary costs to be taken into account in determining the full value of each tender. These include whether a contractor is accepting any depot space on offer from the council or not, and whether it is accepting any leased or purchased plant or vehicles from the council, and also redundancy costs where relevant.

Evaluation of rates

Probably the most critical aspect of any tender evaluation is the comparison of submitted rates (prices) against current market rates for each operation. This necessitates running a market rate model bill. Using accurate market rates is essential. Full account also needs to be taken of specification detail, materials and site conditions.

In relation to grass cutting, accurate assessments of machinery to be used for the various grass cutting regimes is a vitally important analysis. Most authorities outline the total area (square metrage) of grass to be cut. The percentage to be cut by the various machine types (e.g. from 5/7 gang unit to a hand-held strimmer) must be assessed by the contractor. This necessitates detailed visits to each site, or at least the main contract sites.

Such an analysis necessitates experience and knowledge of current market rates for all grounds maintenance operations. A full market rate model bill should be prepared. Then low and high submitted rates need to be analysed. Only then can an overall and objective assessment of the tender viability be made. A good evaluation will be able to assess if, why, and where, a contractor has loaded his rates, i.e. priced too highly or made pricing errors.

Labour resources

Details of proposed manual, supervisory and administrative staffing levels must be part of the ancillary tender information supplied with the tender on specific forms. Such information should, preferably, be broken into summer (say seven-month) and winter (say five-month) periods, due to the significant summer peak and winter trough on grounds maintenance contracts. Separating the winter and summer hours takes account of the fact that most DSOs and all contractors run their workforce on 'annualized hours', i.e. working longer hours in summer and shorter hours in winter.

To accurately compare the proposal with realistic staffing levels, a resourcing model must be run. This will use accurate, realistic standard minute values for each operation in the measured bills of quantity. It is normal to exclude the SoR items from the resourcing analysis. SoR work is not pre-planned and thus may not occur. It is only through the above calculations, and using factors for holidays, sickness, down-time, travel, etc., that a thorough assessment can be made of the viability of the proposed resourcing levels.

Ancillary information

The remaining ancillary tender information to assess normally includes:

- a general work programme;
- organization;
- quality control;
- a working method statement;
- a re-evaluation of the health and safety documents and related codes of practice.

The last item would already have been assessed at the select list evaluation stage, but a condition of tendering may have been that improvements were made to all, or specific sections, of the original submitted documentation.

It is usual to hold a meeting with the lowest pricing contractors to discuss the tender. This allows explanations for prices or manpower resources which are at variance with the market rate or resourcing models. Contractors who had made serious pricing errors would then be allowed to withdraw or stand by their errors and stay in the frame for consideration.

CONCLUSIONS

The Secretary of State for the Environment believes that a decision to reject a lower bid in favour of a DSO will only in very limited circumstances be consistent with the duty of the authority to avoid anti-competitive conduct, and would expect authorities to have specific and well founded reasons for such a decision. Tender evaluations must thus be thorough and objective.

It is clearly a false economy to accept a seriously underpriced or under resourced tender bid. A decision to accept or reject tenders, and especially to reject the lowest tender, must only be taken after careful, thorough and objective analysis. Any such decision can only accurately result from the six stages outlined. Failure to abide by government competition guidelines may well result in forced re-tender.

Chapter 7: summary

by Philip Sayers

This chapter has stressed the importance of thorough tenderer, and tender, evaluation. A relationship which will last five years to ten years deserves through preparation. After all, contract failure is usually an unmitigated disaster, to be avoided if at all possible.

The key points for the chapter include:

- It is false economy to accept a seriously underpriced or under resourced bid
- Over-optimistic prices (or income projections) in tenders need to be weeded out.
- A technical evaluation is needed, e.g. of staff resources, operating practices.
- As is a financial evaluation, e.g. for arithmetic accuracy; accuracy of costs.
- Quality of service delivery is at least equally as important as finance.

Jim Lynch of Strategic Leisure gave an excellent account of the early use of quality criteria in the selection of tenderers and tenders. His view that this type of evaluation would become best practice has been borne out. In Britain, the formal introduction of quality measures has now been accepted in all CCT services. The late 1990s differed from the early 1990s. Now attention can be given to price and quality in the formal evaluation of tenderers and tenders.

The cornerstone of this policy lies in the European Community's concept of 'most economically advantageous tender' (or 'meat' for short). In other words, the tender representing best value for money. The alternative is the lowest price.

The British government published a circular which gave authority to the EU concept. Within England, this is the Department of the Environment Circular 5/96 (published on 2 April 1996). The Local Government Management Board, on behalf of all local authorities, then published keynote booklets to amplify the concept, which was further refined by the Chartered Institute of Public Finance and Accountancy. Reference details are available in Appendix A.

Price and quality assessment will vary from contract to contract: 60% price and 40% quality may be appropriate where there is scope for interpretation by a tenderer. An independent consultant can be a useful arbiter. To remain fair, and not to be anti-competitive, it is essential to be open about evaluation criteria right from the start, i.e. in the public advert. That way, the best contractor and best contract should result.

On efficiency measurement and leisure management

by Gary Crilley, Gary Howat and Ian Milne

'I passionately subscribe to the maxim 'No measurement, no management',' says Graeme Alder, Chief Executive of Leisure Australia (in a personal communication, 1994).

Leisure Australia is arguably the largest management support organization in Australia catering for public leisure centres. Their senior managers believe that managing without performance indicators is much like driving without dashboard instruments, a known destination, arrival time or purpose for the journey. It may be permissible, even recommended, for lazy Sunday driving but inexcusable if you're managing a public leisure centre and wasting council resources, and possibly, disappointing customers.

For these reasons, Leisure Australia has been one of the strongest supporters of innovative applied research work in developing cost-effective and user-friendly performance indicators for leisure managers.

MARKET FORCES

The introduction of performance indicators for Australian public leisure centres was in response to general economic constraints, calls for greater accountability and increased competition amongst facility managers. Public sector emphasis on improved evaluation processes had developed interest in the need for industry indicators to measure :

1. efficiency of services, i.e. best use of resources;
2. effectiveness, i.e. attainment of goals; and
3. appropriateness, i.e. providing services to meet community needs.

This part of the chapter is a brief outline of some of the work done by the Centre for Environmental and Recreation Management (CERM) since 1990 in developing benchmarks for performance indicators of efficiency.

STAGE ONE

In Australia, major initiatives flowed from an approach by Leisure Australia to CERM with a request for joint development of better measurements of facility management. Literature searches of publications in Australia, the UK, New Zealand and North America followed. Initial performance indicators were trialled in three states of Australia and two 'key performance indicators' were adopted to measure the efficiency of operations.

The two key performance indicators of efficiency for Australian leisure facility managers are:

- visits per square metre;
- expense recovery.

'Visits per square metre' are easily calculated by dividing total space of the centre by the total visits per annum.

For expense recovery, total receipts are divided by total operating expenditure. These are multiplied by 100 to arrive at a percentage. For valid comparisons, each centre needs to utilize standard definitions of total space, total visits, total receipts and total operating expenditure. Standard definitions are provided by CERM with the self-administered questionnaire used to collect data.

In addition to the two key performance indicators, a range of 'work-

Table 8.2 Working indicators for efficiency

	Expression	Calculation
Services		
Programme range	Number	Weekly timeslots for programmes
Catchment multiple	Number	Catchment population/total visits
Marketing		
Promotion cost share	%	(Promotion cost/total expenditure) × 100
Promotion cost per m²	$	Promotion cost/total space
Research cost share	%	(Market research cost/total expenditure) × 100
Organization		
Training to payroll cost	%	(Staff training cost/payroll cost) × 100
Direct programming	%	(Direct visits/total visits) × 100
Payroll to labour cost	%	(Payroll cost/labour costs) × 100
Facilities		
Energy costs per m³	$	Energy cost/total space
Equipment value per m²	$	Equipment value/total space
Finance		
Surplus/subsidy(–) per visit	$	(Total receipts minus total expenditure)/total visits
Secondary spend	$	Secondary takings/total visits

ing indicators' was also developed which can assist in understanding the key indicators (Table 8.2).

BENCHMARKING

Benchmarking, in brief, is the process of continuously comparing and measuring your organization against its past performance and industry leaders. This is done to gain information that will help your organization take action to produce a superior performance.

Cooperative compilation of indicators makes the process cost-effective and allows for exacting comparisons. Confidentiality is often an issue and must be managed from the early stages of any benchmarking endeavour.

Confidentiality

Retaining confidentiality of data collected for external benchmarking can be best achieved by having returns handled by an objective third party such as a university research group. This group can then analyse data, provide summaries to individual managers and provide aggregated data to the industry. CERM completed its third Australian survey in 1994 and the 99 respondents were from centres in all states and territories. The results are shown in Table 8.3.

Table 8.3 Key performance indicators of efficiency: Australian public sports and leisure centres (1994)

	Dry centres		
	1000–1999 m² *(n = 16)*	*2000–2999 m²* *(n = 11)*	*3000 m² plus* *(n = 17)*
Visits per m²	40	58	45
Expense recovery	86%	100%	104%

	Aquatic centres	
	Indoor and outdoor pools + *Indoor wet and dry centres* *with outdoor pools* *(n = 35)*	*Indoor wet and dry centres +* *Indoor wet centres* *(n = 20)*
Visits per m²	44	89
Expense recovery	83%	102%

Notes: Visits per m²: the number of visitors to the centre divided by the floor space.
Expense recovery: receipts shown as a percentage of operating expenditure.
n: the number of centres.

The main value to managers of aggregated results (expressed as industry medians) will be to identify any indicators for their centre that are significantly above or below the indicators for similar types of centres.

Exceptional performance

For example, an indicator may be above a median. It is important to know why, especially where exceeding the indicator is desirable. It may be a competitive advantage if strategies can be put into place to sustain this level of performance. This is especially true if this indicator reflects a priority in the centre's current management plan.

Similarly, if a centre manager notes an indicator that is well below a favourable median value, then it is important to identify whether this is a potential problem area requiring correction, or whether it is a result of unique circumstances that apply to the particular centre and cannot be readily changed.

ECONOMIC VIABILITY

This chapter is only dealing with efficiency indicators. It is necessary to remember that they are not the final, or bottom line measure of management performance. They should however, be used for historical and external comparisons which can contribute to quality management.

From the three years of Australian data it appears that the most financially viable centres, with an expense recovery median value of 104%, are dry centres with a floor space greater than 3 000m^2.

The most viable centres with swimming pools with an expense recovery of 102% are those with indoor dry facilities and no outdoor pools.

The financial viability of at least 48 of the 99 centres involved in the 1994 (as in 1992 and 1993) survey is a positive reflection of improved financial management in Australia. A similar study, reported in 1988, found that only 28 of 349 municipal centres recorded operational surpluses.

ATTENDANCES

The other key performance indicator of 'visits per square metre' suggests that in order to match the more viable centres, managers need to consider attracting the equivalent of :

- 89 or more people per m² per annum, to their centre if it includes a swimming pool;
- 45 or more people per m² per annum, if it is a dry centre, 58 if matching the most popular centres is a goal.

This guide should be considered along with other issues such as:

- policies on equity;
- pricing policies;
- external sponsorship;
- management controls on expenditures, e.g. labour.

MARKETING, TRAINING AND DEVELOPMENT

One striking observation from the Australian data relates to promotion cost share and the market research cost share. There is relatively little expenditure on promotion for all types of centres; a range of 1.2% to 2.7%. There is also a near absence of market research, as a percentage of total expenditure, a corresponding range of 0.00% to 0.22%. The values for almost all categories confirm concerns for poor marketing and low investment levels in marketing strategies, an essential activity for sports and leisure centre managers.

A second observation is the conservative amount spent on staff training and development, reflected in the working indicator 'training to payroll cost'. In CERM's 1994 study this indicator (median) for dry centres ranged from 0.9% to 1.6%, and for aquatic centres, from 0.6% to 2.4%, where the 2.4% was a clear exception for one category of aquatic centres.

SURPLUS AND SUBSIDIES

The surplus, or subsidy, per visit values clearly highlight the stronger financial viability of larger dry centres in Australia. Nine of the 17 larger dry centres in the 1994 survey generated a surplus of A$0.11 or more per visit. Neither of the smaller dry centre categories had any surplus income per visit . There is a similar reliance on subsidies per visit for aquatic centres with outdoor pools: only 14 of the 55 aquatic centres in the survey had surpluses of A$0.04 or more per visit.

The apparent benefits of having strong sales and other revenue through kiosks, pro shops, bars or leased amusement machines is evident in the secondary spend values. The relatively high secondary spend per visit for larger dry centres at A$0.57, and for indoor wet and dry centres at A$0. 66, compares to a range from A$0.28 to A$0.34, and A$0.51 for other categories. This is also associated with lower fees per visit and stronger expense recovery indicators.

SUMMARY

These performance indicators of efficiency are only part of the evolving story of measurement and leisure management. Similar performance indicators have been developed by CERM in collaboration with industry. These are for:

- effectiveness via 'customer service quality' (CSQ); and
- appropriateness of service via 'degree of fit' between customer profile and service communities.

In Australia three years of benchmarking provide the following guides for public sports and leisure managers. A manager of a dry centre of $3000\,m^2$ should attempt to exceed;

- 45 visits per m^2;
- 104% operational expense recovery; and
- a catchment multiple of 5.4 or more.

An indoor aquatic centre should attempt to exceed;

- 89 visits per m^2;
- 102% operational expense recovery; and
- a catchment multiple of 10.5 or more.

Managers keen to perform are already using these and other CERM performance indicators as essential information for guiding performance targets. The adoption of these or similar performance indicators of efficiency in New Zealand and the United Kingdom will give international comparisons and incentives capable of raising the quality of leisure centre management. The ultimate winners will include not only our customers and ratepayers, but leisure centre managers who will be recognized as competent professionals.

A full list of references and other publications by the CERM Performance Indicators team are available from, CERM Performance Indicators Team, c/o Dr. G. Howat, University of South Australia, Smith Road, Salisbury East, Australia, 5109. As this book was going to press, CERM is currently finalizing arrangements with the University of Sheffield and ILAM to conduct similar applied research in the United Kingdom to that outlined in this paper.

The London Borough of Newham

by Philip Sayers

The next case study is a world away from Australia, or half a world. It comes from the London Borough of Newham, one of the more deprived multi-racial parts of Britain. Here, great attention is needed to ensure that leisure provision is reaching all sectors of the community equitably.

The case study not only features equitable use. The system used in Newham, also grapples with the thorny issue of defaults and incentives. In English law, defaults cannot be linked to financial penalties. Penalties and defaults cannot mix. Any reduction on a contract value can only be made for exactly calculated costs. This is almost impossible in a leisure management contract.

A different way could be to award extra financial payments for achieving pre-set targets. It is this approach which was largely adopted at Newham. This interesting in-depth case study is provided by Paul Martindill, who is the Leisure Management Coordinator at the London Borough of Newham.

An inner city case study

by Paul Martindill

The Newham's Leisure Services Department is guided by 'The Newham Leisure Services Three Year Plan', and the:

- Race Equality Action Plan;
- Women's Equality Action Plan;
- Disability Action Plan.

The plan also includes the policies contained within the council's overall aims, objectives and values statement. This plan has been subjected to public consultation and is reviewed within the life of every council.

The overall aim of the plan is to ensure that attention is focused upon customer responsiveness and high quality service delivery across all its service activities.

POLICY

The Leisure Services Department in Newham therefore aims to ensure that every resident in Newham is aware of its services, has maximum opportunity to use them and, as a satisfied customer, will return to use them. The main aim of local authority managed leisure centres is to provide a wide range of leisure opportunities for all sections of the local community.

The client

The Leisure Management Client Unit (based within the Leisure Services Department) has wide ranging responsibilities. This includes:

1. drafting the contract specifications, evaluating tenders and awarding leisure management contracts.

The client is then responsible for managing and monitoring the contract to ensure service delivery is to the standard specified in the contract documentation.

In excess of 150 monitoring visits take place each year over the three centres within the borough. Thus the contractors' performance is evaluated, and then reported to committee on a six-month cycle. This evaluation is an assessment of all areas within the leisure management contract, including:

- cleanliness (always a high customer priority);
- health and safety aspects;
- customer complaints and suggestions;
- customer satisfaction levels;
- customer profiles – age, sex, gender, ethnicity, disability;
- service developments.

An example of a service development would be the provision of a new children's soft play area, which was provided following requests from customers.

In addition, the unit also has a more strategic role within the leisure department, in developing sport and recreation across the borough. This includes:

2. market testing development proposals on an annual basis, and then prioritizing expenditure to reflect local demand;
3. developing and submitting bids for lottery funding for new capital developments;
4. working in partnerships with local clubs and voluntary groups to maximize sports development opportunities.

The client role in Newham is therefore much wider than the narrow contract monitoring role that appears to be currently adopted by many other client units.

The three leisure centre contracts in Newham were tendered separately and are currently operated on behalf of the council by the in-house DSO. All three centres combine wet and dry facilities of differing size and age. One includes an outdoor athletics stadium and track.

DEPRIVATION

According to a whole range of studies and statistical surveys, the London Borough of Newham is one of the most deprived boroughs in the country, with high levels of unemployment, high infant mortality, and homelessness. The contract specifications for all three contracts are very detailed. These detailed specifications are provided to ensure a balance between:

- quality;
- equality;
- value for money;

with particular emphasis throughout upon equal opportunity issues.

With increasing financial pressures bearing down on contractors, it is essential that there are also effective mechanisms in place to protect the council's interests as well as to describe them, particularly in areas associated with these equality objectives.

Embodied in the contract specifications is an emphasis on providing customer oriented services which includes:

- a client managed customer comments system;
- customer surveys;
- customer forums;
- customer outreach visits.

These are all designed to ensure that the client is able to measure its performance in terms of customer satisfaction and therefore gauge service quality.

QUALITY PERFORMANCE PAYMENTS

The London Borough of Newham only guarantees payment to the contractor of 85% of the contract tendered price. This represents the guaranteed sum.

The remaining 15% of the contract price represents the quality performance payment (QPP). This is subject to the contractor achieving:

- a high level of customer satisfaction;
- a low cumulative level of default points; and
- the specified customer profile; especially the profile of ethnic minority group users.

The quality performance payment is broken down as follows:

Customer satisfaction	Maximum possible	8%	of contract tendered price
Default points (during a month period)	Maximum possible	4%	
Customer profile	Maximum possible	3%	
Total		15%	

Customer satisfaction

Eight percent of the QPP is directly linked to customer satisfaction ratings which are determined from an annual customer survey conducted by external consultants. Actual levels of customer satisfaction are determined by analysing the results of a question in the survey. This asks: 'Overall, how satisfied are you with the services at the centre?'

This question is asked in addition to questions about how satisfied customers are with specific areas of the service. Examples of specific questions include:

- cleanliness;
- staff friendliness;
- speed of service at reception;
- speed of repairs (e.g. lockers).

Customers are invited to respond by indicating their level of satisfaction on a Likert scale from 'very satisfied', to 'very dissatisfied'. The responses are each weighted as shown in Table 8.4.

Table 8.4 Customer satisfaction weightings on a Likert scale

Very satisfied	+2
Fairly satisfied	+1
Neither satisfied or dissatisfied	0
Fairly dissatisfied	−1
Very dissatisfied	−2

A score of +1.4 is needed to achieve all 8% of the customer satisfaction payment. If the contractor scores 0 or below, no payment is made.

The results of the survey, and customer suggestions, are used to help identify and prioritize capital schemes for improvements, and programming at the three leisure centres.

Improvements

Examples of action to improve customer satisfaction range from staff training on cleaning at all three leisure centres, to the installation of a children's four-storey soft play area at one centre. By way of further examples, the work programme of the client and contractor for the next six months includes:

- replacement of all existing lockers within the three centres;
- converting a basket store room to a relaxation area with sauna and steam cabins;
- resurfacing the athletics track;
- undertaking a range of access improvements to facilitate full access by wheelchair users to the athletics track.

In addition, a bid for lottery funding is to be made for a three-phase project:

- phase I: converting men and women's changing rooms into a unisex changing village. Also reprofiling the swimming pool, to create a large, shallow depth learn-to-swim teaching pool.
- phase II: converting a disused laundry area and changing accommodation to a five-rink indoor bowls green.
- phase III: converting an existing 30.8 metre swimming pool opened in 1933 into a 25 metre pool and, in the remaining part, an under-8s children's interactive wet play area.

Default points

The default points payments are linked to the number of default points issued over a monthly period. The vast majority of these default points are issued during monitoring visits when monitoring officers find specific service areas to be of a lower standard than set in the contract specifications.

If the accumulated monthly default points are below 30, then a 4% quality performance payment is made. This monthly payment reduces by 1% for every increase of 30 default points. At 120 default points, no quality performance payments are made.

Customer profile

The 3% payments are linked to the percentage of ethnic minority customers using the individual centres, as measured by the annual customer survey.

Surveys conducted prior to the start of the contracts at all three of Newham's leisure centres indicated that ethnic minority residents were vastly under-represented as users relative to the borough's population. To ensure that this important equality issue was addressed by the contractor it was decided to link part of the annual contract price to the percentage of ethnic minority customers using the individual centres as determined by the annual customer survey.

Payment is linked to the degree to which the actual percentage of ethnic minority customers meets the targets set within the specification. The targets set within the specification reflect the percentage of ethnic minority customers living in the perceived catchment area based on an analysis of ward demographics – see Table 8.5.

The percentage level of use specified is dependent on the perceived role of the individual leisure centre and the perceived catchment area.

Table 8.5 The ethnic profile across all three centres

	Total attendances	White (%)	White (total)	Asian (%)	Asian (total)	African/Caribbean (%)	African/Caribbean (total)
Apr 92	18 713	71	13 286	11	2 058	14	2 620
Oct 92	14 612	68	9 936	14	2 046	14	2 046
Apr 93	17 283	64	11 061	15	2 592	18	3 111
Oct 93	15 361	74	11 367	10	1 536	12	1 843
Apr/May 94	19 394	60	11 636	17	3 297	18	3 491
Oct 94	17 972	61	10 963	19	3 415	17	3 055
Oct 95	18 930	56	10 601	20	3 786	19	3 597

First, if the centre's facilities were perceived to be of borough-wide significance, with no weighting towards people living locally, then Newham's total ethnic minority population is used to set targets within the contract specification. The proportion of ethnic minorities within Newham is available from the national census data.

Secondly, some centre's are perceived as being of more 'local' significance, e.g. for people living within a one-mile radius of the centre. This data can again be obtained from the census data for the surrounding wards, and an overall average calculated.

Success

There has been an overall increase in the percentage of use by ethnic minorities (see Figure 8.1).

If these results are broken down further it will be noted that the increase is due to an increase in use by Asian, African and Caribbean people, who were all under-represented. Although this increase cannot be totally attributed to the QPP mechanism, it has undoubtedly contributed significantly to the emphasis placed by the DSO in addressing the equality issue by presenting a financial motivation to increasing ethnic usage.

The mechanisms used by the contractor to increase usage include:

- production of a brochure in five ethnic languages detailing all the activities available within the leisure centres;
- the distribution of that brochure to specified outlets;
- regular press releases to the ethnic press;
- outreach visits targeted at specific community groups.

The contractor also actively encourages ethnic community groups to hold major sporting events at the leisure centres. An example would be the two day Asian Games held in June each year.

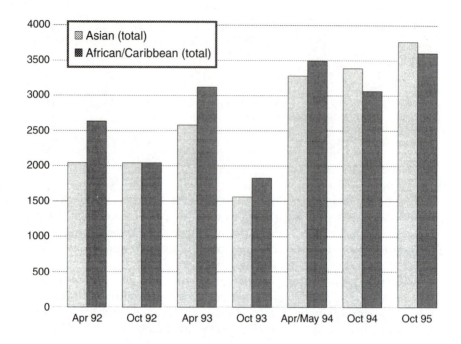

Fig. 8.1 Growth in attendances by ethnic groups across the three leisure centres

This method of ensuring that important equality objectives are protected could be used where monitoring has shown a low usage of facilities by any particular target group, e.g. women, people aged 50+, people with disabilities and young people.

THE CONTRACTOR'S VIEW

It is worth mentioning that despite successes, the DSO in Newham did not initially welcome the mechanisms for performance monitoring.

The value of the quality performance payment system was accepted by the DSO in the original tender submission. The DSO hoped to achieve a 100% contract payment (i.e. all 15% of the QPP). This has led to some problems in the initial stages of the contract. It would be prudent for any contractor to make an assessment of what percentage of the QPP is achievable under normal circumstances, and consequently to base their bid on this information.

The customer profile targets set by the client are based on attracting certain levels of new usage by ethnic minority groups in the borough. The DSO believes that the targets set for this payment would have been fairer if they had been phased in during the years of the contract following the establishment of the existing user base, rather than being immediately based on the perceived catchment area of the facilities from day one. The client would recommend this approach to other clients who are considering using this contract mechanism. With an ethnic profile approaching 50% in the borough, it would also not make any business sense to ignore such a large percentage of the DSO potential market.

Having said that, the QPP has definitely acted as an effective tool in raising performance standards across the contracts. While it does act as a mechanism to claw back some of the potential contract payments, it can equally act as a motivator to the DSO staff in attempting to achieve a minimum number of defaults and the highest level of customer satisfaction.

Chapter 8: summary

by Philip Sayers

In this chapter we have seen two fascinating accounts of performance measurement. Some of the more important aspects of the chapter to highlight include:

- Where there is no measurement, there is no management.
- As contracts progress, a means of measurement is needed to ensure that the contract is being performed, as intended and stated in the specifications.
- With a building contract this is relatively easy to measure.
- The building is built or not, the right materials are used, or not.
- With maintenance and management, it is harder.
- Technical measurement can be made, e.g. length of grass, pool water temperature.
- Measurement is also needed of efficiency, effectiveness, and appropriateness.
- Visits per square metre of pool, and expense recovery from fees charged are two good measurement indicators for a leisure management contract.
- Comparison of 'visits per square metre' and 'expense recovery' with other pools, or leisure centres, provides real management information to motivate improvement.
- There are other equally valuable indicators of performance.
- Expenditure on marketing, training and development indicates commitment.
- An indoor acquatic centre in Australia should achieve at least 89 visits per square metre and 102% operational recovery of expenditure.

In a leisure management contract, attention needs also to be given to policies on equity. There is no point in providing a publicly subsidized swimming pool just for use by the rich.

At the London Borough of Newham in London, specific attention has been given to ensuring equity of use across all sectors of the community:

- Newham aims to ensure that every resident is aware of the leisure opportunities available, and has maximum opportunity to use them.
- Newham believes that satisfied customers will return again and again.

- As well as monitoring key performance measures like cleanliness and speed of service at reception, the client also takes a strategic role.
- This includes actively persuing developments via partnership ventures and helped with lottery funding where possible.
- Newham is a place of great deprivation.
- Specific attention is given not only to customer satisfaction but also the ethnic mix using the leisure facilities.
- A quality performance payment system has been introduced to encourage specific attention by the contractor to:
    - customer satisfaction;
    - adherence to specifications;
    - customer profile.
- With the customer profile, specific attention is given to ethnicity.
- The intention is to try and reflect the ethnic percentages in the local population in attendances in the leisure centres.
- The QPP mechanism has, in part, been instrumental in achieving an ethnic use of the leisure centres which reflects the ethnic populations in the locality.
- With a 42.3% ethnic profile within the borough, the contractor sees the importance of attracting the ethnic market.

The two case studies may be worlds apart, but there is great similarity in the key principles. Great attention should, and can, be focused on customer satisfaction. Also attention can be focused on achieving a use of leisure facilities which truly reflects the ethnic mix of the local population.

Customer satisfaction

Introduction

by Philip Sayers

Straddled between the client and the contractor is the most important person of all, the customer. Offend the swimming pool customer, and he or she will stay away. Both the client and the contractor will have failed. The contractor will feel the effect first. Income will reduce. If the reduction is sufficient, the contract will become unprofitable and the contractor will go under. The client will be left with the unenviable task of finding another contractor to operate the site, pronto.

In grounds maintenance, customers are slightly different. They will not go away. They cannot. Furthermore, they complain in ever-increasing quantity and volume.

The secret of a successful contract is therefore to make a profit, while keeping the customer happy. Both client and contractor have a part to play. Instead of confrontation between the client and contractor, co-operation is far better. Excessive 'tick sheet' monitoring can be self defeating.

A more positive method of contract management for all the three parties:

- client,
- contractor,
- customer,

is to undertake joint customer satisfaction surveys to see:

- what customers want;
- what they are satisfied with;
- what dissatisfies them.

Points of dissatisfaction are particularly important for positive management. Often, simple changes to reduce niggling customer concerns can have a huge beneficial impact on customer satisfaction.

To be accurate, any survey needs to be statistically valid. A representative number of customers have to be sampled if an accurate survey is to result. This is where the next case study takes us and it builds on the experiences recorded in the previous chapter.

The case study in this chapter comes from Darlington. It is an excellent example of cooperative contract management for the benefit of the customer. It is not surprising that Darlington Borough Council were the winners of the annual Sports Council Management Award.

Steve Howell was with Darlington Borough Council and is now a client officer with Hambleton District Council in the north-east part of England. He is an author and lecturer on a number of leisure related subjects and is also a doctoral research student specializing in the performance measurement of leisure services. The chapter provides a clear case study demonstrating how an effective partnership can benefit client and contractor in participation research.

One survey – one aim: a better service

by Stephen Howell

The introduction of CCT to the management of sport and leisure facilities has introduced some dramatic changes to management practices, none more so than the humble practice of participation research.

Often hidden deep in contract specification is the following type of clause: 'The contractor shall be expected to provide user information and statistics and to contribute towards the user and non-user surveys'. This clearly underlines the responsibility of a contractor to carry out participation research. It is the foundation on which we have built our approach to survey and participation work.

The pressures that have led to this approach have been essentially threefold:

1. A more serious approach had to be adopted since the work forms part of a contractual agreement.
2. Market research has become of greater importance in the free market environment of CCT.
3. A greater need has arisen for authorities to monitor those aspects of social policy where implementation now lies in the hands of contractors.

The overall effect of this has been a demand for research which represents a greater validity and reliability than has previously been demonstrated. A demand in which both client and contractor have a vested interest in getting it right.

The practice of participation research is not new to local authorities. However, good quality research probably is. Gone now are the days when we asked leisure attendants to 'get some questionnaires filled in'.

'Surveys? I used to have to do them when things were quiet', one leisure attendant admitted frankly. 'My quota was made up of people who either looked friendly or', he paused a moment, 'those who I thought I would quite like to go out with'. Another leisure attendant highlights some of the short comings inherent in previous research; 'Non-user surveys? I didn't like doing those. You had to stand outside the doors rather than in reception. Very cold in winter!'

The new pressures of CCT meant that Darlington Borough Council needed to grasp the initiative and actively seek an approach which would allow the results of research to hold a level of creditability now demanded of it. In order to inject reliability and validity into our surveys it was necessary to examine in more detail:

Fig. 9.1 'Just another two, then we can go inside and do the users.'

- how we collected data;
- how we analysed data.

The comments of these leisure attendants demonstrate the *ad hoc* manner in which data were being collected. This results in unrepresentative samples. Representativeness is essential, if inferences regarding the population are to be made from samples. Additionally, the problem traditionally encountered in the analysis was one of finding an appropriate method which would fit the level of data. If we were to make any further in roads into understanding participation, these problems need addressing.

REPRESENTATIVE SAMPLING

Participation research is essentially based upon social and economic indicators. These indicators for the main part produce data of a nomi-

Variables

Region of town Type of housing	Age Sex Marital status	Number of children Pre-school child Sex	Household income Employment status

Base or reference categories

Owner occupier Mow/Hum P = C 0.796, D 0.340	Male, married 19–24 P = C 0.291 D 0.571	Male, no children P = C 0.580 D 0.239	Employed £30 000 P = C 0.754 D 0.342

Characteristics which significantly influence participation

	Region of town Haughton 0.582 HarrHill/N Road 0.559 ParkE/BT/Lacs 0.592 NGN/Central 0.595 *Housing* Council tenant 0.625	*Sex* Female 0.722	*Number of children* *by pre-school child* 1 child pre-school 0.354 *Sex* Female 0.740	*Income* <£5000 0.495 £5000–10 000 0.572
CIVIC				
DOLPHIN		*Sex by age* Female, 19–24 0.534	*Number of children* 1 0.350 2 0.483 3 0.431 *Sex* Female 0.322	*Employment status* Unemployed 0.561 Retired 0.217

Lowest probability of participation

	Council house tenant living in Haughton P = 0.373	Males of any age and marital status P = 0.291	Males, 1 child, pre- school P = 0.353	Income under £5000 any employment status P = 0.495
CIVIC				
DOLPHIN		Males any age and marital status P = 0.571	Males no children P = 0.339	Retired any income P = 0.217

Best probability of participation

	Owner occupier living in Mowden/ Hummersknott area P = 0.796	Females any age and marital status P = 0.722	Females no children P = 0.740	Employed with household income over £30 000 P = 0.754
CIVIC				
DOLPHIN		Females 25–34 any marital status P = 0.534	Female, 2 children P = 0.585	Unemployed, any in- come P = 0.561

Figure 9.2 Leisure participation in Darlington. C = Civic, D= Dolphin. Mow/Hum = Mowden/Hummersknott area of town. *P* = probability of participation (see text).

nal or categorical nature. In light of leisure being a complex social behaviour, we wanted to look at leisure participation in terms of a number of such variables:

- sex;
- age;
- region of origin etc.

The level of analysis desired is therefore of a multivariate nature. Mathematically this presents a problem. What we wish to do is to carry out the highest level of analysis, on data of the lowest form.

These problems are challenging, in particular the analysis, but are not insurmountable. In terms of examining usage we found the key to better research lay in:

- probability sampling;[1]
- the use of logistic regression as the method of analysis.[2]

This may sound very technical and difficult, but don't be put off yet!

It may even sound expensive to implement. However, there are a number of pleasant surprises en route. They include the fact that the size of the sample required has nothing to do with the size of the population from which you wish to extract it. The size of the sample and cost of obtaining it are both smaller than may be imagined ($n = 659$). Also the mathematical calculations involved in this can be painlessly achieved by an average desk top computer.[3] Is the effort worth it? Yes it is.

The results are possibly the best indicator for participation we are capable of producing. Figure 9.2 shows how concise the results can be presented. Essentially, running from left to right, it demonstrates four separate models examining different aspects of participation.

Geographical representation

The section labelled variables, indicates what we are examining. For example, the extreme left model examines participation in terms of the region of town lived in and the type of housing tenure held.

Moving downwards to the next row, labelled base or reference categories, shows selected categories of the variables, against which all others are to be compared. The *P* figures represent the probability[4] of participation at the two facilities shown, for those people who are owner occupiers living in the Mowden/Hummersknott (Mow/Hum) area of town. In this case the figure 0.796 for the Civic Theatre and 0.340 for the Dolphin Centre. Here the owner occupiers are the base categories.

Below this are shown the characteristics which significantly influence the probability of participation compared with the base or reference categories. Reading downwards, two boxes are shown representing the two facilities under investigation. Ideally the box should remain empty, as in the case of the Dolphin Centre. This tells us that in terms of participation at the Dolphin Centre the authority would appear to be egalitarian in terms of regional origin and housing tenure.

Variable participation

The Civic Theatre box, however, shows both the variables as influencing participation. The box also lists under them the categories which significantly influence participation. Categories not listed do not alter significantly from the base category, i.e. there were ten regions of which only four are listed as influencing participation relative to the base category. The figures next to these categories show the effect of substituting that category into the base or reference model. For example, the base or reference model shows the probability of participation for an owner occupier living in the Mowden/Hummersknott (Mow/Hum) as being 0.796.

Should we replace Mow/Hum for someone living in Haughton, the effect on the probability is to reduce it to 0.582. Similarly if we replace owner occupier with council tenant the effect is to reduce the odds to 0.625. Theoretically we can calculate the probability for any individual, given their associated categories of the variables. A similar interpretation can also be made for the remaining three models.

A further elaboration of this allows us to identify a best and worst case for each model in Figure 9.2. Having obtained the results it is interesting to note the difference between them, and how differently the clients and contractors utilize them.

CLIENT USES

The client interest is in social policy and promoting the general quality of life for residents. These include for example, concession pricing for the unemployed. This can be examined relatively easily through the probability of participation for that particular group.

Here, the scheme is proving to be effective. The best probability of participation at the Dolphin, in terms of household income and employment status, is for the unemployed. This certainly suggests that removing the economic barriers to participation has encouraged unemployed usage. Similarly, sports development officers can see that region of origin has very little to do with levels of participation.

The assumption: 'that this is a deprived area, therefore we must allocate resources to it', was wrong. A change in strategy towards campaigns targeted on the basis of other personal characteristics is likely to be more effective.

CONTRACTOR USES

The identification of target groups by this method opens the door for highly specific targeted marketing by the contractor.

A good example is the theatre case in which it was possible to juxtapose the results with the population sizes of the various regions. Then calculate that targeted mail drops (costing approximately 70% less), would still maintain approximately 90% of the response.

In addition it became very apparent that use at the Dolphin Centre was child led, which has obvious marketing implication. The effectiveness of the marketing effort can certainly be improved by the use of this type of information.

A PERFORMANCE CULTURE

Changes in the basic structure of how leisure services are delivered in this country, brought about by CCT, have resulted in the creation of a performance and stewardship culture within the industry. Whether you agree or disagree with the basic principles of CCT, the impact on audience and participation research has to be seen as beneficial.

These changes may be seen, as in the above example, as steering us into a world of rigid precision in which accuracy and procedure rule supreme. I am not advocating that the same austere approach be adopted for the management of leisure contracts, for this or any other aspect of performance. All we are attempting to do here is establish a starting point, to provide a basis of fact and knowledge, to which both parties can be in agreement. From this point on flexibility is the name of the game in establishing an effective partnership between contractor and client.

The Centre for Leisure Research[5] has published a report which expresses concern at the nature of most sport and leisure management contracts. In association with that concern, attention is drawn to the lack of non-financial performance indicators to be found within such contracts. The inclusion of clauses demanding participation research will surely go some way to addressing this.

This survey allows the needs of both demand led ideologies and recreational welfare to be satisfied. The results are capable of contributing to what Coalter reminds us was one of the underlining rationales of CCT; to 'increase the consumer orientation of leisure services'.

Demographics

The coming decades hold great shifts in the demographic make up of our population. Darlington will now be in a position in the coming years to monitor how its services are responding to those changes. The contractor will be able to identify their impact in markets. Clients will be able to identify the outcomes of their development work relative to these shifts.

I hope that Darlington's experiences and efforts go some way towards encouraging leisure managers to heed the advice of Coalter who further suggests: 'the future of leisure services will best be secured by going beyond simple consumer based contract monitoring to encompass broader processes which involve citizens'.[6]

When this involves the client and contractor working together the result is, one survey, one aim – a better service.

NOTES

1. Probability sampling gives every person in the population an equal chance of being selected in the sample.
2. Logistic regression is a multivariate technique, capable of handling data of a nominal level, of the form $Y = f(x_1, x_2, \ldots x_n)$ given by $P/(P-1) = b_0 + b_1 x_1 + \ldots + b_n x_n + e_i$. The odds of participation are given by $P/(P-1)$ where P is the probability of being a participant, $b_0 + b_1 \ldots b_n$ are the parameter estimates $x_1 \ldots x_n$ are the independent variables, age, gender, socio-economic group, etc. and e_i is the stochastic term.
3. Logistic regression procedure is available in SPSS for windows, a readily available statistic package.
4. The probability of an event happening is represented by a figure between 1 and 0 where 0 = the event definitely not happening and 1 certainty of the event happening.
5. Sports Council (1993) *Sport and Leisure Management: Compulsory Competitive Tendering*, national information survey report.
6. F. Coalter (1994) 'Leisure services: all to play for', *Journal of the Institute of Leisure and Amenities Management*.

Chapter 9: summary

by Philip Sayers

Every contract needs to satisfy the customer. Both client and contractor take joint second place, to the customer. Indeed, both client and contractor need to satisfy the customer. There is no better way of evaluation than by a customer satisfaction survey. This chapter has shown how:

- In a contract situation customer satisfaction takes on great importance.
- In the free market ethos of CCT, market research becomes more important as well.
- There is also a need for authorities to measure how effective they are being in implementing their social policies.
- Any form of research needs to be valid and reliable.
- Sampling has to be representative of the population being examined.
- For example, the age, sex, and living location of the people being studied, need to be accurately reflected in the sample.
- Large samples are not needed.
- The statistical methods employed can be undertaken on an average desk top computer.
- At Darlington, an assumption that 'this is a deprived area, therefore allocate resources was proved wrong.
- A campaign towards personal characteristics is more likely to be effective.
- Proper representative surveys are good news for the contractor.
- Mail shot costs can be dropped by 70%, yet still maintain high response.
- Client and contractor can work together for the benefit of the customer.
- One service, one aim – a better service.

Addendum to Chapter 9

DARLINGTON LEISURE PARTICIPATION SURVEY

Firstly, some questions about the leisure facilities you use:
Please tick the appropriate box, unless otherwise requested.

1. *Have you ever visited?*

The Dolphin Centre	Yes [ ]	No [ ]
The Civic Theatre	Yes [ ]	No [ ]
The Arts Centre	Yes [ ]	No [ ]
Stressholme Golf Club	Yes [ ]	No [ ]

How often have you visited any of these facilities in the last 12 months?

	Dolphin Centre	Civic Theatre	Arts Centre	Stressholme Golf Club
More than once per week	[ ]	[ ]	[ ]	[ ]
At least once per week	[ ]	[ ]	[ ]	[ ]
At least once per month	[ ]	[ ]	[ ]	[ ]
Less than once per month	[ ]	[ ]	[ ]	[ ]
Once or twice	[ ]	[ ]	[ ]	[ ]
Never	[ ]	[ ]	[ ]	[ ]

Now, some questions about yourself:

2. *Are you male or female?*

Male   [ ]   Female   [ ]

3. *In which age group are you?*

16–19	[ ]	20–24	[ ]
25–34	[ ]	35–44	[ ]
45–54	[ ]	55–64	[ ]
65+	[ ]		

4. *Are you:*

Married [ ]   Single [ ]   Divorced/separated [ ]

5. *Are you registered disabled?*

Yes [ ]   No [ ]

6. *Did you attend school in Darlington?*

Yes   [ ]   No   [ ]

7. *At what age did you, or do you expect to, complete your full time education?*
16 or under   [ ]
17–18   [ ]
19 or over   [ ]

8. *How long have you lived in Darlington?*
Less than 1 year   [ ]
2–3 years   [ ]
4–5 years   [ ]
Over 5 years   [ ]

9. *Do you own or have use of a car?*

Yes   [ ]   No   [ ]

Next some questions about the household you live in:

10. *What best describes your present housing situation? Are you:*
An owner occupier   [ ]
A council tenant   [ ]
A private tenant   [ ]
In residential care   [ ]
Living with parents/guardians   [ ]
Other . . . .

11. *How many children are there in your household* under the age of 16?
0   [ ]   1 [ ]   2 [ ]   3 [ ]   4 [ ]   4+ [ ]

How many of these are aged less than 4 years? . . . .
How many of these are aged 5–11 years? . . . .

12. *Approximately what was your household income before tax last year? (include*
all income to household, not just your own)
Under £5000   [ ]
£5000 to £10 000   [ ]
£10 001 to £15 000   [ ]
£15 001 to £20 000   [ ]
£20 001 to £25 000   [ ]
£25 001 to £30 000   [ ]
Over £30 000   [ ]

Finally a few questions about your occupation.

13. *Are you:*

In employment	[ ]
Unemployed	[ ]
Looking after family/home	[ ]
Retired	[ ]
Not eligible for employment	[ ]
Full time student	[ ]

14. *On average how many hours do you spend working or studying per week, including overtime?*

None	[ ]
Less than 15 hours	[ ]
15–25 hours	[ ]
26–37 hours	[ ]
38–45 hours	[ ]
46 hours or more	[ ]

15. *Does your work involve weekend or evening work?*

Weekend work	Yes	[ ]	No	[ ]
Evening work	Yes	[ ]	No	[ ]

16. *Would you describe your occupation as (or former occupation if not in employment):*

Professional	[ ]
Managerial	[ ]
Non-manual or clerical	[ ]
Skilled manual	[ ]
Unskilled manual	[ ]

17. *What is the nature of the organisation you work for?*

Manufacturing	[ ]
Construction	[ ]
Services	[ ]
Other	....

Thank you for your time
Please return your questionnaire in the pre-paid envelope provided

---

Conflict and collapse

Introduction

by Philip Sayers

There is always an inherent tension in a contract. It starts with the preparations for the tender competition and follows through into the contract period. After all, the contractor is invariably carrying out the work for the least known possible cost. The client is only too well aware of this fact.

There is a real tension for the contractor. The contractor has to satisfy the customer, the client, and also achieve a satisfactory profit. The tension for the client is the ever present fear that the contractor may not be carrying out the work as specified. Cutting some corners here and there, rather than cutting the grass. The sheer amount of detailed paperwork relating to the contract also brings its own tensions.

CONFLICT MANAGEMENT

A good contractor, and a good client, spend an inordinate amount of time positively managing the contract situation. Good contract management demands maturity, ever present reasonableness, and more than anything an ability to see the other person's point of view. Easier said than done.

Mature management also demands that both parties need to play by the rules. At least open conflict is manageable. The view of each party is open and clear.

Sometimes, the client or the contractor may not be playing by the rules. The desire to play hidden games intensifies as the pressure mounts within the contract situation. For example, where a large contractor has many contracts across the country, pressure can come from the knock-on effect from contracts which are going badly. What the contractor loses on one contract, he tries to make up on other contracts.

Problem resolution

Contract management is littered with disputes. The ones which make the courts are but the tip of an iceberg. But it is all too easy for the client or the contractor to totally believe that they are in the right. Invariably both have weaknesses. It is a foolish person who believes that they are all right, and the other party is the one who is all wrong. It is far better perhaps to avoid confrontation, if possible.

This chapter provides two very different case studies. The first case study highlights a dispute between a client and contractor which went all the way to court. The court and legal processes then took an unusual turn.

The second case study looks at one contractor in depth. It is an amazing story originally told in full in Parliament itself. Many local authorities in the country suffered from the collapse of this contractor. Indeed, any authority suffers from the sudden cessation of any contractor. A planned termination is much easier to manage.

Malcolm Gilbert is a solicitor specializing in contract dispute work. Over a number of years of experience he has developed a healthy respect for the commercial impact of litigation. Here, he shares some thoughts on a particular dispute.

Litigation – is it worth it?

by Malcolm Gilbert

One of the consequences of the CCT regime is to extend the potential for contract disputes of the type experienced for many years by the civil engineering fraternity. Arbitrating and litigating contractual disputes involves the application of tremendous amounts of resources, including money, for those involved. Very often the resources to be applied exceed the sums at risk.

A brief look at a dispute in Plymouth may persuade other local authorities to think carefully before committing themselves. The dispute concerned a grounds maintenance contract with an estimated value of approximately £1000 000 per annum. The contractor was a European company, operating through a UK subsidiary. A parent company guarantee had been given, backed by a European bank.

The specification was output based. The contract conditions included the usual provisions allowing the client to serve:

- remedial action notices (RANs),
- performance failure notices (PFNs),

to support the monitoring of contract compliance. The client was empowered to terminate the contract in the event of a specified number of PFNs being served in any calendar month, or in the event that a specified aggregate number of PFNs were served over a three-month period. The actual numbers are not significant.

DISPUTED DEFAULTS

What is significant is that the client and the contractor took opposite views as to the interpretation of precisely how many PFNs were required to trigger the right to terminate under the aggregation formula. The client was not satisfied with the performance of the contract and sought to terminate on the basis of the aggregation of PFNs over a three-month period. The contractor disputed the termination, alleging:

- first, that insufficient PFNs had been served to trigger the right to terminate; and
- that in any event, of the PFNs served, a proportion were defective or invalid.

The contractor issued proceedings in the High Court claiming damages, including:

- loss of profit;
- the recovery of liquidated sums, such as wasted hire and rental fees for plant.

The contractor did not seek to obtain an order requiring the client to continue performance of the contract.

THE HIGH COURT

The client chose to defend the proceedings in the High Court and not to require the dispute to be dealt with by way of arbitration. Strictly speaking, the client would have been within his rights to insist that the dispute was arbitrated and could have applied for the High Court proceedings to be stayed, pending a reference to arbitration. However, it was very soon clear that the dispute could turn upon the interpretation of the number of PFNs required to allow the valid termination of the contract under the aggregation formula. It was, therefore, felt that the dispute would be better dealt with by a High Court judge, as opposed to an arbitrator.

Given the nature of the contractual dispute, the matter was to be dealt with as Official Referee's business in the High Court. Although a part of the High Court, the Official Referee's list is a specialized section of the judiciary concerning itself particularly with disputes of a contractual nature. As a part of the procedure in the Official Referee's list, a judge is allocated to the matter at the commencement of the proceedings and a timetable for development of the case for trial is given early. This allows the parties to the dispute to be aware of the steps that have to be taken to prepare the matter for a trial, normally a fixed date trial.

Usually, in a complicated matter, the programme for preparation of the dispute will be for a 12- to 18-month period. The programme will allow for the exchange of witness statements and for the preparation of experts' reports. Another significant stage in the proceedings will be the preparation of a list of documents by each party, such list to be exchanged within a date specified by the programme. Official Referees are not known for adopting a flexible attitude to parties to litigation who do not comply with the programmed timetable.

... at a high cost

The way in which Official Referees discharge their business has a wonderfully concentrating effect upon the minds of parties to litigation. From a very early stage in the proceedings, litigants find that they must allocate resources almost exclusively to the preparation of the case.

THE EUROPEAN NATIONAL COURT

In the particular dispute between Plymouth and the European contractor, the matter was complicated by the parent company guarantee. The English courts had no jurisdiction over the guarantee. It became necessary therefore to commence proceedings in a European national court in order to enforce payment of the sums due under the guarantee.

These important proceedings were commenced and the City Council was successful in recovering sums due. The amount of the guarantee was substantial and worth recovering, but the proceedings in the European court were, none the less, an unwelcome distraction from the High Court proceedings.

PERFORMANCE FAILURES

In the event, the initial instinct to allow the proceedings in the High Court to proceed, and not to insist on arbitration, was quite correct. Not only were the client and contractor at odds as to an interpretation of the aggregation formula, but so were opposing Counsel and Queen's Counsel. In

Fig. 10.1 No one could agree on how to validly terminate the contract

fact, no two views coincided on the number of PFNs required to validly terminate the contract. The interpretation of the appropriate contract condition was made the subject of a preliminary point dealt with by the judge in advance of a full trial. The point went against the City Council.

At this stage, without prejudice discussions took place between the client and the contractor and the proceedings were settled. The settlement sum, which must remain confidential, was not an inordinate figure taking into account the amount of the contractor's claim. It was, none the less, a sufficiently large settlement to allow both parties to walk away with their honour intact.

KEY ISSUES

The City Council has learnt a number of lessons from the dispute

Contract conditions

Contract conditions have to be worded extremely carefully. Formulae allowing for termination dependent upon the service of a number of PFNs are still incorporated into City Council conditions. However, they are now simplified, so that the possibilities of conflicting interpretations are minimized. Anything that overcomplicates the process has to be avoided.

Pre-tender meeting

A pre-tender meeting is now held with potential contractors. This allows an opportunity for contractors (including the DSO) to seek clarification of any of the contract conditions. This is a very helpful exercise allowing for potential disputes to be headed off at the outset.

Early legal advice

On any occasion where a client considers himself to be dissatisfied with the performance of the contract by a contractor, the matter is referred to the legal department at a very early stage so that advice can be obtained as to the best way to manage the problems being experienced. This advice will include commercial considerations as to whether, in practical terms, the dispute is one which ought to be taken to litigation or arbitration.

In conclusion, I would say that the decision to terminate a contract, thus inviting litigation or arbitration, or indeed the decision to litigate independently of termination of a contract, is one which should not be taken lightly.

A client officer who feels that his work would be made easier by the termination of a contract should be aware that the legal process is more likely to add to his burden than bring immediate relief.

Contract collapse

by Philip Sayers

The next case study is in relation to leisure management contracts. At the start of CCT, very few companies were specializing in leisure management contracts. Many of the big national companies stated publicly that they did not intend to get involved in these new public sector contracts. And they didn't. A number of leisure management contract companies did start up, however, in response to the supply of these new contracts. Many of these companies started with a few key personnel derived from local authority leisure departments. Over the years many of them have slowly expanded and grown, in a difficult market, to achieve substance and a reputation for the delivery of quality services.

Others have come and gone since the start of CCT. They have failed due to a variety of economic reasons, which have forced their closure. One of the leisure management companies which failed was Contemporary Leisure plc. Its methods of operation were questionable from the start.

The rise and fall of Contemporary Leisure plc was succinctly stated in a House of Commons parliamentary debate. The transcript which follows (pp. 167–172) is taken verbatim from that Parliamentary Session, as recorded in the official report of the House of Commons Parliamentary Debates; commonly known as Hansard (Friday 3 February 1995, column 1388).

The speaker initially was Mr Mike Gapes, Member of Parliament for Ilford South. The reply was provided by the Parliamentary Under Secretary of State for the Environment, Mr Robert B. Jones.

Extract from Hansard debate on Contemporary Leisure

Mr Mike Gapes (Ilford, South): I wish to raise today a serious issue which has implications for local government nationally and for standards of behaviour..

....

Mr Gapes: ... The debate also has implications for standards of behaviour in public life. In 1988, the Conservative Government introduced the Local Government Act 1988 which forced local authorities to put out their contracts for leisure services to competitive tender by 1 January 1993. That move is now being followed by steps to force white collar and professional jobs out to compulsory competitive tender.

A number of companies were set up – many of them by former or serving local authority staff – explicitly to compete for those leisure management contracts. One such company was Contemporary Leisure, which was originally incorporated on 4 December 1989 as Leicester Ltd, a shelf company. Its directors were David James Bryant, the former director of leisure of Westminster city council and director of leisure of Leicester city council, and Thomas Kiernan, who was the area manager of recreation services for the London borough of Camden until early 1990.

On 26 February 1990, Leicester Ltd changed its name to Contemporary Leisure. In September 1990, Bryant and Kiernan were joined as directors by Douglas Stewart, the direct of leisure at Hackney council. As the BBC 'File on Four' programme revealed on 31 January 1995, while Stewart was still the director of leisure at Hackney and a director of Contemporary Leisure, Contemporary Leisure did paid consultancy work for a company called Whitewater – Britain's own Whitewater scandal – and Hackney council gave Whitewater a contract for the refurbishment of the Kings Hall leisure centre. Publicity material released by Contemporary Leisure in an attempt to gain local government contracts mentioned that Whitewater Leisure Ltd was one of its clients.

On 18 June 1990, the shareholders of Contemporary Leisure were listed as Douglas Stewart, with 94 ordinary and 3,900 preference shares; Tom Kiernan, with 94 ordinary and 3,900 preference shares; and Robert Hulbert with 95 ordinary and 3,900 preference shares. At that time, Mr David Bryant had 15 ordinary shares which by 1992 had increased to 110 ordinary shares, with 3,900 non-preference shares and 34,000 preference shares.

The 'File on Four' programme revealed this week that Robert Hulbert was deputy director of leisure at Glasgow city council at the same time as he was a shareholder of Contemporary Leisure, but he did not declare that interest. It was also revealed how in 1991 Contemporary Leisure had attempted to get contracts from Bolton council by deception and had falsely claimed to have contracts with Erewash council and Glasgow council. Mr Hulbert was subsequently sacked by Glasgow city council for gross misconduct over the matter.

Within three months, Mr Hulbert was working for Contemporary Leisure under the false name of John Smith. However, Mr Hulbert's association with Contemporary Leisure was to prove embarrassing for the company because it raised concerns among other local authorities with which the company hoped to win contracts, and Mr Hulbert was later bought out. The 1993 accounts of Contemporary Leisure reveal that the profit of the group before exceptional items of taxation was £77,519. The footnote revealed a payment of £95,000 as an exceptional item, giving an overall loss of £17,481. That exceptional item was an

> " ex gratia settlement agreed to be paid to a former employee and related professional expenses."

That employee was Robert Hulbert.

The accounts revealed also a net cash inflow of £428,000 and a net cash outflow of £685,000, leaving a £235,000 deficit that had to be financed by issuing £102,000 in shares and a new £100,000 bank loan. Mr Hulbert's departure and the earlier departure of Douglas Stewart, the three directors in

1994 were David Bryant, Thomas Christopher Kiernan and Charles Michael Bartholomew, who was appointed on 24 June 1992.

In 1994, a fourth director listed was Moneytime Ltd – an investment company with 15 shareholders that owned 41,000 shares in Contemporary Leisure in 1994.

The company, using its network of contacts, worked hard to win local government leisure contracts. By 1993, it had won contracts to manage leisure facilities for Three Rivers district council, the London borough of Redbridge and for Croydon, Bournemouth and Kingston upon Thames. It also won contracts for ground maintenance with Bromley and Elmbridge, and a catering contract in Bath. It expanded into managing the Harlow theatre and the Tropicana swimming baths in Weston super Mare owned by Woodspring council. It even set its eyes on growth in Canada, where it won a contract.

The company had big plans to diversify into activities in which it claimed 'expertise' – ground maintenance, theatre management, leisure developments and management of leisure facilities overseas. In the company's 1993 annual report, its chairman, David Bryant, stated:

"Within three years the company has made remarkable progress. It has gone from four employees to over 1,000, moved from a loss of £20,000 to an operating profit in leisure management in the UK of £122,000, achieved an annualised turnover of over £15 million, is a significant investor in leisure facilities, has great financial stability and is probably the largest unlisted leisure management company in Great Britain. The company is now medium sized and international. The achievement was marked by Contemporary Leisure become a plc."

Within a few months, the company was in serious trouble.

Cash-flow problems mounted. There were discussions with a number of councils to reschedule payments over the winter of 1993-94. Mr Hulbert's association with the company was ended. Complaints started about high chlorine levels and algae in Redbridge swimming baths, smelly changing rooms, the pools being too cold, run-down supplies and lack of cleaning materials. Staff in Croydon had to use a cash-and-carry to buy in bulk because they could not obtain items from the company. Redbridge council had to step in twice to force the company to bring the pool up to scratch following complaints from local swimming clubs.

The company's association with the London borough of Redbridge – my local authority – began in 1991. The then ruling Conservative group agreed to put the management of the council's three swimming pools out to competition for a six-year contract. Contractors were invited to tender on 18 March 1991. Four companies, including the council's direct services organisation, registered an interest.

Under the relevant legislation, Redbridge was required to allow all tenders, even if they were considered unsuitable. In the event, only two bids were received. City Centre Leisure and Saxon Moore Leisure did not submit tenders. An internal tender evaluation was carried out by council officers. The lower tender, of £654,000, was received from Contemporary Leisure. The other tender was from the council's own direct services organisation – involving no redundancies – and was £142,000 more expensive, coming in at £796,000.

Contemporary Leisure was, according to the evaluation exercise, a newly established company with only two weeks' experience of running leisure facilities. When it was inspected by council officers, it had no track record. The official report entered a great many caveats and warnings, yet the Conservative group on Redbridge council voted to give the tender to Contemporary Leisure. The minutes record the Labour group's opposition to the decision.

The council hoped to save a great deal of money, but it recognised in its documents that the exercise would cost it £101,000 in redundancy payments in the first year. In the long term, however, it thought that there would be savings. Because of the subsequent problems, those savings have turned to dust.

The following year, Contemporary Leisure won the contract in Redbridge for the management of the golf course, again pipping the direct services organisation, whose bid came in second of the many that were received. Redundancy notices were issued to local employees, as was a six-year contract.

In Redbridge, things seemed fine for a few months, but by January 1994 the company was getting behind with its payments. Redbridge was owed a considerable amount of money, and the company was calling for a rescheduling of payments through the winter to try to deal with its cash flow problems.

It was agreed at the initiative of the then chair of the recreation committee, Councillor Hyams, that that could be done; but by September 1994 it had become clear to many people in Redbridge council that the losses being made on the golf contract were undermining the company and that there were still problems with the swimming pools. Urgent discussions were held, and by November it was clear to Redbridge council – it had already become clear to a number of other councils, including Croydon, which had already made representations as early as August 1994 to the Department of the Environment – that things with Contemporary Leisure were going very badly wrong.

When Redbridge contacted the Department of the Environment for advice on what to do, the council hoped that the Department would move quickly. Regrettably, at that stage it did not, although DOE officials have been helpful, in this matter, to a number of councils in recent weeks. I wish, however, to register my concern that there was no early action before the company collapsed and was put in the hands of the administrator.

These councils were concerned about protecting their facilities – swimming baths, golf courses, and so on – but under the 1988 Act it appeared that they would have to shut down those operations and cut their services. That is why they urged the Department to take action before Contemporary Leisure went under. That did not happen. On 5 December, the High Court placed an order on the company, and an administrator was appointed. The company's employees in Redbridge and elsewhere were written to and told that they were being made redundant.

This traumatic event caused enormous anguish for people in the run-up to Christmas. Then, my local authority and others had to try to see what could be done to resolve this problem. My council found the situation worse than it had feared. Redbridge council expects to have to pay up to £200,000 this financial year to sort out the mess. It had to pay unpaid wages to many of the workers of Contemporary Leisure. It faced possible liability for bills to utilities which had not been paid by Contemporary Leisure. It has discovered that stocks of cleaning materials, toilet rolls and other items had been run down by the company throughout the period that it had been in control.

Redbridge, like other authorities, had a bond, but it is not clear whether the bond will be sufficient to meet the costs that the authority faces. At a time when it faces cuts in its standard spending assessment and a potential £8 million to £10 million deficit over the next year necessitating cuts in services and an increased council tax, the authority is being hit by a company set up by the former director of leisure of Westminster council, which, ironically, is benefiting from its SSA while Redbridge is being punished.

Councils thought about withdrawing from contracts. However, if they had withdrawn early, they would have lost their bonds. Many councils got together as early as the autumn of 1993. A Contemporary Leisure users' group was set up to co-ordinate the position of councils that had problems with the company.

Contemporary Leisure thought that it could escape from the problem. It started to approach local authorities to propose an alternative. Mr Bryant had been the director of leisure at Westminster council in the mid-1980s. The assistant director at that time was Roger Bottomley. Both men were intimately involved in the affairs of Westminster council in the 1980s. Bottomley, like Bryant and some others in local government, had seen the opportunities open to councils through compulsory competitive tendering. With a number of Westminster colleagues and others, they set up a company called City Centre Leisure to launch an in-house bid for Westminster's leisure contracts. They were successful in getting one of them and the other was won by a small company called Civic Leisure.

City Centre Leisure subsequently lost its Westminster contract, which meant that it was looking for new work. To meet the problems of the ex-Westminster director of leisure, David Bryant, and his company Contemporary Leisure, and given the potential of City Centre Leisure, being run by his deputy, Mr Roger Bottomley, Mr Bryant proposed that City Centre Leisure should take over the contracts of a number of local authorities that had been previously won by Contemporary Leisure.

As *Leisure Week* revealed in its issue of 18 November to 1 December 1994, City Centre Leisure eventually decided to pull the plug on the arrangement. It was not able to deal with the possible start-up costs that would be incurred; in any event, many local authorities were extremely unhappy at the proposal.

Difficulties are being faced throughout the country. Thirteen local authorities and thousands of employees have faced difficulties, insecurity and financial loss. There are some people who face the prospect of losing a great deal of money. That is all because of legislation that enables CCT to apply to leisure services. Is it a one-off problem or is the Minister going to tell us that the difficulties are due to overstretch and bad management within a particular company?

We need some assurances from the Government. Will the Minister recognise the need to change their position on companies that default on their contracts? Will he assist councils that are left to pick up the pieces? There is no provision for default by notice, but companies can default by termination of a contract, leaving terrible problems.

When are the Government going to table the exemption orders for Redbridge, Croydon and the other authorities which they need legally to do what they have had to do to pick up the pieces? Under the present legislation, the authorities have to re-tender the contracts, presumably next year. Will the Minister allow Redbridge the time needed for the negotiations between the political groups about the re-tendering process in an authority with no overall control? What plans does he have to prevent this happening in other forms of CCT?

Above all, will the Minister refer the issue of CCT in local government to the Nolan committee? There are serious questions to be asked about the role of people working for private companies while still serving, or immediately after having served, as local government officers. Does he agree that there should be no provision to allow shareholding or the acceptance of directorships or consultancies by senior local government officers in or with any company in a related sphere subjected to CCT? What is good for the ministerial goose is good for the local government gander. Many of us are concerned about the way in which CCT has developed. There is a whiff of corruption and some form of local government mafia. I should be grateful for some ministerial reassurance.

The Parliamentary Under-Secretary of State for the Environment (Mr Robert B Jones): The hon. Member for Ilford, South (Mr Gapes) has raised a number of issues and put me under some pressure of time to reply, but I shall do my best. He has anticipated at least part of what I was going to say, in that the collapse of Contemporary Leisure or any private contractor does not discredit compulsory competitive tendering any more than it would discredit the competition process generally.

It is a fact of commercial life that companies come and go. In this instance, the failure of Contemporary Leisure seems to have occurred because of the particular management of the company. It had entered into unfavourable contracts and overstretched its resources. I noted what the hon. Gentleman said about the company's circumstances and, if he has reason to believe that there has been any improper behaviour or fraud, he should refer the evidence to the police.

As for the general temptations of local government officers, there are already adequate safeguards against corrupt dealings between them and private contractors. It is illegal for officers not to declare a pecuniary interest in contracts, and the safeguards would be necessary whether or not tendering was compulsory.

Of course, other companies, those which are competent and competitive, remain active in local government CCT. Most CCT contractors, whether private sector or in-house, operate without serious problems, providing quality services and value for money.

It is extremely important to keep the collapse of Contemporary Leisure in perspective. First, only a handful of local authority contractors have folded or withdrawn since CCT began. Secondly, council in-house teams are themselves not immune from commercial pressures and the consequences of mismanagement; nor should they be. They operate under financial constraints and have to meet a statutory financial objective. They sometimes fail to do so and I am sure that the hon. Gentleman will be aware of the fact that, if an authority does not deal promptly with the financial problems of a direct organisation, my right hon. Friend the Secretary of State can use, and has used, his powers to intervene. Intervention can take the form of a direction requiring work to be re-tendered or even for the authority to cease carrying out the activity.

There are certainly lessons to be drawn from Contemporary Leisure's demise about how authorities should go about putting work out to tender. They should not be going blindly into arrangements with contractors but should, as a matter of course, be protecting themselves against possible failures by assessing the financial health of tenderers. They should also investigate the resourcing of contractors' bids, and contractors in turn should be open to reasonable requests to justify the details of their proposals.

It is a misconception that CCT requires authorities to accept the lowest bid, regardless of whether it would deliver the service described in the specification. It is true to say that authorities need specific and well-founded reasons if they are going to reject the lowest bid. Quality is an important consideration, especially in the management of sports and leisure facilities, and I accept that authorities will want to have regard to that factor in assessing bids. Any authority may wish to reject a bid that fails to meet the specification or is from a company in an unsustainable financial position.

If, despite those precautions, a service provider collapses, it can, of course, lead to difficulties, especially when the service is high profile, provided directly to the public. Some authorities affected by Contemporary Leisure's collapse have been able to assign the work to other private contractors. Others have had to bring the work in-house while the contracts are being re-tendered. My Department has co-operated with those authorities to legitimise their position by arranging an order exempting them from the CCT regime. I am grateful to the hon. Gentleman for what he said about the co-operation of officials. We are proposing to exempt nine authorities affected by the collapse, until the end of March next year, which is ample time for re-tendering.

My officials were in touch with the affected authorities when Contemporary Leisure's difficulties were first apparent. They made clear to them that if the company withdrew from contracts any application for a temporary exemption from CCT, pending re-tendering, would be treated sympathetically. Within a matter of days of the Department's being told that contracts with Contemporary Leisure had been terminated, we wrote to the authorities telling them that Ministers were minded to make an order in their favour – the so-called letter of comfort. Procedures are now in motion for making the formal exemption order.

Under present legislation, an authority would be acting ultra vires if it undertook work without first having exposed it to competition, even if it takes the work on temporarily while re-running the tender exercise. A specific exemption order is needed from the Secretary of State to legitimise a council's position. Further legislation would be needed if authorities were to bring services back in-house temporarily without the Secretary of State's sanction in circumstances such as the financial collapse of a contractor or his total failure to perform to specification. I would certainly be prepared to consider such a change, but I would need to be satisfied that any new provision would not be misused so that, for example, an authority overlooked satisfactory arrangements with an alternative private sector provider in their haste to bring the work back in-house.

Councils in any case should routinely make plans for dealing with contingencies. Also, if appropriate, they should ensure that they are safeguarded against any possible financial loss by arranging for the contractor to enter into a performance bond. Authorities adopt those safeguards as a matter of course.

The authorities who have brought Contemporary Leisure's work back in-house can do so only for a short time because the CCT legislation requires them to put the work out to tender again. The authorities should seize the opportunity for advantages in the process. There are some 15 or so private sector companies known to be in the field who may be keen to bid. Indeed, there may be more. My Department has commissioned an analysis of potential markets in certain service areas and its main conclusion is that firms bidding for local authority contracts are only a small proportion of firms that are capable of bidding. Authorities can only gain from taking steps to maximise competition.

The authorities have an opportunity to review and update specifications and to encourage imaginative approaches. They should not let their experience with Contemporary Leisure deter them from looking closely at what the private sector can offer.

It is open to authorities to make arrangements direct with private contractors and there are examples of authorities doing so. On the other hand, there is nothing in the present legislation preventing authorities from inviting bids from the private sector which involve some investment in facilities as well as the provision of a management service. If private contractors want a longer contract period in which to recoup their investment than is available under the contract in the legislation, a variation can be offered to them once a contract has been made.

In the latter half of last year, my Department issued several consultation papers dealing with various aspects of the guidance on competition procedure, including the length of contract periods and the use of performance bonds. I am aware that some sports and leisure contractors are particularly keen to have extended contract periods for their activity.

I am pleased to say that we received a very good level of response to our consultation exercise and my Department will be making amended regulations and revising the guidance currently included in circular 10/93.

Where necessary, proposals will be subject to further consultation. The intention will be to consolidate the guidance available on CCT services by autumn 1995 and, wherever it makes sense, to bring into line the guidance on blue and white collar services.

I hope that the matter has been set in context for the hon. Gentleman and I hope that he will contribute his thoughts to the consultation process being undertaken. Meanwhile, I hope that my comments will be helpful to him and his council.

Question put and agreed to.

Adjourned accordingly at nine minutes past Three o'clock.

Chapter 10: summary

by Philip Sayers

The first case study highlighted the costs in time and effort to pursue a contract dispute through the courts. Some of the key aspects of the case include the following points.

- With CCT, there is the potential for contract disputes.
- Arbitrating and litigating contractual disputes involves much work and money.
- At Plymouth, the client and contractor took opposite interpretations of the termination procedure, where there had been performance failure.
- Counsel and Queen's Counsel were also at odds over interpretation.
- A High Court case came, at high cost.
- The English courts had no jurisdiction over the parent company guarantee.

Fig. 10.2 Initial financial offers may not be all they seem

- As a continental European contractor was involved, proceedings then had to be commenced in a European national court.
- Subsequently, both parties settled out of court and each emerged with honour intact.

Lessons learnt from the dispute include:

- Contract conditions and termination clauses need to be simplified.
- Simplified documentation reduces the chances of conflicting interpretations.
- Pre-tender meetings with potential contractors allow for clarification.
- Where there is likely to be a dispute, the earliest legal advice is needed.
- A decision to terminate a contract should not be taken lightly.
- Where termination is considered by a client officer, beware; the burden placed on the client officer is likely to increase.

The second case study follows the rise and fall of a new leisure management company. Established with experienced officers from local government, the company set about tendering with vigour. A contract was entered into in Canada, before the company began to unwind. A few unwise personnel practices, linked to financial difficulties led to the company collapsing.

A few of the key lessons to be learnt from this study are now outlined:

- Contract confidence is not helped by key personnel adopting false names.
- Rapid company growth may hide an underlying financial weakness.
- The cash flow of the company should always be checked.
- The track record of the company is important in initial assessment
- A low bid may not be so low when account is taken of redundancy costs.
- CCT is a government imposed legal process.
- Government (DoE) approval is needed to any variation of the statutory processes.
- If a company suddenly ceases trading and a council takes over to keep services running, the council becomes liable for its debts.
- CCT is also a political process, and still subject to debate in Parliament.
- In commercial life, companies come and go.
- There is therefore risk.

- Assessment of the quality of a contractor, is as important as the price offered.

Care and attention is needed at all times in contract situations. Complacency by either client or contractor can lead to events taking a turn of their own.

Chapter Eleven

Divorce

Introduction

by Philip Sayers

Contracts are usually offered to the lowest bidder, as established via a competitive tender. Great elation is experienced by the winning contractor. Everyone is congratulating everyone else. They did it. They beat off all the other competitors. Winning at anything is always euphoric. Champagne corks pop. The morning after is different.

The winning contractor is left wondering 'was the price we tendered too low? Did the other contractors have a higher price because they knew something we didn't?' It is too late to ask. Invariably the winner has bitten the bullet and started the commissioning period.

It is one thing to win a tender, quite another, to operate a contract profitably for a period of between five to ten years; and at the lowest known cost. Of course, there are casualties both in the public and private sector. If a DSO makes a loss, at least the authority normally has time to retender. This is not so with a contract operated by a private sector company.

Where a private sector contract fails, it can make the news. And not just for financial reasons. Invariably, termination is abrupt. Public services are suspended and disrupted. Time does not allow for a considered take over. The contractor has to terminate here and now with a pack of creditors in hot pursuit of their money.

This chapter is based on some very telling case studies. Agonies in their time become highly valuable learning material in due course.

FLARES

There are a number of key indicators that all is not well. Regrettably, like divorce, the last person to realize what is happening is often the partner, in this case the client. Yet there are certain key events which can highlight the coming disaster. An experienced leisure operator should be able to read the signals.

These signals are rather like flares from a sinking ship. Amazing though it is to us nowadays, but the flares fired from the *Titanic* were simply misunderstood by other shipping in the area. They thought that the *Titanic* was having a fireworks display. Some fireworks display. The ship was sinking, and sinking fast. The catastrophe could have been lessened by just the one ship coming to the aid of the stricken vessel.

But emergency signalling was in its infancy. The messages were just not understood. And who could blame any other captain? After all, the *Titanic* was unsinkable. The hype of the time ensured that everyone knew that nothing untoward could happen to the *Titanic*. Partially as a result of the *Titanic* disaster, emergency signalling is now recognized by all shipping around the world.

Contracts in many services are now in their infancy. This is especially true of contracts now subject to compulsory competitive tendering. Messages between client and contractor can be, and are, misunderstood, frequently.

Contract collapse in areas subject to compulsory competitive tendering is also a new experience. With a confident contractor in charge of the contract, possible failure is invariably not even contemplated by the client. Why should the client have any doubts? After all the celebration of the contract win, after all the hype of the company's public relations people; the last thing the client will be expecting is a failure.

The scene is set for catastrophes of titanic proportions. Messages are misunderstood, or not even recognized. A contract professional cannot allow distress signals to go unnoticed. A grounds maintenance contractor pulling out on a Friday is bad news. It is little short of catastrophic if that weekend the county cricket team are playing at home. Similarly with the abrupt closure of a swimming pool on a Friday. The weekend's takings are lost. And that is the least of the worries. Customer confidence is badly shaken. It will take time to regain that confidence. In the meantime, attendances and income drop.

Watch out

So it is essential in contract management to constantly look out for hidden distress signals. If any of the following happen, trouble is brewing:

- The contractor is late in paying wages.
- All sorts of minor adverse bits of gossip abound.
- Suppliers of goods and services to the contractor complain about not being paid.

- The same suppliers then come to the council asking to be paid directly.
- Requests are made by suppliers to miss out the contractor in the payment chain.
- Maintenance is not carried out properly by the contractor.
- The contractor becomes obsessed with the need for short-term income.
- The contractor then neglects essential expenditures to maintain the long-term health of the contract .
- The contractor is only interested in short-term issues.

This chapter follows two interesting case studies where contract collapse led to immediate difficulties. In both cases, urgent attention had to be given to rescuing a leisure service before customer confidence had been terminally wounded, and before the complaints to the council rose to an unmanageable crescendo.

The first case study comes from the London Borough of Croydon. Faced with an immediate termination of a leisure swimming pool contract late on a summer Friday afternoon, the council had to act quickly but with forethought.

The case study is provided by Reg Harrison, the Chief Officer at the London Borough of Croydon who was thrown in at the deep end, so to speak. Reg has been a council member of the Institute of Leisure and Amenity Management for many years. He was President of the Institute in 1995/96, the highest acclamation to be bestowed on an Institute Member.

Going bust

by Reg Harrison

Winning contracts is only the first hurdle. Successfully delivering the contract conditions over several years is an even greater headache. Some winners turn out to become losers, both in the private and public sector.

In Croydon we had early experience of a contractor terminating late on a Friday afternoon. The detailed background reasons for the withdrawal of the leisure operator were mainly financial. However, these are not of prime importance for this part of the book. The main purpose is to deal with the problems that arose. Suffice it to say that a meeting took place finishing at 4 pm on a hot summer Friday afternoon in late August. At the end of the meeting, a 25-year management agreement was terminated, with effect from one hour later. This meeting took place only one and a half years from the commencement of the contract. Legal actions are still likely to arise from this decision.

THE WATER PALACE

The Water Palace, Croydon was a £10.5 million design, build and manage project. In essence, the Palace was a state of the art swimming pool and water health spa opened in 1990. The scheme was agreed and set up prior to current CCT legislation being in place.

It was envisaged as a private sector scheme. However, it was funded totally by the local authority and controlled by a central department of the council.

THE FIRST TWO HOURS

At the meeting referred to, the leisure operator advised the council that without additional council funding they would go into voluntary liquidation. The council decided that this would be the best course of action. There were doubts about some of their staff, and another new manager was soon to commence work. This was the third manager in a period of less than 18 months.

We therefore advised them that the agreement was terminated and that the company was required to dismiss all its staff in line with the liquidation. It was also envisaged that, as CCT would require the centre to be put out to contract again, we did not want to be encumbered by any

Fig. 11.1 Immediately on hand over security and insurance are essential

long-standing employment or servicing contracts, especially as the management of the centre was causing local concern.

For the previous 24 hours a locksmith had been kept on permanent standby to ensure that if trading ceased all external locks could be changed immediately. This would in turn allow new insurance on the building and its contents, to be put instantly into place. This became an extension of our existing insurance cover, bearing in mind that the previous operator's insurance ceased with liquidation.

At the same time, security from our own department was put around the building. We were anxious to ensure that all the contents of the building other than private belongings were intact when we took over. In the event this presented no problem. Nevertheless, this was essential to protect our assets, bearing in mind that the building and its contents had been paid for by Croydon Council. There was in fact a fair amount of cash on the premises.

Normally in cases of liquidation of a company, all assets, bank accounts, etc. are put in the hands of an appointed company with immediate effect. This prevents further loss to shareholders, creditors, and others.

Service utility undertakings were notified to ensure that continuation of fuel, water, etc. was maintained during the hand over. All meters were checked pending official transfer readings.

AND THE FIRST TWO DAYS

It was a weekend. The first two days were thus a Saturday and Sunday. Apart from keeping a security presence in the building, staff directly employed by the council with the council's other DSOs, were immediately seconded to take over and run the complex until further notice.

Staff interviews

All previous staff were to be notified immediately, where possible, by their employer of their redundancy. They were offered interviews by our staff with a view to re-employment if we deemed that they were both suitable and required. At that time the number of staff employed was unknown. It turned out to be well in excess of 100. Many of these were not on duty. In some instances some staff were only found up to a week later when they reported for duty. Throughout the weekend and following week, therefore, interviews took place to assess future staffing requirements.

Our caution in appointing staff was due to the fact that many of the staff were known to be inexperienced. In some instances they were known to us, having left our own previous employment. During this hot weekend the air conditioning system broke down. This only added to our discomfort. A heating engineer with computer expertise was required to put it right.

Keeping customer goodwill

Commencing on the Friday evening security staff were employed to intercept all customers arriving. Each customer was offered a special complimentary ticket for a free visit within the following six weeks. During the weekend this amounted to somewhere in the region of 6000 tickets. Although this cost us much lost future income, it was deemed to be a goodwill gesture for the future success of the centre. Subsequently many of these passes were presented at future visits.

Many of the weekend visitors had come a long distance and were obviously disappointed. However, the polite interception, rather than just a 'closed sign' was greatly appreciated. The security staff encountered no hostility throughout the weekend period, much to our relief.

The centre was found to contain a lot of money. The final count amounted to around £46 000. £40 000 of it was in cash, mainly coin. This had to be ferried away in security vehicles. The actual count of all monies from machines, etc., throughout the building took a very long time.

An inventory

Throughout the weekend an inventory of the building contents was made with special reference to the bar and catering areas. Welcome help was given to us by Fairfield Halls, our fellow catering department within the council. The food and drinks valuation was £40 000. Contained within the store was a large quantity of beefburgers (28 000) which in due course took us several months to use up. But what should have been an asset turned into a liability because they turned out to be of doubtful quality containing everything except beef.

Large stocks of liqueurs and spirits were also present. Some of these were taken away for sale elsewhere. However, they had been purchased above our normal purchasing prices. These items therefore could only be used elsewhere at a loss. Likewise a large quantity of wine was also found, of extremely poor quality. This was ultimately poured down the drain. This was under strict auditor's supervision, when the bottles blew! We had in fact tried using some of the red wine at a luncheon with disastrous results.

In a complex the size of the Water Palace, plant and machinery comprise a very large element. Even the previous staff remaining were not fully familiar with its servicing and operation. This, however, is an unusual set of circumstances, which is unlikely to occur in a long established centre.

Press and public relations

Throughout the weekend there was a spate of press and public enquiries. We saw confidence and promotion of the centre as an essential exercise to assure everybody that we were opening for business 48 hours later. The closure occurred during the latter part of the school summer holidays and in hot weather conditions – the worst time to close a leisure swimming pool which relied on a constant stream of casual visitors.

For several months after the closure, people were still enquiring as to whether the centre was open. In essence, bad news travels quicker than good. The local press, and national leisure press filled many column inches with what was a good topical story.

We re-opened on Monday morning on a wing and a prayer. The last few days of the school holidays were extremely busy and difficult. Except for engineering reasons, no other closures have taken place. In effect the 48-hour close down served both to:

- establish a new staffing structure;
- provide a legal break period.

The legal break clause was to ensure that we inherited no contractual or financial commitments from the previous management.

SUBSEQUENT PROBLEMS

Legal ownership of some of the contents was, however, in dispute. This was especially true of office furniture and equipment, some of which was reclaimed by the previous management as not forming part of the council's assets.

A fitness suite under the name of 'Busy Bodies' was in operation and had been since the date of opening. A patent solicitor's letter was received claiming discontinuation of the title which was already a registered trade name. It transpired that the previous operating contractor had been notified about this, but had taken no action. The name therefore had to be changed and all publicity, advert boards and the like discontinued. This just added to the daily run of routine problems.

Contracts with suppliers

The company had entered into a number of contracts with suppliers. These all ended when the operating company went into liquidation. Many of the supplier's services and goods were no longer required by the council.

Some of the contracts had been entered into under the name of the parent construction company and also the leisure subsidiary, as well as the operating company. Some suppliers therefore claimed that we could not cancel the contract because it was only the operating company that was in liquidation and not the other two companies. This move was successfully resisted and all contracts deemed to be terminated.

In many instances the council had its own contracts for supply of goods and services, often at more commercial rates.

Machinery and equipment

The condition of machinery and equipment gave concern. Some had not been serviced or maintained since installation. Some had also been totally immersed in water during a major flooding incident. This was still the subject of an insurance claim for damage and loss of income. The manufacturers' warranty on equipment can be invalidated by inadequate maintenance or treatment. Maintenance records of equipment were often non-existent.

Complimentary tickets appeared to have been issued by the operating company without record, and continued to be presented for some time after.

Staff suitability

Many of the retained staff were not adequately trained for pool-side safety. An emergency training programme had to be introduced to establish a standard appropriate to the local authority. This factor was of great importance in helping to assure the public that a high safety standard was in operation.

To help staff identity, special T-shirts had been produced with the Water Palace logo. This enabled easy identification. Unfortunately they had also been sold to the general public which caused one or two embarrassing moments for our staff. We therefore have had to completely revamp uniform designs.

The credit card authorization for the previous operating contractor was personal to them. Therefore, for a while, 'cash only' ruled until a new authorization could be established. This took longer than expected but quickly established customer confidence.

Licences

The building had no fire certificate. Some of the wiring for lights and alarms was questionable. Emergency work was needed to ensure that insurance cover was not invalidated. The liquor licence name plate was still in the name of the first manager, who had left some time previously.

The publicity arising from the earlier management of the centre had produced a lot of local comment and political criticism at a time when public confidence and increased attendances were required. This has since been addressed by a public promotion exercise via leaflet distribution, press publicity and posters together with changes to the pricing structure. Pricing is, and always has been, a local authority responsibility.

WHAT TO WATCH OUT FOR

On the basis of my experience the following are the key points for future examination:

1. Tight monitoring of the contract by qualified leisure client staff especially regards staffing and operation of centres. Special attention to be given to health and safety procedures with frequent on-site inspections.
2. Close security of financial aspects and accountancy procedures with an agreement on banking arrangements. Close watching of income and expenditure trends to detect early variation from estimated budgets before crisis points are reached.
3. Scheduled maintenance programme for all equipment and fittings. Possession of plant maintenance handbooks and computer programs, bearing in mind the high sophistication of modern computerized plant and equipment in a large building complex. Regular physical checking of the maintenance programme. (Remember who owns the equipment at the end of the contract.)
4. Ensure all contracts entered into by the operator including franchises, concessions, etc., are made in one company's name for periods not exceeding the lease duration unless by prior agreement with council.
5. Maintain an updated inventory of all furnishings, fittings and equipment, and its condition to ensure there is no dispute at a later stage. Require an annual stock take to include condition as some items will experience rapid wear and tear.
6. Where advanced customer bookings or contracts are involved, especially including pre-payment of fees, a complete record needs to be held and inspected regularly to cover for the unforeseen happening in the future.
7. Do not just count stock of consumable items and assume adequate quality. Check on quality, shelf life and storage conditions. Wasted stock valuation can soon escalate with large quantities passing their sell-by date, especially with food hygiene regulations.
8. It seems impossible to insure against failure. Therefore the prime concern is to rapidly re-establish a service to the public. Without continuity, confidence is quickly lost.
9. Public confidence is worth a lot in cash terms, in the longer term.
10. Take great care with parent company guarantees and bonds. In a volatile market, changes to company structures during the life of a contract can lead to possible financial exposure for which no cover is held. Well run, reputable companies should be capable of obtaining external guarantees to safeguard the local authorities assets.

FINALLY

Undoubtedly the existence of an in-house DSO enabled a 'rescue oper-ation' at very short notice to take place. Without the ability to step in and pick up the reins, the local effect both politically and leisure amenity wise, would have been much greater and doubtless with considerable longer-term financial implications.

My thanks are due to all the loyal staff involved together with the support of the chairman and members of the parks and recreation com-mittee who gave backing during an extremely difficult period.

Emergency planning

by Philip Sayers

The second part of the chapter provides an emergency plan to use when a contractor suddenly terminates a contract. As with all of the book, it has derived from real life experience. It is provided by David Goldstone who is the Senior Youth and Community Officer at Wiltshire County Council.

As it becomes increasingly apparent that a contractor failure may occur, it becomes increasingly important to make adequate contingency plans. What follows is a simple checklist, based on the solid foundation of experience.

Emergency planning for a contractor failure

by David Goldstone

A leisure facility under contract may have to be taken back, or a contract terminated early. This may be on the initiation of the contractor or the client. It might mean that you will have to work without the contractor's help or support. Either can happen with little warning. There are a number of factors which need to be taken into account so that you are prepared.

The purpose of any take-over must be to:

- keep the facilities open if possible;
- minimize any shutdown necessary;
- cause least inconvenience to the public;
- cause minimum loss to the council;
- protect assets.

CONTINGENCY PLANNING

If the contractor left right now, how vulnerable would you be? What bills are outstanding? How can you minimize these risks? Could you manage the centre's systems now? Do we have a plan? Or has the contractor instituted his/her own systems/computers? Shouldn't you be trained?

A viable contingency plan necessitates the ability to arrange for staffing cover:

- a manager;
- all other staff.

Therefore, designate a named member of your staff now who will take on the role of manager, in an emergency. Don't wait for the emergency to happen. Likewise be ready with other staff including: receptionists, sports assistants, bar and catering staff, cleaners, grounds staff if needed.

In an emergency take-over, there follows the interesting and important issue of the contractor staff. Can you use them? Are employment conditions protected? Do you have to take on the staff on the same terms and conditions? Are conditions of service and contracts available?

Are you insured if you take over? Insurance is needed for:

- monies;
- the building;

- equipment;
- public liability;
- employees.

A possible take-over procedure if you terminate a contract would include the following:

1. Council decisions: arrangements for council members (i.e. councillors) to take the necessary legal decisions, i.e. committee decisions are required. It is a policy and financial matter for the council to take. Officers should advise. Legal advice is essential.
2. Serve notice: agree time for notice to be served, and ensure that all possibilities are covered: head office by fax, personal delivery, registered first class delivery, sites by personal delivery to contract/site managers.
3. Have your team ready: they will have to include finance/cashiers/audit as they are used to coping with cash and inventories.
4. Break the news: two senior client-side officers are needed to break news to contractor's site managers and invite them to call their staff together to break news. Client officers to have details of contractor's telephone numbers, if needed by contractor's staff.
5. Compassion: allocate a member of the client team to each member of contractor staff while they pick up personal effects only, and leave the premises. Do this as compassionately as possible to help them cope with the news. Suggest all questions be addressed to the contractor.
6. Keys: all keys to be returned to the designated officer, receipted, identified and tagged.
7. Hand over: invite the contract manager to help smooth the transition by checking and agreeing (signing) all records. A simple audit of cash on the premises, meter readings, etc. is needed.
8. Reception: ensure you have a senior person in reception to deal with all enquiries about take-over. Refer to legal department and press office. Post notices and supply handout explaining new situation to customers. Normal procedures if possible.
9. Bar: close immediately (until the licence is transferred). Empty gaming machines, record income and switch off.
10. Services: contact telephone and other services immediately to arrange reading of units and reconnect in your name.
11. Stock valuation: catering and bar, shop, equipment, contractor owned/leased equipment. Ensure you record any company

records, books, etc. on the premises.
12. The property department: the property section of the authority needs to complete structural, electrical and mechanical checks throughout the property and arrange for locks on outside doors to be changed; arrange for alarm codes to be altered.
13. Finance/audit: a new suite of books is needed so that systems can continue. Do you know what systems are in operation? Can you take over the contractor system, or do you need to introduce your own?
14. Legal: contact has to be made with licensing authorities regarding; liquor, gaming, and entertainment licences, etc.
15. Press release: a press release is essential with continual updates, especially in the first few days.

On-going attention is necessary to: staffing levels, commitments/bookings, to provide letters to regular users/clubs and contact suppliers and sponsors. A time period is required for retendering. No doubt changes would be advisable to reduce vulnerability/exposure.

Picking up the pieces

Introduction

by Philip Sayers

A contractor in debt is a liability. It matters not whether the contractor is in the private sector or an in-house DSO. Both will deliver poor services, will record losses and lose contracts. Before termination is considered, any worthwhile client will tolerate some poor performance. To a certain extent, an operational contractor is better than a terminated one. All the work and uncertainty of taking on a new (and often unproven) contractor is a decision not to be taken lightly.

However, when a contractor starts to run up losses, then only the contractor can arrest the deficiency. At the end of the day, customers and the client can only give clarion calls to wake up the contractor to impending doom. Some contractors hear. Some do not. And so, every year, some contractors go bust. We have seen the mess they leave behind earlier in the book.

It doesn't have to be this way. Liquidation is not the only course of action for a failing contractor. Instead a contractor can fight back:

- address the issues leading to unprofitability;
- jettison loss makers;
- restructure;
- re-organize;
- critically re-assess all costs;
- balance all expenditures with a greater level of income.

This chapter highlights examples where managers have fought back and where the inevitable has not been accepted, where loss has been turned into profit. Clarity of thought has over-ridden sentiment and subjective judgements.

This is a chapter of champions.

Best business principles are enshrined in these case studies. Tough decisions are taken. These are decisions which hurt. Decisions which anger those adversely affected. Decisions which knock lifestyles sideways, as inevitable dismissals take place. But these are also decisions which limit the damage. Instead of all jobs being lost, only a few go. Instead of another bankruptcy being declared, losses are contained. The new contractor emerging from the process is much the stronger.

One word of warning. Everyone involved in turning round an unprofitable situation feels the heat of the kitchen. Anger and annoyance are the least of it. Perhaps walking away from it all and letting the contract go bust is an easier option after all. It is a soft option not chosen by those highlighted in this chapter.

The first case study was initially highlighted in the monthly publication *Local Government News*. Telling commentaries on CCT and contract issues are regularly featured in this publication which is freely available to all who manage and have an interest in local government services. As with all contributors, more details of *Local Government News* is available in Appendix A.

Brian James now supplies a dramatic account of how a DSO, on the brink of despair, pulled things round. Brian is Director of Works at Torfaen Borough Council in Gwent, south Wales. When he began employment with the council, the Works Department of which he was to become director was heading for an accumulated trading deficit of nearly £1 million. And it was getting worse.

Liaison Committee was considered inappropriate for the effective management of a contracting organization. The council agreed to the creation of a new smaller Direct Works Board. This board comprised a group of eight influential, dedicated and commercially aware members (councillors). None were renowned for their passiveness or timidity. A difficult period lay ahead and the appointment of a progressive board was considered a major priority to effect the recovery.

In the absence of the necessary commercial expertise within the department at the time of the building maintenance tender submission, the council had engaged consultants to advise on the preparation of the in-house bid. In their submission the consultants, quite rightly in my opinion, did not take account of the section's prevailing low productivity and high overheads. They based their rates on competitive, market-led principles. After the tender was submitted the consultants departed, leaving an ominous statement in their final report; 'We will gladly leave the implementation of the contract to the new director'.

Fight back

On appointment, my initial cursory assessment of the extremely competitive tender rates revealed they were substantially below those which were required to sustain the department's overheads and productivity levels. The Finance Controller, Hugh Brooks, developed an in-house computer program to determine the optimum performance criteria necessary to meet the tender requirements.

He established that:

- overheads would have to be reduced by 30%;
- labour rates reduced by an average of 25%;
- productivity needed to simultaneously increase by up to 30%.

I considered that with draconian belt-tightening measures, coupled with full trade union and political support, the required 30% reduction in overheads was achievable. However, my wishful expectation of reducing labour rates by 25% was made substantially more difficult. The workforce had previously learned 'through the grapevine' that the consultants prepared tender had actually allowed for a 9% labour increase. To this day I have yet to reconcile this element of the tender submission. Suffice it to say, our negotiations with the trade unions and workforce, to reduce labour rates to the required competitive levels, proved totally futile.

The majority of the workforce were fully convinced that the perpetrator of such a ludicrous suggestion should have been permanently committed to an institution for the mentally insane. Unfortunately, time

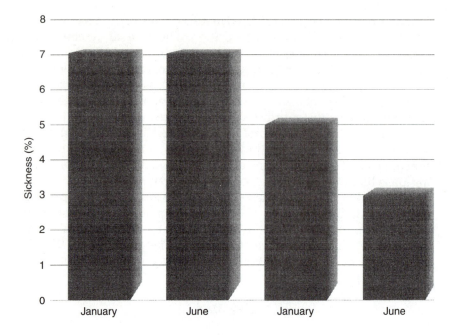

Fig. 12.1 Sickness levels could, and did, reduce

was not on our side to enter into protracted negotiations. The new contract had been running for eight weeks. By continuing with the status quo we were still paying the original high, unaffordable labour rates. We estimated we were losing up to £1000 per day. We were now rapidly approaching a crisis situation whereby it had become increasingly clear that a negotiated settlement would not be forthcoming.

TERMS OF EMPLOYMENT

At that time, we felt the only remaining course of action open to us was to take the bull by the horns. This meant terminating the contracts of employment of all the section's employees. Simultaneously, we offered new contracts that were affordable within the tender rates. We were extremely reluctant to take such drastic action. It contravened all our principles. However, we genuinely believed we had no other option. It was a gamble. If it proved unsuccessful we would have plunged the section, and probably the whole department into oblivion.

The notices were issued on a Friday. New contracts were offered from the following Monday. It was the longest weekend I have ever experienced. Yet, to our absolute astonishment and relief all the section turned up for work on Monday. They got on with their jobs as if nothing had happened. This was the turning point of the department's fortunes and the most critical element towards recovery.

Undoubtedly, in my opinion, the catalyst to the section's eventual but reluctant acceptance of the new terms was the department's GMB Trade Union Convenor, Dave Burton. He had worked tirelessly over the preceding weeks. He was both forceful in support of his members' position as well as rational. He was an invaluable mediator between the two potentially warring factions. But our unilateral action was never accepted by the trade union.

The following months saw protracted negotiations on a compensatory package. We believe both sides emerged with honour from these negotiations. Most importantly, 200 jobs were saved.

The rationalization of the department's Highways and Sewers section proved substantially less traumatic and confrontational. The desired results of reduced labour rates and improved productivity were rapidly secured.

OVERHEADS

Concurrent with the rationalization of the two main contract areas, the blitz on overheads continued unrelentlessly. When I was initially appointed, it was suggested that the Direct Works Department had too many staff and that the proverbial axe would have to be unceremoniously wielded.

In reality however, I found an uniquely slim structure well into an advanced stage of anorexia nervosa! Repeated previous vain attempts at reducing overheads, had focused largely on reducing staff numbers as the obvious solution. However, by critically examining every single invoice charged to the department over a period, I identified the real problem.

We were being grossly overcharged for various commodities and services. Some of the most notable examples included:

- disproportionately high computer charges;
- astronomic rent on a stores building remote from the main depot;
- outdated plus-payments to selected staff;
- guaranteed minimum pay adjustment;
- cross-trade flexibility payments;
- inadequate plant hire control and materials purchasing policies.

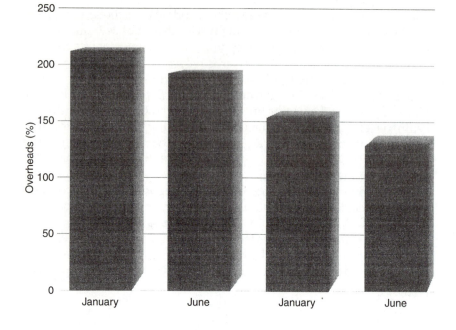

Fig. 12.2 Oveheads reduced when overcharging was weeded out

To give one detailed example of an overhead, the guaranteed minimum pay adjustment was costing £100 000 per annum.

Guaranteed minimum pay adjustment

In the local government national conditions of employment, building tradesman are guaranteed a bonus level of 12.5% of their weekly wage. However, in Torfaen we had a cash-based productivity incentive scheme, whereby the tradesmen were paid cash values for each job they carried out from a predetermined schedule of rates display.
For example:

Hanging an internal door	£8.00
Fitting a new Yale lock	£1.50
Fitting a new bath	£35.00

At the end of each week, tradesmen have to add up their accumulated earnings from the scheme. If their total actual earnings from the scheme are below the guaranteed minimum bonus (GMB) level of 12.5%, we were obliged to make up the difference, i.e. the guaranteed minimum payment adjustment.

Consider a hypothetical situation.

Carpenter:	Basic pay	=	£200/week
	Bonus 12.5%	=	£25
	Total guaranteed minimum pay	=	£225

However, consider a situation whereby in a given week a carpenter fixes 20 doors (£160) and 10 Yale locks (£15). He would have actually earned £175.00 from the cash based scheme. We therefore have to make good the difference, i.e. £225 – £175 = £50.00! Once these, and other areas had been addressed, overheads rapidly plummeted. The desired 30% reduction was quickly achieved.

INCOME

Of equal significance was income recovery, or rather, the lack of it. The absence of contractor oriented commercial expertise within the department probably accounted for under-recovery of an average of 10% across all contract areas. Once the problem was identified we quickly appointed an experienced commercially-aware and contractor trained commercial manager, Carl Phillips. This critical appointment has not only allowed us to realize our original goal of a break-even situation on all contracts, but the additional income being generated could well eliminate the accumulated historic deficit during the current financial year.

One of the more satisfying results of this appointment and other recent senior appointments, is that some departmental staff who previously appeared to lack the necessary commercial guile and self-motivation, have suddenly blossomed into competitive animals. We now have a commercially orientated organization as good as any DSO or most contracting companies in the area.

We are now able to look forward to the trials and tribulations associated with the local government reorganization in Wales from a position of genuine strength as well as with a great deal of optimism for the future.

Turnaround in grounds maintenance

by Philip Sayers

The second case study in the chapter concentrates on a specific grounds maintenance issue. Again, it clearly shows that an adverse situation can be turned around by a clear understanding of a situation and a commitment by everyone involved to improve. It is provided by Michael Burgess who is the Grounds Contractor Manager at Stevenage Borough Council in Hertfordshire.

His commercial acumen, built up over years of operating profitable grounds maintenance organizations, was put to good use when he inherited a less than ideal situation on commencing employment at Stevenage. Arresting a deteriorating situation is never easy. It always has to be accomplished faster than seems possible.

From weeds to winners

by Michael Burgess

In the first round of CCT, the in-house grounds maintenance DSO won the contract for 80% of Stevenage Borough Council's work.

In its first year of operation, the contract started to make losses. As a result, work programmes slipped and the number of default notices for non-performance soared. In order to address these issues and maintain job security for the workforce, new working practices were introduced. High output machinery was purchased which in turn produced significant savings in labour requirements.

Improvements in costs and performance went hand in hand with staff training programmes.

This improved the quality of work across a variety of areas such as tree surgery, sports management, and maintenance of cemeteries, parks, children's playgrounds, sheltered accommodation units and a golf course. It provided a secure base from which to successfully tender for the contract which included all the grass cutting of highways and housing areas within Stevenage, which was the final 20% tranche of the Councils grounds maintenance contracts.

During this time, the Council's nursery was used merely as a storage yard for grounds maintenance materials or items other departments did not need. The nursery was previously a walled garden for a manor house, sited in Shephalbury Park. It consisted of two 40-foot long glasshouses within an acre of grounds. The output at the nursery was geared to produce summer and winter bedding plants for floral displays. It only met the needs generated by the contract.

A CATALYST FOR ACTION

During the third summer, vandals broke into the nursery and caused some £8000 of damage. The need to spend money on new stock and repairs was the catalyst required to review the operation of the nursery. The assessment provided two options:

- Closure of the nursery, resulting in one redundancy and changing to a system of buying in bedding plants ready for planting in summer and winter.
- Investment over and above the £8000 required in remedial work in order to compete with the private sector.

The latter option was chosen. A process of improvement was begun.

First, disposal was arranged of all the redundant items stored at the nursery. The rubbish had accumulated from both the client and contractor. Therefore, the disposal costs were divided equally. Next, the client section ensured the security of the nursery by authorizing capital expenditure to rebuild parts of the perimeter wall together with new gates.

The contractor purchased new heating and irrigation systems for the glasshouses and built four new polythene tunnels. The road and pathways were hard surfaced, and compost and storage bays provided.

BENEFITS

Over the course of a few months the nursery was transformed into an efficient and professional operation. The main benefits to the council are:

- The morale of the staff has improved. There is increased commitment to a high standard of work. As a result the contractor bedding displays won first prize for the 'Stevenage in Bloom' competition. This is a competition arranged on an independent basis with a highly successful local garden centre, the Roger Harvey Garden World.
- The quality of the bedding displays has encouraged companies in the town to sponsor roundabout bedding displays. This has reaped the following rewards:

  Dagenham Motors (Ford Main Dealers)   £30 000 over 3 years

  Other companies are queuing up.

  In subsequent years, the combination of this commercial partnership and council led endeavour, resulted in the town being awarded the regional 'Anglia in Bloom' top award.
- The client has purchased 3000 trees and shrubs. This allows replacement plants to be planted, on a schedule of rates basis by the contractor. This creates large savings because the client can authorize gaping up of shrub beds when teams are carrying out routine maintenance. Such a policy reduces duplication of work on both sides.
- The efficient organization of the nursery has encouraged the contractor to compete for large multi-site landscape schemes. In the five months since the changes, the contractor has submitted 12 tenders and been successful in 11. This has resulted in nearly £9000 of savings for the council and is detailed more fully below:

Value of planting contracts won by the DSO £50 200
Value of next lowest tender bids £54 000
Direct saving to client section £ 3 800
DSO profits from planting contracts £ 5 000
Total savings to the Council £ 8 800

- Future improvements to save money and increase turnover include opening the nursery to the public and also reducing the purchase price of stock from trade nurseries by up to 15% by entering into contract grow partnerships.

Both the client and the contractor have benefited financially through the development of the nursery.

However, perhaps the greatest benefit, is to see different sections of the council working closely together. This has resulted in client – contractor barriers falling. There is indeed a common commitment to a quality service provided to the residents of Stevenage.

Chapter 12: summary

by Philip Sayers

This chapter has given some vivid accounts of how loss making enterprises have been turned round by hard work and tough decisions. At Torfaen, in south Wales, a massive loss making enterprise proved to be a catalyst for action. Some of the key elements for success can be summarized:

- A loss making enterprise needs immediate attention or else extinction is inevitable.
- Consultants can help provide industry-wide, up to date, comparative costs.
- Then the hard work of implementation begins.
- With a local authority DSO, political commitment is needed.
- Officer acumen is also essential.
- As is the willingness and commitment of the Unions and workforce.
- Tough decisions which hurt, need everyone to pull together.
- At Torfaen, overheads had to be reduced by 30%.
- Labour rates needing reducing by 25%, and productivity improved by 30%.
- Reductions were achieved by addressing each cost area.
- An under-recovery of income also had to rectified.

The catalyst for action at Stevenage in Hertfordshire, was an attack of vandalism in the plant nursery. A re-appraisal of the nursery was made:

- In essence, the nursery could be closed down or radically improved.
- It was decided to improve. Both client and contractor did their share.
- Morale improved.
- Quality of work improved.
- The town and council started to win awards for the quality of their displays.
- Real financial savings were made by both client and contractor.

Perhaps the key point to emerge from both case studies, is the fact that a determination to positively address adverse situations can lead to real benefits to the organization. It just takes commitment.

Profitable management

Introduction

by Philip Sayers

Successful contracts demand shrewd commercial acumen. The announced annual profits of a large company are but the tiny tip of a massive iceberg.

Profits are created by constant daily attention to disciplined detail. The old saying 'look after the pennies, and the pounds will look after themselves' still holds true. Exacting attention is needed to every penny of income and expenditure to build towards annual profits.

In every industry, there are norms for productivity and profitability sometimes called 'key ratios'. Successful companies operate well within those norms or key ratios. They shave pennies off here and there. This in turn saves pounds, which builds success and builds profits.

Large chains of retail companies trading in our High Streets keep a close tally on daily income. They know next day what income was taken the day before. The national headquarters know the income taken at all outlets by noon the following day. Trends can quickly be spotted. Where the income to expenditure ratio is outside the norm, it is quickly noticed. Less successful companies are invariably less cost conscious.

KEY PRINCIPLES

The catering industry is one good example where constant attention to trading figures leads to profit. For leisure centres operating within a contract situation, a profitable catering business unit provides a valuable source of 'secondary spend' by the customer. And there is little or no client control of prices. The customer dictates. The catering manager has to generate revenue through selling products which satisfy the customer, while stringently managing all costs, to create a real net profit.

GROSS PROFIT

The catering industry uses the standard terminology of the business world. A key term is gross profit. It is a most important key principle to grasp.

Gross profit (or GP) is:

- the net (ex VAT) total income;
- less (or minus) the cost of purchases.

This gives a concrete standard from which to work.

For example, a caterer may buy a large raw hamburger and bun for £0.45. It sells for, say, £1.00 plus VAT when cooked. This gives a gross profit of 65% (£1.00 less, or minus, the £0.45 spent purchasing the raw burger and bun).

A TRADING ACCOUNT

A trading account for catering should be quite simple. It is most important to calculate all figures exclusive of VAT and similar sales taxes and other taxes. A trading account would comprise:

- net sales revenue, i.e. income excluding VAT;
- cost of sales, e.g. purchases of beer, crisps, burgers, orange juice, etc.

net revenue from sales – cost of sales = gross profit

Now, from the gross profit, payments are made for the:

- staff costs, e.g. counter staff, cooks, staff serving behind the bar;
- overheads, e.g. rent, heat, light, head office expenses.

That leaves a financial surplus which is called the net profit. In the public sector, the word profit is still sometimes frowned upon. The net profit can therefore sometimes be called the revenue surplus.

Well that part is easy. The difficult part is first, to achieve a good level of net (i.e. ex VAT) spend per visitor/customer, say, £0.75p to £1.00 per customer; then to get the key ratios right.

The percentage spent on purchases, and the percentage spent on staff, largely determines the profitability of the enterprise. It differentiates the successful catering contractor from the unsuccessful one.

PERFORMANCE BY PERCENTAGES

Within the trading account, gross profit, staff costs, overhead costs and operating profit should each be expressed not only in sterling values (£s), but also as percentages of net sales revenue. These percentages are the key ratios.

KEY RATIOS

For a catering outlet operating as an efficient business unit, key ratio percentages could be of the following order.

Given that net (excluding VAT) sales revenue is the 100% income base; then the following key ratio's should be achieved:

- cost of sales (purchases):   35–45% of income
- gross profit: 55–65% of income
- staff costs: 25–35% of income
- overheads: 5–15% of income
- profit or surplus: 5–25% of income

Thus for every £100 (excluding VAT) taken over the bar counter then, say:

- £40 will pay for the purchases;
- £30 for staff;
- leaving £30 for overheads and surplus.

Actual percentages will vary from operation to operation (e.g. bar sales or food sales).

Close attention is needed to ensure these percentages remain constant. A weekly stock take is necessary. This is followed by the production of a weekly trading report. This will provide a running tally of profitability, wastage and the like. A monthly stock take by an outside specialist company provides an independent analysis if desired.

The next case study is a fascinating account of a story of doom turned round into a story of success. As with a number of case studies in this book, contract confidentiality precludes identifying the site.

Although catering is the subject of the case study, the principles are equally applicable to all industries. For example, in grass cutting, costs are incurred on:

- machinery and equipment;
- staff costs;
- overheads and surplus.

The same three elements of cost are true for:

- leisure management;
- refuse collection;
- vehicle maintenance;
- security work;
- white collar professional work, e.g. accountancy;
- all contracts.

An exacting and continuing attention to all varying costs is essential. The case study also highlights the benefits of employing a consultant for a specific task and for a specific length of time. It is provided by Peter Ranson, who is Managing Consultant of the Peran Consultancy Group.

The consultancy group has particular specialist expertise in catering within leisure locations. One of the performance improvement tools developed by Peran Consultancy to help meet clients quality and gross profit management needs is 'The Food and Beverage Manager's Toolkit'. This specialist software application calculates input, then compares the achievable, the actual, and the budgeted, gross profit levels. It also provides tools to break down and analyse unacceptable variances.

Catering for profit

by Peter Ranson

The introduction of CCT saw the DSO of a large local authority in southern England win the contract to manage the large local authority-owned leisure complex. The complex contained:

- swimming pool - the wet side of the centre;
- sports hall
- squash courts } the dry side of the centre
- fitness suite.

However, the DSO became dissatisfied with the quality and financial performance of their catering operations. The catering consisted of:

- a combined wet-side café and bar, i.e. adjacent to the swimming pool;
- a dry-side restaurant, i.e. away from the pool;
- a dry-side bar, also away from the pool;
- two banks of vending machines.

One of the banks of vending machines was in the wet-side foyer and one in the dry-side foyer. Both were in prime selling locations.

For historical reasons, the dry-side restaurant and bar operations were contracted out to a private company. All vending and the wet-side catering operations were directly operated by the DSO as part of their leisure centre operations management contract.

BUSINESS ACUMEN

Problems arose. This was despite the fact that the DSO had a young catering manager in the post. His previous experience was as a deputy manager in a High Street brand commercial catering operation. The reasons why the problems arose with someone with this background are explained by the way that large catering chains tend to operate.

With national and multinational catering chains, the high level business and operations management skills tend to be vested in a small number of specialist people at head office. It is these specialists who conceive and create the concepts and the product ranges. Then they develop the quality, operations and business management systems necessary to control the business. The concepts are then rolled out throughout the chain.

The person appointed as manager of the operation is trained to do what the company needs, i.e. to run the branch within the highly structured environment created by head office. Branch manager is not the best title; chief operator would often be a more accurate and descriptive job title.

When this type of manager finds him or herself in an unstructured environment, as in the case of this leisure centre, there is a struggle to cope with all the responsibilities of the job. This is because many of the elements of the job are beyond the manager's training and experience. Many managers cannot create the structure necessary for their own business to be successful. They have never been taught to manage a business in the full sense. They can operate a given code of instructions. They cannot manage and juggle a whole range of activities and orders.

Specialist advice

Yet employing someone on the pay-roll, with all the necessary high level specialist skills and experience, is expensive. This is particularly true when the specialist skills are often only necessary for a limited period to establish, say, the structure, systems and procedures. After this setting up phase the person must either be fired or retained. Dismissal can be messy and traumatic for all concerned. It is also expensive. If the specialist is retained, the employer is paying a hefty premium for skills and knowledge which are no longer required month after month. Furthermore, even the best in-house specialists can become inward-looking, incestuous in their thinking, stale and out of touch.

Using specialist consultants can be a cost-effective way for leisure business managers to get the support and assistance often needed to achieve the twin goals of quality and profitability. This is particularly true when a catering operation is:

- being established;
- in need of rejuvenation.

A STRATEGY

Specialist catering consultants with the requisite skills were therefore appointed by the DSO in question, to carry out a review of the catering operation. They prepared a series of reports. Recommendations included:

1. The creation of business management structures. Among other things, this included specialist food and beverage management software, to achieve full quality and cost control.

2. That the DSO bid for the contracted-out part of the catering operation when it came up for tender. This would enable catering to be properly integrated into, and coordinated with, the leisure centre's core activities.
3. A change in catering emphasis, so that in the short term:-
   - the more formal style of a restaurant service be changed into a self-selection café style which would be more in keeping with the informality of a leisure centre;
   - the café product range was enhanced with premium priced, premium products, to enhance the quality perception of the menu;
   - that opportunities would thus be provided for customers to spend more on products which yielded a higher gross profit (GP);
   - active promotion of the sales of those high GP products;
   - vending machine sales should not be allowed to substitute their low spend, low GP purchases, for the high spend, high GP opportunities available in the cafés.
4. In the longer term, consideration needed to be given to:
   - locating one or two vending machines in remote areas of the building in order to capture customer spend (revenue) that would otherwise simply bounce away and be lost to the DSO;
   - creating a kiosk in each foyer to serve a very carefully developed selection of hot and cold hand-held food and beverages;
   - keeping the kiosks open for a longer working day, possibly even opening the kiosks for the same length of time that the centre was open;
   - developing the wet-side café product range so that it complemented the range of kiosk offers;
   - then limiting the café opening hours;
   - adding to the dry-side bar (which sold only liquor), a range of hot and cold food and beverage products which would complement the range of kiosk offers.

Finally it was suggested that the dry-side café (ex restaurant) be converted into a dedicated and branded function suite, with its own entrance. This would develop the opportunities to attract non-leisure centre related function business.

ACTION

The young manager decided to leave. The consultants assisted in recruiting an experienced, highly professional manager. A step-by-step approach to testing and implementing the consultant's recommendations was then adopted. This is an on-going process which will take a number of years to complete.

The following progress has been made:

1. When the dry-side catering contract (which was previously managed by the private sector catering operator) came up for tender, the DSO with consultancy support, bid successfully for the contract.
2. The product range and associated promotions were continually developed.
3. Specialist software was purchased (the Food and Beverage Manager's Toolkit).

There were significant benefits from the changes.

SUCCESS

The gross profit previously had been between 46% and 54%. On average, the gross profit was 50.3%. This level of gross profit was well below what was achievable. The 'Food and Beverage Managers Toolkit' software program calculated that a 67.7% gross profit was in achievable. An encouraging 66.2% was in fact achieved. This was an improvement of 15.9%. No mean feat!

Strict attention to cost control and an improved product range benefited the contract immensely. The total annual catering revenue was £425 000. The gross profit previously had been £214 000. The gross profit subsequently was £281 000 – an improvement of £67 000 per year clear profit. The table below illustrates the position.

	£	%
Before	214 000	50.3
After	281 000	66.2
Improvement	£67 000	15.9%

VENDING OR KIOSK?

The proposal to replace vending machines with a kiosk was regarded as the most radical. The assessment as to whether to change to a kiosk was helped immeasurably by an unplanned and unexpected event. A safety problem with the floor in front of one of the banks of the vending machines resulted in the closure of the machines for some three days until the floor could be repaired and made safe. Thus no income was

Table 13.1 Gross profit analysis

	Cost price (p)	Selling price (p)	Gross profit (p)	Gross profit %
Typical purchase from vending				
Packet of crisps	14.0	29.8	15.8	53
Can of coke	18.5	42.5	24.0	56
Total	32.5	72.3	39.8	55
Typical purchase from counter				
Large fries	15.0	72.3	57.3	79
Large coke	21.8	119.1	97.3	82
Total	36.8	191.4	154.6	81
Net benefit:	+4.3	+119.1	+114.8	+26%

Note: all prices here are shown in pence; net of VAT, calculated to the nearest tenth of a penny.

received from the vending machines for those three days. Café sales went up by 45%.

The key question was; did profit increase or fall during the period when the vending machines were unavailable? There was a loss of vending sales of £85 per day. This equated to a loss of gross profit of £38 per day. However, there was a 45% gain to the café. Total sales of £215 were made on a typical day. This yielded a gross profit of £142.

Everyone was surprised and delighted to realize that the gross profit had improved by 21% or £104 per day! Extrapolated on an annual basis, this would give a profit improvement of £37 800. Thus the case was made.

No successful caterer can afford to ignore a potential profit opportunity of nearly £40 000 per year. The opportunity stems from the significant difference between a typical purchase from the vending machines and one from the café. Table 13.1 illustrates these differences very graphically. Quite clearly, the spend per customer in this example almost tripled from £0.70 to nearly £2.00.

CONCLUSION

Although neither a scientifically controlled experiment nor a comparison of average purchases, this anecdotal evidence illustrates:

- the benefit of premium priced, premium products, yielding a high GP;
- the importance of service delivery through an appropriate retail platform;

- the importance of ensuring the retail area is in the right location within the centre;
- the shortcomings of vending as an effective commercial retail platform;

if available spend is to be captured!

Now the DSO plans to implement on the dry side:

- a kiosk adjacent to the foyer with terraced seating overlooking the main sports hall;
- enhancing the bar to make provision for a substantial range of food;
- developing the branded function suite in the ex-restaurant area; and
- detailed proposals have been drawn up accordingly by the consultants.

The additional financial return from investing in this dry-side development is conservatively projected to be as follows:

Figure 13.1 The DSO cannot outperform the private sector

Total catering revenue	=	£293 600
Gross profit (GP)	=	£187 000
Wages	=	£ 88 100
Purchases	=	£ 29 400
Profit to share	=	£ 69 500

The catering operation has turned around.

Historically at best, the catering operation had broken even. Often it had lost money. It is now a robust and routine profit contributor. It always had that potential. It is now set to be an even greater income generator and profit centre within the leisure centre. The profit from catering is available for reinvestment. The positive financial contribution from the catering operation makes the DSO significantly more competitive when tendering under the rules of CCT.

Chapter 13: summary

by Philip Sayers

The catering industry provides clear examples of commercial management. Studying the financial accounting practices used in catering, allows us to see real live examples of successful management methods in practice. Some of the practices highlighted in the chapter are now summarized:

- The concept of gross profit is an essential principle to grasp.
- Gross profit is the income from sales, less the purchase cost of those sales.
- Profits are created by constant daily attention to disciplined detail.
- Key ratios are an all important management tool.
- Key ratios include the cost of purchases, and staff costs relative to the resale price.
- The cost of purchases should be about 35–45% of the reselling price.
- Similarly, staff costs should be between 25–35% of the retail sale price.
- This then leaves between 20 and 40% to cover overheads and provide a net profit.
- In a leisure centre and swimming pool environment, careful consideration needs to be given to the location of the catering facilities.
- Careful consideration needs also to be given as to whether a kiosk or vending machines are the best form of delivery for the customer, and for profit.
- Consultants can offer helpful advice, for a 'one-off' payment.
- An additional gross profit of 26% is possible from 'over the counter' catering, positioned in the right location, compared to vending machines.
- In the case study detailed in the chapter, an increased net profit of £70 000 is anticipated from changes proposed to the catering outlets.

Key ratios are important in all areas of commercial management. In grounds maintenance, some of the principal costs include machinery and staff. In leisure management, specific attention is needed to the costs of heat and light, staff costs and constant income monitoring. The case study from Broxbourne gave a good example.

Each industry differs. Each industry has its own key ratios and benchmarks. Anyone wishing to succeed in a competitive environment needs to give constant attention to the principal costs and incomes in their own area of operation.

Addendum to Chapter 13

ABC CATERING: LEISURE CENTRES
LONDON: 7 day Trading Period from 06 Feb to 12 Feb inclusive
Actual v. Achievable and Budget

	ACTUAL	ACHIEVABLE	VARIANCE to Actual		BUDGET	VARIANCE to Actual	
NET REVENUE	£8401.97	£8411.02	−£9.05	−0.1%	£8500.00	−£98.03	−1.2%
Opening stock: Feb 05	£3531.50	£3531.50	£0.00	0.0%			
+ Stock Purchases	£3675.08	£3635.93	£39.15	1.1%			
− Closing Stock: Feb 12	£3918.78	£3918.78	£0.00	0.0%			
COST OF STOCK	£3287.80	£3248.65	£39.15	1.2%	£3250.00	£37.80	1.2%
- Staff Meals	£207.44	£207.44	£0.00	0.0%	£200.00	£7.44	3.7%
- Wastage	£101.24	£101.24	£0.00	0.0%	£75.00	£26.24	35.0%
COST OF SALES	£2979.12	£2939.97	£39.15	1.3%	£2975.00	£4.12	0.1%
GROSS PROFIT	64.5% £5422.85	65.0% £5471.05	−£48.20	−0.9%	65.0% £5525.00	−£102.15	−1.8%
Opening stock	7.5 days' supply	7.6 days' supply					
Closing stock	8.3 days' supply	8.4 days' supply					
Customer numbers	8305 persons				8500 persons	−195	−2.3%
Visitor numbers	12 976 persons				13 100 persons	−124	−0.9%
Market penetration	64.0% (Customer/Visitor)				64.9% (Cust/Visitor)	−0.9%	−1.4%
Spend per customer	£1.01 (ex VAT)				£1.00 (ex VAT)	£0.01	1.2%
Spend per visitor	£0.65 (ex VAT)				£0.65 (ex VAT)	£0.00	−0.2%

Market orientation

Introduction

by Philip Sayers

Prior to the introduction of CCT, there were fears that it would lead to public leisure services becoming more market oriented.

It was felt that it would be difficult to protect the social objectives of the service within the contract specification. The contractor would have an incentive to act in a more commercial manner. If it was difficult to protect the social objectives of the service it would be difficult to justify its existence as it would not be doing anything different to the commercial sector of leisure provision. This was obviously of concern to those who worked in the public sector and felt a commitment towards the service that it provided.

At a more general level, it was a concern of those who did not share central government's commitment to a more market led economy. They felt that CCT was a tool designed to force local authorities towards central government's approach. This suspicion was reinforced by the compulsory element. At the same time as CCT was being introduced central government was imposing spending restrictions on local authorities as part of its strategy to reduce public sector spending.

This chapter considers whether CCT is politically neutral or whether it inherently leads to a more market oriented service. It then considers the impact of financial constraint on the process of CCT within local authority leisure services.

Client v. contractor, customers and costs

by Geoff Nichols

The client – contractor split imposed by CCT sets up two different groups with two different interests. Within the CCT process a balance is achieved between the interests of the two groups. In theory there is little difference between the interests of the DSO and a private contractor. The objectives of the two are now both related to financial performance. The client is the custodian of the social objectives of the service. Thus the balance between the interests of the client and contractor, corresponds to the balance between social and market led objectives.

Measuring social objectives ...

To ensure that the social objectives are achieved, the client officer first needs to know what the aims of the service are.

These aims then have to be translated into specific policy objectives. These need to be measured by performance indicators and related to specific measurable targets. The client needs to be able to build these targets into the CCT specification and to ensure that the financial reward of the contractor is related to their achievement.

A more detailed description of this process with a specific example is provided in the Sports Council's research report, *Developing Sport Through CCT* [1]. In the example given by the Sports Council, a strategic aim which represents a general social objective, is to make sporting and recreational opportunities available to all sections of the community regardless of race, sex age or ability. Within this, a more specific objective is to increase participation by women. The intention is that women users of a leisure facility should be representative of the proportion of women in the catchment area.

To achieve this, there are a set of policies to be implemented at the facility level and specific actions to be taken. A policy might include price incentives for women or crèche provision. A specific action might include introducing a women's only session. A relevant performance indicator would be the number of women participating over time. A specific target might be increasing numbers from a specified level by 50% over the first year.

..... and building them into the contract

So to incorporate this into a CCT specification the client officer would first have to know what the general objective of the service was and plan how to achieve it. This is termed strategic level planning. The client would then have to state in the contract the sessions that were to be run and the prices to be charged. To set realistic targets the client would need to know how many women were already using the facility.

Fig 14.1 Outputs have to be measurable, measured, monitored and be realistic

To measure the achievement of objectives, an information system would have to be in place that could show how many women used the facility. The contract would have to include some means of relating this performance indicator to the subsequent payment to the contractor. The level of planning described here, and good information systems, are a prerequisite for CCT to be able to meet social objectives. So it is all important to think through the aims and objectives and then tie these requirements into the specifications.

INCREASED MARKET ORIENTATION

Of the sport and recreation management contracts awarded after January 1992 in England, 84% went to the DSO [2]. This means that in general the same people were managing the facilities before and after CCT.

In contracts won by the DSO a more market oriented approach from the contractor would require a change in attitude of the DSO managers. The contract had to be loose enough to give the facility manager a degree of discretion over prices and programming that allowed a more market oriented approach to be developed. The facility manager had to have an incentive to become more market oriented, either in the form of increased income to him and his staff directly, political capital or job security.

Thus within CCT there is a balance between what the client has to do to ensure that social objectives are achieved, and what the contractor might wish to do and be able to do, to make the service more market oriented. Another factor affecting this balance is the possibility that the client might actually want the service to become more market oriented. In this case the contractor might be given greater scope to express a market orientation. This will be considered in the discussion of the impact of financial constraint.

STRATEGIC PLANNING

As the Sports Council point out in their guidance on the incorporation of sports development objectives into CCT, leisure departments' strategic planning was at an embryonic stage prior to the writing of the first round of contracts. This meant that client officers did not have clear guidance on what the objectives of the authority were in providing leisure services and how they were to be achieved. Therefore the majority of contracts restricted themselves to describing the service as it existed prior to CCT.

Client officers would be aware of the general political stance of councillors and the implications of this for the general orientation of the service. However, rarely had this been developed into a strategic plan that said how the objectives would be achieved and measured.

The Sports Council survey [2] found that 47% of authorities in England had a general leisure strategy. However, it is likely that this gives an over-optimistic picture of the level of planning. These strategies will have been at variable stages of development. The survey found that it was relatively common for authorities to specify general policy objectives for target groups. But it was much less likely for these to be supported with specific target figures. This made the specifications meaningless. One reason for the lack of specified target group outputs was that client officers did not know how many people in these target groups used the facilities before CCT. Therefore any targets might have been unrealistic.

Outputs

The lack of specific output targets meant that client officers did not have to deal with the situation where targets had not been met. Experience of client officers who have had to deal with situations where private sector contractors have not met the conditions of the contract suggests that it is sometimes difficult to default the contractor. More often the client ends up acting as a free consultant to the contractor to help solve the problem.

For example, one contractor's tender document had stated that there would be a duty manager at the facility all the time. In practice the client officer found that the duty manager in the mornings had been replaced with a cleaner with a mobile phone. When the client officer asked the contractor why this was, they told him that they were short of money. They wanted to save the expense of a manager at slack times. The client also asked about the development of the marketing plan that the contractor had outlined in their presentation to councillors. The local manager said he knew nothing about this. He then consulted a road atlas to assess likely local markets.

In this situation the client felt it would be futile to default the contractor as poor financial performance would only be compounded. The process of terminating the contract and appointing a new contractor was considered too expensive. Thus the best option was for the client to help the local manager improve the management of the facility.

This might illustrate the need for client and contractor to work together but it also illustrates the difficulties in rectifying a contract situation where the contractor is not meeting the specification. Perhaps financial defaults and bonuses related to target outputs will be more viable in the second round of contracting. The Sports Council have not given guidance on good practice in ensuring that target outputs once set, are achieved, beyond stressing the importance of the relationship between client and contractor.

For a client to ensure that social objectives are incorporated into the contract, requires:

- an advanced level of planning;
- a good quality of information;
- an ability to ensure that set targets are achieved.

These were not present in the first round of contracting. Quite apart from these attributes the client also required the skill to write a contract that would achieve what was required. This was not always achieved as the officers were all doing this job for the first time.

For example, a long and detailed contract, written for an authority that was keen to ensure social objectives were met within CCT, was found to be inadequate when a private company unexpectedly won the contract. It is likely that other similar contracts were also inadequate but this was never revealed because the contract was won in house.

Private sector contractors

Private contractors were inevitably profit oriented. On the other hand they were also keen to develop a good working relationship with the client. It was not in their interest to have an antagonistic relationship with the client. They realised that this would make working difficult. The relationship required a degree of give and take. However, they were keen to exploit market opportunities wherever the contract allowed them to do so.

Contracts won by private sector companies were nearly all in authorities who were favourably disposed towards the private sector. Here contracts tended to allow the contractor greater scope for altering pricing and programming.

DSO contractors

DSO managers had to change their attitude to the service while they were preparing their tender. This depended on how worried they were about the potential competition.

One DSO manager felt that the threat of competition was considerable. He reported that, 'all the advice we were given ... was to cut costs. You basically have to cut back on staff and staff costs' [3]. Another DSO manager in a similar authority said that, 'we did not budget for the specification. We tendered to keep our jobs'. In the same authority the client reported that his DSO manager was extremely worried about the outcome of the contracting process. The greater the perceived threat of competition, the more the DSO manager was pressurized to become cost conscious.

Antagonism

Sometimes antagonistic relationships that had developed between DSO and client in the preparation for CCT had unanticipated consequences. One authority had employed a new DSO manager for his business acumen in the preparation for CCT. When the manager realized that there was no threat of competition, he put up the cost of the DSO bid to award himself a pay rise. Hard bargaining was required to inject a greater sense of realism.

The national survey [2] found that the average number of bids submitted for leisure management contracts was 1.7. This was the second lowest figure for any contracted service. There was an average of 5.4 expressions of interest for all CCT tenders, e.g. refuse, grounds maintenance and the like. For leisure management, therefore, the threat of competition was much greater than the actual competition. Competition was concentrated in the authorities that were politically friendly. Contractors did not want the hassle of working with an antagonistic authority. Thus the degree to which DSO managers were required to change their orientation of the service in preparing for CCT varied with the perceived threat of competition.

While operating within the contract the attitude of the DSO managers towards the service became more market oriented. The degree of this change reflected the:

- political nature of the authority;
- effectiveness of the client – contractor split;
- relationships between individual officers;
- the attitude of individual managers.

WORKING THE CONTRACT

Working under a contract has ensured that DSO managers are much more financially aware. This is illustrated in the book *Managing a Leisure Management Contract* by Rogers and Chaytor [4]. Writing from the perspective of DSO managers, they state that key points are to encourage:

- increased commercial awareness;
- increased financial awareness.

DSO managers have a much greater awareness of the financial implications of their decisions. This is due to better financial information. Also
and crucially, their performance is now measured in financial terms in
relation to the contract.

But does increased financial awareness mean that managers will
change their approach? In an authority that welcomed competition and
had an effective client contractor split one DSO manager reported that,
'my objectives have changed. Previously my point of view was "yes, I
am doing a good job, and it looks good to the public". I now have to
look at it as, "I am doing a good job, and it looks good to the public,
but also that I am running an efficient business"'.

Public service or profit?

The same manager continued, 'if I am going to be giving support to special income groups, the unemployed and similar people, I cannot do it
off my own back. I cannot do it all by myself. I just cannot cut down
on the activities that generate income. Now if I were expected to do that
... I have to have added financial support from the council. They have
got to have variations in the contract' [3]. This manager had to change
the approach to programming in the leisure centre.

Another DSO manager was employed in an authority that was politically opposed to CCT. He commented that, when deciding what new
sessions to put on, it was 'Anything that will bring in more money. The
difference between the fact that the contractor is a contractor (opposed
to a public sector manager) is putting on activities that will generate
more money'. However, in this authority the client – contractor split was
not so clean. There was still an underlying feeling in both the client
and contractor that they were both there to provide a service to the
public. This was illustrated by the flexible way money was allocated for
minor improvements to facilities. This might come from the client or
contractor budget, depending on which was most healthy.

In a similar authority, a client officer described the same shared commitment. 'At the end of the day, the client and contractor are working
to the same end, the improvement of the service to the public'. But he
added: 'it is not always like this in other facilities and people forget
that they are public servants'.

So public sector managers have not metamorphosed overnight to private sector managers. However, CCT makes them much more aware
of the financial consequences of their actions. The degree to which a
DSO manager adopts a private sector orientation reflects the political
climate in their authority.

As the client officers have not managed to set targets of performance that measure use of the facilities by specific groups, and which are related to social objectives of the service, the only targets that remain are financial ones. These are the ones by which DSO managers are being judged and which will therefore motivate their performance.

DIFFICULTIES OF CONTRACTING FOR SOCIAL OBJECTIVES

There are other factors affecting the balance between social objectives and a market orientation.

The experiences of the first round of contracting suggest that it has been harder for the client to ensure that social objectives are achieved than it has been for the contractor to pursue a more market led orientation. Contributory factors have included the distinctive characteristics of leisure services, compared and contrasted to other contracted services.

1. The objectives of providing leisure services are diverse, unclear and difficult to measure. They may include: the attraction of tourism, the reduction of anti-social behaviour and the improvement of the quality of life among others. This means that it may be difficult to achieve agreement on the objectives and their priority in an authority. Therefore it was difficult to apply even the first stages of the planning process, as advocated by the Sports Council.
2. There is a greater need for flexibility in a service that is meeting leisure demands that are susceptible to change. A four- to six-year contract that is tightly specified will have to be frequently renegotiated to allow the programming and pricing to be altered. On the other hand, a contract that allows the contractor greater flexibility will inevitably allow a more a market oriented service to be developed. The quotes earlier from DSO managers illustrate how variations in the contract are required if the DSO manager is to introduce new sessions for disadvantaged groups.

   On the other hand, where there is flexibility, the first consideration of a DSO manager when introducing a new session is whether it will generate extra income. Interviews with twelve client officers revealed that the initiative for the vast majority of new sessions comes from the contractor rather than the client. This indicates that once the contract is written the client side tends to think that apart from monitoring, their job has been done until the next round. Meanwhile the contractor is continually looking for new ways to increase income.

3. Users of the service are paying directly when they pay entrance charges. There is also the potential for secondary spending on refreshments and equipment. This gives greater scope for DSO managers to increase income by changes to programming, pricing and other management decisions.
4. Private sector contract operation was an infant industry with no large established companies bidding for contracts when CCT was first introduced to sport and leisure management. This meant that in choosing a private contractor there was a very limited track record by which to judge companies. It was easier to choose one that was not able to do the job. Some companies had few financial reserves to act as a cushion if they encountered difficulties meeting the contract obligations.

FINANCIAL CONSTRAINT

This analysis suggests that, while in theory there was an even balance between social objectives and a more market oriented service, within CCT, in practice it favoured a move towards a greater market orientation. This trend has been increased by the impact of restrictions on local authority spending.

A recent survey indicates that up to the start of CCT, real spending on leisure by local authorities increased. However, over the subsequent three year period, a majority of leisure departments experienced a reduction in their budgets. The average reduction was 10% and the most severe was 40% [5]. This had an impact on councillors' attitudes to the service and the approach of client officers. Councillors show little interest in the generation of performance indicators that show non-financial outputs of the service. Rather, their major concern is with financial performance, which is measured more accurately as a consequence of CCT.

A client officer in a traditional Labour authority describes how: 'the only concern to councillors now, having got through the initial CCT process, is whether the contract is performing or not in line with its central government (DoE) requirements and also how the contract compares to budgets. That is the overlying concern at the moment: financial information.'

Financial targets

DSO managers have been under great pressure to meet financial targets. In turn, client officers have been more prepared to allow a degree of flexibility in specifications to enable contractors to respond more quickly to market opportunities.

A client officer reported how: 'to deal with budget reductions the client is paying the contractor less. Hence the facility managers less. To allow for this there is a liberating of the contract which allows the contractor more flexibility over pricing, marketing and opening hours.' Thus in the operation of the contract, financial constraint has led to a more market oriented service.

It may also have affected the preparation for CCT and the awarding of contracts. The delegation of a senior officer to write contract specifications, and other preparations for CCT, were expensive at a time when financial constraint was already having an impact. A shortage of resources to write effective contracts, and to devise a sophisticated selection procedure to choose between tenders, led in some cases to selection of inappropriate contractors. A client officer who was in this position described how, when councillors saw the price of the lowest tender, 'Their eyes popped out of their heads. It was like manna from heaven'. The officer himself was sceptical of the financial viability of the tender. However, the manager did not have a sufficiently well developed selection process to reject it, despite his reservations. His reservations proved to be justified.

Financial constraint will also affect the awarding of contracts in the next round. Authorities who are unable to afford the cost of refurbishing facilities will try to negotiate contracts with private sector companies. The contract will require the company to invest capital funds for improvements into the facility. This will be in exchange for a longer and less tightly specified contract which will thus allow the company to recover its investment. This in turn will lead to a more market oriented service.

Is greater market orientation ...

While it appears that leisure services are becoming more market oriented, is this at the expense of social objectives?

The analysis of the information available before CCT, implies that the Audit Commission was correct when it criticized local authorities for being unclear about their objectives and reasons for subsidy [6]. This means that it is not possible to say exactly what was being achieved before CCT and how effective local authorities were at doing it. Therefore it is also not possible to say how exactly the outputs of the service differ before and after CCT and if social objectives have been sacrificed. Rogers and Chaytor [4] illustrate that in many cases social and financial objectives are compatible.

... at the expense of social objectives ?

However, there are instances where they are not. For example, it is very difficult for sports development sessions to be set up using leisure centres on mid-week evenings, when more revenue can be gained by aerobics or football. Similarly a sports development officer reported that relatively small price rises for economically disadvantaged groups deterred participation. These price rises had been imposed as a consequence of CCT and financial constraints.

Overall, it is the impact of financial constraint in combination with CCT that is likely to have the greatest impact on an authority's ability to achieve social objectives. In one authority this was the reason why general policy objectives were not backed up by specific targets. The authority could not afford to specify a service that would achieve them. In another, eligibility for the concession scheme had been reduced to save money. The direction of development of the service now appears to be financially led, as is reflected in nearly all new programme initiatives coming from the client side.

However, it is possible that CCT might provide the stimulation for improved planning and improved information systems, in the way advocated by the Sports Council [1]. This will enable authorities to be more specific about:

- what their objectives are;
- how they will achieve them;
- setting targets;
- measuring if the targets have been achieved.

If this happens authorities may become more effective at achieving social objectives while at the same time allowing facility managers to exploit market opportunities and reduce the overall subsidy of the service.

IMPLICATIONS FOR THE CLIENT

Improved planning and improved information systems are vital if social objectives are to be effectively incorporated into the CCT specifications. This is the major conclusion of the Sports Council report [1].

Councillors need to be persuaded of the need to invest in new information systems. This is on the basis that if you don't know what the service is achieving, it is difficult to be effective at doing it and plan for improvements. Similarly, objectives of providing the service need to be clarified. If these are not clear it is difficult to measure if they have been achieved, and to plan the actions to achieve them.

The information systems need to be robust enough for output targets to be related to the contractor's performance and reward. New contracts need to recognize where there is a conflict of social and financial objectives and to protect social objectives with a tight specification where it is necessary to do this. On the other hand, contractors should be given sufficient scope to react to market opportunities where this will not affect social objectives and might generate extra revenue to cross-subsidize them.

NOTES

1. Sports Council (1994) *Developing Sport Through CCT*, London: Sports Council.
2. Centre for Leisure Research (1993) *Sport and Leisure Management, Compulsory Competitive Tendering National Information Survey Report*, London: Sports Council.
3. Chapman, J. (1992) *The Impact of Compulsory Competitive Tendering on Local Authority Leisure Managers*. Dissertation submitted as part requirement for MSc in Sports and Recreation Management, University of Sheffield.
4. Rogers, P. and Chaytor, S. (1994) *Managing a Leisure Management Contract*, Harlow: Longman.
5. Taylor, P. and Page, K. (1994) *The Financing of Local Authority Sport and Recreation: A Service Under Threat?*, Institute of Sport and Recreation Management, Melton Mowbray
6. Audit Commission (1990) *Local Authority Support for Sport*, HMSO London.

Chapter 14: summary

by Geoff Nichols

The introduction of CCT into areas of sport and leisure management led to fears that social objectives would be jettisoned. There was fear that the imposed need for profit would over ride social objectives.

- To incorporate social objectives into the contract there needs to be clarity over what the social objectives are; and how they will be achieved.
- This clarity can be achieved through strategic planning.
- Ensuring social objectives are achieved in a contract requires measurable performance indicators.
- The achievement of social objectives through the contract is the responsibility of the client officer.
- The major objective of the contractor is financial performance.
- In the first wave of CCT, social objectives were not adequately protected in the contract.
- This was because of inadequate planning, in-house experience and poor information on what the service was achieving.
- In the future, improved planning and information systems should improve the ability of client officers to build social objectives into CCT contracts.
- However, continued financial constraint will increase pressures towards a more market oriented service.

Peace in partnership
or working at a relationship

Introduction

by Philip Sayers

Partnerships of recrimination and remorse are all to easy to slip into. It takes a lot more effort to develop a positive partnership.

Partnerships which work, have to be constantly maintained. Constant give and take. It is an odd fact of life that everyone sees when, where, and what they themselves 'give'; but never what they 'take'. And that is how things go wrong: the 'give' is always too apparent to the giver. But that is life. We all live in a world of our own perceptions. Our own versions of reality. Any partnership involving two or more parties is based on perceptions. There is plenty of scope for differing perceptions. Furthermore, partnerships based on contracts won in open competition, always have an inherent tension. Work has to be undertaken at the lowest price.

There are not two, but three interested parties in a contract:

- customer;
- client;
- contractor.

The customer comes first.

Without the customer, there would be no work for the client or the contractor. Yet often the customer has little say in the relationship. The customer is often too small. For example, in a grounds maintenance contract, the giants of the contract are the client and the contractor. The customers are the thousands of residents who benefit from the service. It is hard for them to have a coherent and collective voice. Thus the attention to customer surveys in the earlier chapters.

When customers group together into say a club, then they do have an effective voice. The three-way partnership becomes more meaningful and real. Sports clubs are good examples of where the customer gains an effective voice. The sports club often has the ability to bring as much pressure to bear on a situation as the client or the contractor. Indeed, a sports club will have more clout. If a sports club is able to develop an effective link with the elected members of an authority, then the sports club can readily bring ever increasing pressure to bear. As with any relationship, sports clubs can have a positive or a negative effect on the situation.

A golf club based at a municipal golf course is a good example. Some golf clubs have a stranglehold on the use of some public courses. Every benefit is given to the regular club player, with little thought for the casual player. Yet at some public golf courses, a wider community based partnership has been developed. Here, there are many partners involved.

With a public 'pay and play' golf centre the contractual relationships can be very complex. These include:

1. Customers: casual golf players, and golf club players.
2. Grounds maintenance: client staff responsible for specifying high standards, and contractor greenkeepers who have achieve these high standards.
3. Management: the leisure management client who sets fees and charges, sets the bookings policy, and the like; the on-site manager, often the golf professional/shop manager, who actually takes the bookings and charges the correct fees.
4. The caterer who provides the bar and restaurant.

The client and contractor roles may be combined or separated depending on local circumstances. But there will remain the clearly identifiable roles. All can pull together; or pull apart.

The next case study is an excellent example of all parties pulling together. None of the parties had anything readily available to give. And yet, they all had everything to gain.

A little common sense and a lot of organizational acumen by the client, allowed the partnership to flourish. Anyone for golf?

The case study is provided by Steven Chaytor. Steven is the Leisure Management Officer in Middlesbrough responsible for all contract and non contract facilities plus the catering contract. He is also co-author (with colleague Phil Rogers) of the book *Managing a Leisure Management Contract* published by Pitman for ILAM.

A hole in one: success at the golf course

by Steve Chaytor

A golf course is a living, breathing organism. It is ever changing, growing and developing. It is sensitive to the volume and frequency of use by golfers of varying ability and also with players of varying regard for the etiquette of the game.

For this reason, it is important that golf course management extends beyond simple grass cutting. And even beyond the undoubted skills of the experienced greenkeeper who maintains the course from season to season, and year to year. It is necessary to plan for future developments and attempt to predict and pre-empt potential difficulties.

Middlesbrough Municipal Golf Course is operated by Middlesbrough Leisure, the in-house contractor responsible for managing the leisure facilities subject to CCT. The grounds maintenance function is performed by the authority's DSO. They are the nominated subcontractor within the bid for managing the leisure facilities within the borough.

The main contract is monitored by the client section of Middlesbrough Leisure Services. In order to maintain proper control over the grounds maintenance element, the specialist client section of the department, responsible for all other grounds maintenance contracts, performs a monitoring role on behalf of the main client. It is these three parties – grounds DSO, leisure client, and grounds client, which have the greatest impact on the management of the course.

There is a fourth interested party, the golf club. The club operates as a semi-autonomous, but formally constituted body, at the golf centre. Importantly, it has the ability to raise its own funds through club membership and fund raising ventures.

The course is relatively new, opened in 1977. It is built on a tight, clay-based soil which suffers from drainage problems. It also presents difficulties in growing trees and shrubs and establishing strong grass root growth. Against this background and with around 65 000 rounds per year, the course is under enormous pressure. The staff are under equal pressure to maintain and improve standards.

DEVELOPMENT PLAN

Middlesbrough Leisure has produced a development plan for the course which goes beyond day-to-day maintenance. It looks at the changes that are required to help it thrive in future.

The plan emerged as a five-stage process:

- identifying the areas to be developed;
- establishing priorities – short, medium, long term;
- allocating responsibilities for actions;
- identifying funding sources;
- action.

The whole process was assisted by the way in which the course is managed. This means that there are four contributing parties, each able to play a part and take responsibility for some element of the plan. These four parties are the:

- leisure management contractor;
- grounds maintenance subcontractor – the council's DSO;
- grounds maintenance client – giving specialist advice;
- club – a separate body based at the golf centre.

Each has been able to play a significant role in the development plan and the implementation of individual elements.

FIVE KEY STAGES

The identification of development needs was carried out by discussions with club members. The club does not necessarily represent the views of all players. However, the club does give a thorough overview. It is often able to give quite specific views on how the course could be improved from a customer/player perspective.

In addition, monitoring reports from the client, delivered through weekly meetings with the leisure contractor and grounds maintenance subcontractor, identified areas of technical deficiency or schemes which require further specialist analysis.

Identification of development needs

A development group with representatives of each party guided the work and acted as a monitoring and evaluating forum. A detailed sketch plan of each hole was drawn up by the leisure contractor and grounds maintenance client.

This plan of the golf course included the following components:

- tee extensions required, with artificial tee mats (purchases required);
- details of desired pathways to prevent wear and tear;

- indications of desired planting schemes;
- locations for course signage and course furniture;
- areas in urgent need of drainage improvements.

Discussions identified that the course now required improved teeing areas because of the vastly increased use of the course since it originally opened. A number of areas were being established as pathways or desire-line footpaths. Other areas were quite obviously in need of improved drainage. They were all identified.

Planting schemes were discussed from an aesthetic point of view and as a means of 'directing traffic' along desired pathways. Advice on the suitability of particular plant and tree types was given by the specialist client. The signage scheme which emerged was a direct result of discussions with club members and an accumulation of comments given to the course wardens by pay and play users.

Because of the evidence of more substantial and structural drainage problems, it was also decided that an in-depth study into the course, its drainage, soil conditions and green construction should be commissioned. This was commissioned by the specialist grounds maintenance client. It involved the employment of a sports turf consultancy. They made long-term recommendations for fundamental improvements to the golf course and its construction, after a detailed survey of the course using a number of technical performance measures which gave scientific support to the recommendations.

Establishing priorities

The specialist consultants' report is obviously a significant document with medium- and long-term consequences. However, the financial implications of implementing the recommendations mean that action on these schemes is dependent on external funding or a long-term commitment from the authority. However, many of the other issues identified by the development group were achievable in the short term. Indeed, some of these issues were absolutely necessary in order that the contractor, Middlesbrough Leisure, could continue to provide a quality service for customers.

In year one of the contract, the following works were identified as priorities:

- purchase of four winter tees;
- the extension of three specific blue tees (the most used 'tee of the day');

- three significant areas of planting;
- improved tee signing and waste baskets.

In year two of the contract, further priorities were:

- two more winter tees;
- extension of two more blue tees;
- the laying of two pathways;
- a local drainage system in a particularly badly affected area of the course.

These priorities had been established by the development group from the initial needs which were identified. However, a second factor also influenced the decision: the ability to finance particular schemes.

Funding ...

Middlesbrough Leisure won the right to manage the leisure facilities of the town against genuine competition. Consequently, the ability to generate massive surpluses is not there. All work has to be completed within a tightly tendered figure. In addition, the town has been consistently hit by Government spending restrictions. This has meant that the funding of the development scheme has been a patchwork of contributions and a very tightly controlled investment programme.

... and apportioning responsibility

In year one for example, the materials for the tees and the winter tees were purchased through contract surpluses. The labour for these works was provided by the grounds maintenance subcontractor within their contract price.

In the same year, the tee signage was supplied by a specialist course signage company which paid for the installation through advertising. Again, the grounds maintenance subcontractor supplied the labour for the work.

In year two, one of the pathways was paid for entirely by the club. Some club volunteers helped the maintenance staff to lay the path.

The local drainage laid in year two was completed by a private contractor and paid for by contract surpluses.

The major course survey was then instigated and paid for by the leisure client. In year four of the contract, a financial package identified contributions from the:

- grounds maintenance client;
- leisure management contractor;
- golf club;
- grounds maintenance contractor.

These contributions has enabled a further £30 000 worth of drainage work to be undertaken. The drainage works were identified by the survey, and are to the standards suggested in the consultants' report.

This approach has enabled the course and the customers to benefit from a steady and consistent programme of development. It has seen the most significant improvements to the course for many years. Having established the plan and the priorities, it means that whenever funding becomes available, there is a plan of development to refer to which has the approval of all parties. This saves time and enables a quick response.

Action

Action is linked to finance and to the weather and ground conditions which prevail at the time. On occasions, the three do not coincide. However, having a plan which is agreed means that the work can be more responsive and adaptable.

However, action is a key word in the development plan.

Fig. 15.1 Players benefit from partnership

Golf course users want to see things being done. They want to see development and improvement even if it is slow and incremental. Inaction is seen as a crime.

The work completed in four years is valued at £65000 excluding some labour costs. This has been found from different sources. More importantly, it has been completed because of effective partnership, discussion and consultation. A common purpose has been established in which each partner has a stake and influence. The chief beneficiary has been the golfer. If the golfer is a beneficiary, then so is the contractor and the local authority.

CONSTRAINTS

Clearly, with four principal partners involved in any situation, there are bound to be times when there are conflicts of interest and differences in emphasis. The club, while representing the golfers, also tend to be biased towards the needs of competition golfers. This is not always the same priority which the leisure manager will have, as he seeks to accommodate more pay and play customers.

Equally, there are conflicts of priority and interest between the contractor and maintenance subcontractor. Middlesbrough has had to work very hard to ensure that the rate of return of the subcontracts is not compromised by development work. The contractor after all, is trying to get as much work done as possible within the contract price. This has largely been accommodated by a flexible approach to staffing which has enabled the leisure manager to redirect maintenance staff to development work.

Changing from maintenance work to development work can be accommodated if:

- time and workloads permit; or
- a 'trade off' is accepted.

For a successful trade off, one type of maintenance work will be substituted for some other element of development work. There have been many 'interesting' discussions and debates between the client and contractor partners, but the end result has been progress and (yes, that word again) action.

Occasional tensions between the principals are not unusual. In some authorities it has led to the dissatisfaction of customers who see apparently simple things going wrong on their golf course. It is undoubtedly a difficult path to steer. However, it is a path which, with persistence, can achieve significant results.

Chapter 15: summary

by Philip Sayers

The more clearly defined roles since the client–contractor split brought about by CCT, has helped to focus on the development issues, particularly in terms of responsibility and ability to act.

Establishing clear areas of responsibility has enabled a much more effective partnership to emerge which means that golfers at Middlesbrough Municipal Golf Centre can look forward to a steady programme of improvements over the coming years.

The key essentials of this successful partnership include:

- The clarity of thought to look beyond day to day affairs.
- The leisure client manager actively developing partnerships.
- A five-stage process to develop and implement the plan.
- All four partners have a clear role to play.
- Identifying the most pressing needs, e.g. better tees and paths.
- Establishing priorities; a shopping list was prepared.
- Next, the all important cash and resources had to be found.
- Resources included: voluntary labour and sponsorship.
- Some cash was kindly contributed from the contractor's annual surplus.
- Finally, there was actual action on the ground.

In this case study the conflicts and constraints ever present in a contract situation were put to good use. The principal beneficiary were the main golf players - club or casual.

Appendix A: List of addresses

Broxbourne Borough Council
Grundy Park Leisure Centre
Windmill Lane
Cheshunt,
Herts EN8 9AJ

Broxbourne Borough Council has a Conservative administration which fully supports the ethos of open competition on a level playing field. It has been at the forefront of local government and management change and wants to deliver a high quality service to all its customers.

Chartered Institute of Public Finance and Accountancy
3 Robert Street
London WC2N 6BH

CIPFA have provided on-going detailed advice in respect of all CCT services by means of many publications. Their document *The Contract Documents used in CCT* (1996), links to the government circulars on CCT procedures and quality.

City of Plymouth
Civic Centre
Plymouth PL1 2EW

Plymouth, the major district council in the south-west of England, obtained unitary status under local government review in 1996. With a population of approximately 250 000 Plymouth has major areas of open space. The City Council has attracted a good deal of competition for its blue collar services. Although adopting CCT as an important element of service provision in a major city, Plymouth has maintained a policy supportive of the provision of in-house services.

Darlington Borough Council
Contract Services
Vane Terrace
Darlington DL3 7AX

Darlington Borough Council is situated in the south of County Durham in the north-east of England. It provides an extensive range of leisure facilities including a large sports centre, arts centre, theatre and a golf course and maintains a number of parks throughout the borough. It serves over 110 000 residents and took on unitary status in 1996.

Department of the Environment

This is the government department responsible for local government, and CCT in particular. Their publications can be obtained from Her Majesty's Stationery Office (see HMSO).

East Hampshire District Council
Penns Place
Petersfield
Hampshire GU31 4EX

East Hampshire District Council serves a population of approximately 106 000 within an area of 199 square miles from just to the south-west of Farnham in the north, to Rowlands Castle some 25 miles to the south. It is an Area of Outstanding Natural Beauty with nearly 60% of the area being designated as such.

Gillespies – Environment by Design
Edmund House
Wood Street
Altrincham
Cheshire WA14 1ED

Gillespies is a national-based multi-disciplinary practice, established in 1962, which provides a broad base of expertise in the fields of landscape architecture, urban design, planning, architecture, graphic design, ecology, forestry, land reclamation, and landscape management. The practice offers comprehensive advice on the opportunities and problems posed by environmental change.

HMSO Publications Centre
PO Box 276
London SW8 5DT

Government publications and DoE circulars can be obtained from HMSO in London and other major cities.

Institute of Leisure and Amenity Management (ILAM)
Lower Basildon
Reading
Berks RG8 9NE

ILAM is the professional body for leisure professionals. ILAM represents every aspect of leisure, cultural and recreation management and is committed to the improvement of management standards. Further details are available on page xi.

Knight, Kavanagh and Page
Bank Chambers
Market Place
Bury BL9 0LQ

Knight, Kavanagh and Page are a leading UK consultancy on sports development and related management issues. They have worked with a number of local authorities on development strategies and specific planning for compulsory competitive tendering.

Landscape Management Consultants
Frog Lane
Pickmere
Knutsford
Cheshire WA16 0JG

The consultancy specializes in advice to local authorities on all aspects of grounds maintenance CCT, including:

- the writing of full grounds maintenance contract documentation;
- detailed select list evaluations;
- objective and independent tender evaluations;
- running contract management workshops for client sections;
- advice on cost effective landscape management regimes and methods.

Leisure Australia
12 Greenhill Road
Wayville
South Australia 5034

Leisure Australia is Australia's largest management support service to public sports and leisure services.

Local Government Management Board
Layden House
76-86 Turnmill Street
London EC1M 5QU

By focusing on management and human resource issues, LGMB helps local authorities to be more effective in their work, the way they deliver services and the way they provide democratic leadrship in their communities. It has provided much help to local authorities with CCT, including the publication *Quality in the Balance* (1995).

Local Government News
Hereford House
Bridle Path
Croydon
Surrey CR9 4NL

Local Government News is the UK's leading technical monthly for professional local authority officers. It circulates, free of charge, to senior personnel in the technical departments of every council in Britain. Key areas of coverage include the environment, amenity, building and construction, landscape and design.

London Borough of Croydon
Crosfield House
Mint Walk
Croydon
Surrey CR9 1BS

Croydon is the largest of the 32 London boroughs with a population of 320 000. It was formerly a market town on the southern edge of London, but today is a bustling residential and business community, stretching from the hilly North Downs in the south to Norbury in the north. It is well provided with open space and leisure facilities including the Fairfield Halls and a modern library and museum.

London Borough of Newham
Leisure Services Department
292 Barking Road
East Ham
London E6 3BA

The London Borough of Newham aims to ensure that every resident in Newham is aware of its services, has maximum opportunity to use them, and as a satisfied customer, will return to use them. The main aim of local authority managed leisure centres is to provide a wide range of leisure opportunities for all sections of the local community.

Middlesbrough Borough Council
Middlesbrough Municipal Golf Course
Lad Gate Lane
Middlesbrough
Cleveland TS5 7YZ

Middlesbrough Council became a new unitary authority in April 1996 following local government reorganization. The authority serves a population of around 150 000. The new department of Community Development, Leisure and Libraries includes youth services, adult education, community development and libraries along with the components of the old Leisure Department including parks and leisure management. The leisure DSO has operated successfully since January 1992 and now also manages all non-contract facilities.

The Municipal Journal
32 Vauxhall Bridge Road
London SW1V 2SS

The Municipal Journal is the leading news weekly for senior local government managers with particularly strong coverage of contract management and compulsory competitive tendering issues.

Peran Consultancy
103 Layston Park
Royston
Hertfordshire SG8 9DY

The consultancy group has particular specialist expertise in catering within leisure locations. One of the performance improvement tools developed by Peran Consultancy to help meet clients quality and gross profit management needs is: The Food & Beverage Manager's Toolkit. This specialist software application calculates input; then compares the achievable, the actual, and the budgeted, gross profit levels. It also provides tools to break down and analyse unacceptable variances.

Stevenage Borough Council
Department of Leisure Services
Danestrete
Stevenage
Herts SG1 1HN

Stevenage was the first new town to be designated after the second world war, in 1946. It has a population of over 76 000 and is situated some thirty miles north of London. Leisure activities provided by the Borough Council include 10 parks, a golf complex, a sailing centre and a large range of indoor and outdoor sports and recreation facilities. The council's goal is 'Aiming for Excellence'.

Strategic Leisure Consultancy
West Hall
Parvis Road
West Byfleet
Surrey KT14 6EZ

Strategic Leisure was started in 1988. Within four years Strategic Leisure had shot into the small group of consultancies that are the market leaders. Always strong in the public sector and active leisure, the company rapidly built a matching strength in commercial leisure and tourism, and is now equally at home in all these fields. Not only do Strategic Leisure teams from the UK tackle overseas assignments, but the company has offices in mainland Europe, Australasia, and South-east Asia.

Torfaen Borough Council
Central Works Depot
Panteg Way
South Pontypool Industrial Estate
New Inn
Pontypool
Gwent NP4 0LS

Torfaen Borough Council is situated in south-east Wales and has a population of approximately 93 000. The authority is committed to providing high quality direct services and the direct works department operates a semi-autonomous contracting unit within the organization.

On local government reorganization in April 1996, Torfaen Borough Council amalgamated with a disaggregated portion of Gwent County Council to create a new unitary authority; Torfaen County Borough Council. The new authority's Contract Services Department, comprising 1100 staff with a turnover of over £15 million, manages all the authority's DSOs including Leisure and Sports Management.

University of New South Wales
The Australian Graduate School of Management
Sydney
NSW 2052

The Australian Graduate School of Management (AGSM) provides management training and research in the field of business management. Part of the University of New South Wales, the AGSM provides programmes in management, as well as having established two national centres with industry and government support.

The University of Sheffield Leisure Management Unit
Hicks Building
Hounsfield Road
Sheffield S3 7RH

The Leisure Management Unit at Sheffield University specializes in applied postgraduate management education. It runs three postgraduate programmes; MA and Diploma in Leisure Management, MSc and Diploma in Sport and Recreation Management, and MA and Diploma in Arts and Heritage Management. The unit also recruits postgraduate research students and is active in conducting research and consultancy in the leisure industry.

University of South Australia
Salisbury Campus
Centre for Environment and Recreation Management (CERM)
Smith Road
Salisbury East
South Australia 5109

CERM is a research centre of the University of South Australia. The performance indicators team is primarily concerned with applied research in best practice in public sports and leisure centres. CERM have been developing benchmarks for performance indicators of efficiency since 1990. Initial performance indicators were trialled in three states of Australia. Then two 'key performance indicators' were adopted to measure the efficiency of operations. As this book was going to press, CERM was finalising arrangements with the University of Sheffield and ILAM to conduct similar applied research in the United Kingdom to that outlined in this paper.

The University of Sydney
Graduate School of Business
Bldg C37
NSW 2008 Australia

The Graduate School of Business, The University of Sydney, provides management education relevant to industry and government. Drawing on the academic traditions of Australia's oldest university, students are encouraged to question and move beyond conventional wisdom. In particular, consideration of the future business environment and the needs of business and government lies at the heart of all the management programmes offered by the school.

Wiltshire County Council
Education – Youth and Community Services
Grosvenor House
26 Churchfields Road
Salisbury
Wiltshire SP2 7NH

Wiltshire is one of England's largest inland counties. It has more prehistoric relics than any other county. There is the gigantic circle of Stonehenge, and its prototype of Woodhenge. Wiltshire now has a rapidly developing local economy characterized by an increasing diversification in economic activity.

Appendix B: Outline of a tender

An outline of the main parts to be expected in most tender and contract documents.

1.   Instructions for tendering

A formal statement of how to go about submitting the tender.

2.   Form of tender

Quite brief; this is the actual tender, the formal offer.

3.   Financial summaries

This is the summary of anticipated income and expenditure in leisure management tenders. Otherwise, just expenditure.

4.   Draft form of contract

Brief; this is the actual written contract, when signed.

5.   Conditions of contract

The rules or conditions by which the contract will be operated.

6.   Form of bond

This is a guarantee from a third party, to honour the contract, if the appointed contractor should fail.

7.   Form of insurance

Covers the contractor for normal risks.

8.   Specifications and activity programmes

Many pages of specific work instructions, and activity scheduling to be provided, e.g. school swimming 9.30 - 11.30 am, in a leisure tender; grass cutting daily on the bowling green in a grounds maintenance tender.

9.   Schedule of rates

These are provided to help price events, or works, of a 'one-off' nature.

10.   Parent company indemnity

Where a small subsidiary company wins a contract this form will ensure that the parent company is responsible for any costs arising through the failure of that smaller company.

In addition there are appendices. These will include plans and maps; some demographic information about the area; recent income trends; current fees and charges; samples of forms in use etc.

Appendix C: Glossary of terms

BoQ (Bill of quantities) These bills quantify the tender. In a grounds maintenance tender, for example, the bills will show that there are say 10 playing fields each of 10 hectares in size. Note: absolutely exact quantities need to be stated. For a leisure contract, the exact floor area will be stated, the quantity of water in the swimming pool to be heated, and all other quantities relevant to the contract and more particularly to the price to be calculated by the tenderer. Accurate bills of quantity lead to exact like for like tenders being received – the very basis of successful competitive tendering.

Client The local authority (and its officers), who award and run the contract.

CCT (Compulsory competitive tendering) The legal requirement (thus compulsory) to seek competition via tenders and specifications to deliver services in the most economically advantageous manner – often the lowest tender.

In Britain a local authority cannot employ its own staff to carry out certain activities (e.g. grounds maintenance, the management of leisure and housing services), unless that work has been subject to a competitive tendering process, and the local authority's in-house contractor has won the tender in a fair competitive process against any other bidders.

The implementation of CCT in a practical setting is explained in the book *Managing Sports and Leisure Facilities: A Guide to Competitive Tendering*, written by Philip Sayers and published by E & FN Spon.

Contract documentation   This is the package of documents supplied by the authority which details all the contract requirements of the authority, and how the management and maintenance operations will be carried out and controlled.

Contractor   The tenderer who submits the winning tender bid and is awarded the contract thus becomes the contractor.

DoE (Department of the Environment)   The government department charged with the task of introducing and monitoring the whole CCT process across Britain.

DSO (direct service organization) A council's own in-house contractor, where the staff are employed directly by the council. The DSO will be most usually just one of a number of tenderers bidding for a tender.

Franchise   With a franchise contract, the client meets the debt charges and external maintenance costs of the buildings. The franchisee meets other costs.The franchisee retains income from all users and pays a fixed fee (or rental) to the client. It is this fixed fee or rental which is stated in the tender. Catering contracts are often a good example of a franchise contract. Sometimes the fee is not fixed; see the definition of income sharing contracts.

Income sharing   With an income sharing contract, the contractor retains all income from users (especially in a leisure contract) and uses this and the fee from the client to meet costs and provide profit. The contractor pays a proportion of the income received from users to the client irrespective of whether or not the operation is profitable. Often the income will not be shared until after the income projected in the tender submission has been achieved.

Sometimes, a 'profit sharing' guarantee will be agreed. However, the calculation of profit can lead to disagreement. Income sharing is a much more certain way to share in the success of a contract.

n n = the number of units in a survey. For example in the Australian survey, $n = 18$, i.e. 18 leisure centres.

Profit sharing   See income sharing

SDO (sports development officer)   An officer (or officers) employed by a local authority to develop sports within the local community, and most likely involve those people in the community who have not traditionally been involved with sports. SDOs are often involved with outreach work within the community as well as providing sessions within leisure centres. They also help coordinate, and encourage, new groups to become established in their chosen sport.

SMVs (Standard minute values)   The time a task takes to accomplish, expressed in standard minutes, e.g. the time taken to mow a bowling green. These standard minutes are defined by a work study assessment. SMVs vary from place to place but are becoming progressively more standard. SMVs across the country will never be fully equal, for example due to the difference in soil and terrain types.

SoR (Schedule of rates)   Literally a schedule of rates – a list of prices. Often used when quantities are not known in advance of the tender (see bill of quantities). In a grounds maintenance tender, SoRs can often account for 20% of the work (sometimes more). They can also be very variable in value (i.e. price) at the tender stage and thus bring a degree of uncertainty into the tender bid. Thus the number of schedule of rates items should be reduced to an absolute minismum.

An example of a schedule of rates item would be tree pruning in a grounds maintenance tender. The number and size of trees to be pruned in any one year will not be known in advance. Thus a tenderer may be asked to price for pruning say 10, and 100 medium size trees (up to 10 metres high). By contrast a playing field is a known and unvarying quantity, Therefore the tender will seek a price for say the *xyz* playing field which is 10 hectares in size, and is to be cut 10 times per year.

Tender   The actual bid made by the tenderer, in accordance with the contract documentation, and the tendering instructions.

Tenderer   A person, company, or council who completes the tender and returns it to the authority (e.g. a catering contractor).

TUPE (Transfer of Undertakings (Protection of Employment) Regulations 1981)   This is the UK implementation of the European Community 'Acquired Rights Directive'. TUPE has been the subject of intense debate, government edict, and court room battles. Put simply, the regulations try to protect the terms and conditions of employees (pay, hours of work, etc.), at the time of tender and at the moment of the transfer of an undertaking from one organization to another. It is not as easy as it sounds. The conflicting views have led to legal challenges.

As far as competitive tendering is concerned, any tenderer would be wise to allow for the transfer of existing employees at the time of tender and contract commencement. Although each tender does differ. Exact enquiries need to be made by the tenderer at the time of tender and expert legal advice should be sought, as in all matters relating to contracts and competitive tenders.

Ultra vires An action which is beyond an authority's or organization's legal powers.

VCT (voluntary competitive tendering) The same principles apply as in all competitive tendering (see compulsory competitive tendering). However, in VCT, the compulsory element is absent. The advantage with VCT is that both client and contractor are willing parties to the tender process and the subsequent contract.

Index

Acknowledgements x
Action plan for partnerships 237
Addresses/contacts 243
Antagonism 224
Attendances, measurement of
    132
Audit Commission criticisms 230
Autonomy, lack of 60

Benchmarking 131
Bendigo, Australia 24
Bill of quantities 253
Bonds
    danger in loss of 169
    importance of 173
Bonus schemes 201
Break clause between contracts 183
Broxbourne Borough Council 243
    winning a leisure contract 96
Budget restrictions 50
Bureaucracy 58
Burgess, Michael xi
    winning ways in grounds
        maintenance 203
Business acumen 211
Business plans 90

Cash limitations 58
Catering for profit 211
CCT *see* Compulsory competitive
    tendering
Challenge
    by an aggrieved contractor
        116
    reducing the likelihood of 114
Chaytor, Steve xi
    success at the golf course 236
CIPFA 243
Clarity 88
Client
    establishing the role of 53
    explanation of 253
    meets contractor 46
Client role 136
Client, contractor, customer 146
Client and contractor harmony
        205
Clientside 66
Clubs 236
Coalter 154
Collusion 22
Commercial
    awareness 226

Commercial *cont.*
practices for the DSO 53
pressures 171
Community involvement 45
Company
formation 167
growth 168
termination 169
Compulsory competitive
tendering
benefits of 25
in Britain 12
different approaches 67
explanation of 253
introduction to 15
preparations for 66
Conditions of contract
in dispute 161
word carefully 164
Conditions of service 16
Conflict
management 159
and use of the default system
56
Conflicting interests 70
Constraints and cooperation 241
Consultants
cost effective advice 212
for mediation 61
Contemporary Leisure 166
Contingency planning 188
Contract
collapse 166
concept 41
conditions 164
going bust 179
the life of a 13
planning 39
Contract documents 251
Contractor
assessment of 171
establishing in-house 53
explanation of 254

for landscape maintenance
46
Contributors xi
Converging interests 72
Cost effectiveness 41
Crilley, Gary xi
and efficiency management
129
Croydon, London Borough of
246
contract collapse at 179
Customer
needs 16
orientation 137
profile 140
satisfaction 146
satisfaction assessment 138
surveys 156
Customer, client, contractor 234

Darlington Borough Council 244
customer surveys and better
services 148
Declaration of Interest
avoid misunderstanding 30
be early 27
Default
clause 56
disputed 161
points 140
in practice 56
Demographic change 154
Department of the Environment
(DoE) 244
a legal challenge from 117
Depression, the 1920s and 1930s
8
Deprivation 137
Development
in contracts 66
parameters 84
plans 236
for sports, explained 81

Dispute management   159
Distress signals   177
Divorce   176
Domberger, Professor Simon   xii
  a tender business   24
DSO
  closure threatened   195
  explanation of   254
  fighting back   197
  lack of autonomy   60
DSO manager's attitudes   225

East Hampshire District Council
    244
  sports development
    implementation   79
Ecological management   42
Economic
  climate   94
  depression   8
  viability   132
Edwardian era   7
Efficiency measurement   129
Efficiency via CCT   16
Elmbridge Borough Council   111
Emergency planning   187
Employment
  conditions   8
  erosion of security   25
  terms of   198
Equality issues   135
Ethical
  behaviour   32
  guidelines   23
Ethnic profiles   141
European National Court   163
European Union legislation   114
Exemption Order for CCT   171
Expenditure control   105
Expense recovery   130
Extinction faced by a DSO   195

Failure of a contract   185

False name   167
Fears   17
Financial
  evaluation of tenders   109
  targets   229
Financial constraint
  adverse effects of   73
  coinciding with CCT   230
Fire certificate   184
Flares for failures   176
Franchise   254
Future, analysis of   95

Gapes, Mike, MP   167
Gilbert, Malcolm   xii
  litigation, is it worth it?   161
Gillespies, Environment by
    Design   40
  from landscape concept to
    contract   244
Glossary of terms   253
Going bust   179
Goldstone, David   xii
  emergency planning   187
Golf course management   236
Goodwill of customers   181
Gross profit
  an analysis   215
  explanation of   208
  percentages   209
Grounds maintenance   44
Grundy Park Leisure Centre   96

Hansard   166
Harrison, Reg   xii
  going bust   178
High Court proceedings   162
Hopes of CCT   15
Howat, Dr Gary on efficiency
    measurement   129
Howell, Stephen   xii
  and measuring customer
    satisfaction   147

Improved information 15
Improvements for customers 139
Income
    at a leisure centre 104
    sharing 254
    for sports development 72
    targets 105
    under recovery, rectified 201
    unrealistic 119
Increasing attendance and income
    104
Increasing income 228
Insider advantage 30
Institute of Leisure and Amenity
    Management (ILAM) 245
    further information on 245
Interests
    conflict of 70
    converging 72
    declared 27
Inventory of contents 182
Invitation to tender 114

James, Brian D. xii
    from loss to profit 194
Job insecurity 18
Jones, Robert B., MP 170

Key contractor indicators 196
Key financial ratios 209
Key reference indicators 134
Keynes, John Maynard 8
Knight, Kavanagh and Page 79
    contact address 245
Kwan, Ian xii
    a tender business 24

Landscape Management
    Consultants 120
    contact address 245
Landscape management plans 48
Landscape planning 41
Legal advice

always obtain your own x
always seek early 164
Leisure
    participation by demographics
        150
    strategy 223
    survey 156
Leisure Australia 246
Leisure management
    specifications 63
Liability – limitation of 183
Licences 184
Liquidation of a company 180
Liquidation, fight back from 197
Litigation, is it worth it? 161
Local Government Management
        Board (LGMB) 126
    contact address 246
Local Government News 194
    contact address 246
Logistic regression 151
Loss to profit 195
Lynch, Jim xiii
    tender evaluation 111

Maintenance and management
    44
Management
    measurement of 130
    military 7
    model specification 80
    specification 86
    by unemployment 8
Market forces 129
Market orientation 220
Marketing
    for a leisure centre 102
    percentage of expenditure 133
Martindill, Paul xiii
    quality performance in a
        contract 136
Measuring performance 127
Mediation 61

Middlesbrough Borough Council 247
  partnership at the golf course 236
Milne, Ian on efficiency measurement 129
Minimum standards 118
Mission statement
  in general 93
  for a leisure centre 97
Moffatt, Duncan xiii
  grounds maintenance tender evaluation 120
Monitoring 136
Morale booster 204
Most economically advantageous tender (MEAT) 114
  EU and quality 126
The Municipal Journal
  100 years ago 5
  contact address 247

n, explanation of 254
Newham, London Borough of 247
  quality performance in a contract 135
Nichols, Geoff xiii
  introduction to CCT 15
  market orientation and CCT 221
  sports development within CCT 66
Non-performance 55
Non-user surveys 148
Nursery profitability 205

Objectives
  clarification of 15
  for a landscape contract 42
  for leisure 228
  social 73
  for sports development 76
  for young people 83

Open selection of tenderers 32
Operational plans 92
Opportunities
  in a leisure centre 99
  marketing 74
  as part of a SWOT analysis 94
Opportunity costs 71
Options 85
Outline of a tender 251
Outputs 224
Over-optimism 119
Overheads, waging war on 199

7 Ps 102
Parliamentary question and answer 167
Participation research in leisure 148
Participation survey 156
Partnerships 234
Peran Consultancy 210
  contact address 247
Performance
  in Australia 129
  culture for leisure 153
  failure disputed 163
  failure notice 161
  measurement 127
  percentages 209
Performance bond
  danger in loss of 169
  need for 172
Performance indicators
  for leisure 134
  for sports 83
Personalities get in the way 52
PEST audit 97
Phased improvements 139
Philosophy in a specification 66
Plant nursery rejuvenated 204
Plymouth, City of 243
  the burden of litigation 162
Political climate 98

Poppy, Mark xiii
  winning ways for leisure
    management 97
Pre tender meeting 164
Press and public relations 182
Press interest 29
Pricing
  assessments 115
  negotiated 69
  the specification 86
Private sector contractors 225
Privatization
  fears of 17
  of landscape work 46
Probability sampling 154
Problem resolution 160
Productivity
  incentives 200
  in parks 203
  problem areas 196
Profit
  and the business plan 90
  for the DSO 54
  gross 208
  in jeopardy 193
  key principles 208
  net profit 208
Profit or public service? 227
Profit sharing 254
Profitable management 207
Progress indicators 84
Provider 64
Public service or profit? 227
Purchaser 64

Quality evaluation 113
Quality landscape 44
Quality payments
  by the client 138
  the contractor's view 142
Questionnaire for customers
  156

Ranson, Peter xiii
  contact address (Peran
    Consultancy) 247
Rectification notices 56
Red tape 58
Redbridge, London Borough 168
Redundancy, compulsory 46
Redundancy costs 169
Redundancy and re-employment
  181
Reeves, Nick xiv
  preparing a business plan 92
Relationships
  deterioration of 19
  professional 75
  and resentment 57
Representative sampling 149
Resource assessment 123
Restructuring 196

Sampling 149
Savings
  on a contract price 6
  turns to profit 205
Sayers, Philip xiv
  a century of contracting 1
  impact of personalities 51
Schedule of rates
  explanation of 255
  in general 122
Scott, David xiv
  naturalistic landscape 41
Secondary spending 229
Secondary spend in catering 216
Selection of tenders
  criteria 32
  by price 28
  and by quality 113
Shared responsibilities 240
Sheffield University 249
Sickness, management of
  198

Social objectives
    measuring 221
    policies 73
Social perspectives 97
Specifications
    an example 83
    managing 63
    pricing 86
    sports development 67
    tight 77
Sports Council 68
Sports development 66
Sports Development Officer
    (SDO) 255
Staff resources 100
Standard minute values (SMVs)
    explanation of 255
    in grounds maintenance 124
Stevenage Borough Council 248
    winning at grounds
        maintenance 203
Strategic
    planning 223
    priorities 93
Strategic Leisure Consultancy 111
    contact address 248
Strategy
    for catering 212
    for a leisure centre 104
Strengths
    in a leisure centre 98
    as part of SWOT 94
Stress 60
Strikes 11
Subsidies 133
Suitability of staff 181
Suppliers, contract termination
    183
Surpluses 133
Surveys of customers 150
SWOT
    analysis 94
    in a leisure centre 98

The 7 Ts 100
Take-over procedure 189
Target groups 153
Targets
    for a leisure business 94
    for leisure customers 139
Team building 100
Team effort 52
Technical evaluation of tenders
    109
Technology 98
Tender
    analysis 33
    assessment 115
    evaluation 119
    explanation of 257
    MEAT and the EU 114
    most economically
        advantageous (MEAT) 126
    not accepting the lowest 116
Tender documents, an outline 251
Tender prices
    at Bendigo 28
    at Elmbridge 117
Tenderer
    becomes a contractor 90
    evaluation of 109
    explanation of 255
Tendering process 26
Tenders
    analysed 116
    minimum standards 118
Termination – be prepared 188
Terms of employment 198
Threat of competition 226
Threats
    as part of SWOT 94
    in a leisure centre 99
Titanic 177
Torfaen Borough Council 248
Trade offs 241
Trades union convenor 199
Trading accounts 208

Trading report 219
Training 203
Training costs 133
TUPE
    at Broxbourne 101
    explanation of 255
    in practice 121
    and pensions 123

Ultra vires
    an example of 171
    explanation of 256
Unemployment 8
University of
    Sheffield 249
    South Australia 249
    Sydney 38, 250

Valididity of projections 113
Value for money
    100 years ago 6
    in grounds maintenance 28

in leisure 117
Variable participation in customer
    sampling 152
Variation orders (VOs) 63
Vending or kiosk? 214
Visits per square metre 130
Voluntary competitive tendering
    an example 45
    explanation of 256
Voluntary liquidation 179

Warrington New Town 40
Water Palace, Croydon 179
Weaknesses
    in a leisure tender 99
    as part of SWOT 94
Wiltshire County Council 250
    contingency planning 187
World-wide tendering 3

Youngs, Chris xiv
    management specifications 80